Dedicated to the memory
of David Rocastle
(1967–2001)
and
Kevin Campbell
(1970–2024).
You did so much for us.

BLACK ARSENAL

Club, Culture, Identity

BLACK ARSENAL

Club, Culture, Identity

EDITED BY CLIVE CHIJIOKE NWONKA
AND MATTHEW HARLE

W&N
WEIDENFELD & NICOLSON

CONTENTS

Contents

EDITORS AND CONTRIBUTORS

CLIVE CHIJIOKE NWONKA is Associate Professor in Film, Culture and Society at University College London, and a Faculty Associate of the UCL Sarah Parker Remond Centre for the Study of Racism and Racialisation. Nwonka is the co-editor of the book *Black Film: British Cinema II* (2021) and author of *Black Boys: The Aesthetics of British Urban Film* (2023).

MATTHEW HARLE is a writer and curator from Islington, North London. His work explores cultural histories, cities and identity in books, exhibitions and events. He has worked at the BFI and Barbican and is now Curator of Artistic Programmes at the Warburg Institute. He attended his first Arsenal game in the 1993–4 season.

LES BACK is a sociologist and journalist. His books include *The Changing Face of Football: Racism and Multiculture in the English Game* (with Tim Crabbe and John Solomos, 2001) and he wrote '"When you score you're English, when you miss you're Black": Euro 2020 and the racial politics of a penalty shoot-out' published in the journal *Soundings*. He's from South London and a Millwall fan.

STARDIOUS CHRISTIE was born in Finsbury Park and attended his first game as a schoolboy in 1973. He has lived in Islington ever since, working as a heating engineer and chef, selling jerk chicken, burgers and hot dogs outside the stadium since 2016. He was a fixture of Arsenal's Clock End terrace from 1976 until the mid 1980s.

REUBEN DANGOOR is a British artist who creates work heavily influenced by current affairs and British culture. His work has been exhibited at Tate Britain and the Design Museum, and has been covered across the *New York Times*, *GQ*, *Evening Standard*, Netflix, BBC News, Channel 4 and Sky News.

PAUL DAVIS is the former Arsenal midfielder who made 447 appearances for Arsenal between 1980 and 1995, winning the First Division League title in 1989 and 1991. He worked as a coach at the Arsenal Academy, later joining the PFA and the Football Association as a senior coach and educator.

STEPHEN DAVIS was born in Hackney and moved to Jamaica in early childhood; he returned to London when he was nineteen as an Arsenal supporter. He was a maintenance worker at Highbury Stadium from 1999–2001.

CELIA FACEY is an Arsenal in the Community Youth Coach. Having worked with the club since 2007, she was given a Premier League Kicks 'local legend' award in 2022 for her work in Islington.

DAVID FORREST is Professor in Film and Television Studies, and Deputy Vice President for Education at the University of Sheffield. David's research explores the histories and practices of British social realism through film, television and literature, and the relationships between screen and literary culture and region – he is the author of a number of books and articles on these topics. He is an Arsenal fan from West Yorkshire and has supported the club for over thirty years.

PAUL GILROY is Professor of the Humanities and founding Director of the Sarah Parker Remond Centre for the Study of Racism and Racialisation at University College London. His books include *The Black Atlantic* (1993), *Against Race* (2000), *Postcolonial Melancholia* (2008) and *Darker Than Blue* (2010). Gilroy's is a unique voice that speaks to the centrality and tenacity of racial orders and inequalities in the modern world. He first attended an Arsenal home game in 1966.

RODNEY HINDS is currently the sports & features editor of *The Voice* newspaper. In 1999 Rodney was co-editor of *Black Pearls: The A–Z of Black Footballers in the English Game*. Thereafter he penned his second book, *Black Lions: A History of Black Players in English Football* (2006).

SEAN JACOBS is associate professor of international affairs at The New School. He is the founder/publisher of Africa is a Country, a website for criticism, analysis and new writing. His book, *Media in Post-apartheid South Africa: Postcolonial Politics in the Age of Globalization*, was published in 2019. He was born in Cape Town, South Africa, where he worked for the Institute for Democracy in South Africa and as a journalist. He has been awarded Fulbright, Shorenstein, Commonwealth, Africa No Filter and Shuttleworth fellowships.

TARIQ JAZEEL is Professor of Human Geography and co-Director of UCL's Sarah Parker Centre for the Study of Racism and Racialisation. He is also founding co-director of UCL's Centre for the Study of South Asia and the Indian Ocean World. He writes on postcolonialism, critical human geography and South Asian studies. His recent books include *Postcolonialism* (2019) and *Subaltern Geographies* (co-edited with Stephen Legg, 2019). He is currently writing a recent history of British Asian dance music.

Editors and Contributors

MATTHEW JOSEPH is a former professional football player and current academy coach at Arsenal. A former Arsenal and England youth player, he played over 400 games in the Football League and worked as a coach at the Football Association.

Brothers **FEMI AND TJ KOLEOSO** make up two of the Mercury Music Prize-winning jazz quintet **Ezra Collective**. From North London, both are lifelong Arsenal supporters.

AMY LAWRENCE is the Arsenal correspondent for The Athletic. She was the *Observer*'s deputy football correspondent for over a decade. She has also written a number of football books, mostly about her specialist subject of Arsenal. Her most recent book *89* was in 2019. She also worked as the producer on a documentary of the same subject, entitled *'89*, which was released by Universal Studios.

GAIL LEWIS is a psychotherapist, academic and co-founder of the Organisation of Women of African and Asian Descent (OWAAD). She was Presidential Visiting Professor at Yale University, Women, Gender and Sexuality Studies (2021–22), Reader Emerita of the Department of Psychosocial Studies, Birkbeck College, and Visiting Professor of Women's, Gender and Sexuality Studies at the London School of Economics.

JAMES McNICHOLAS is a sports journalist who has been writing about Arsenal for the best part of twenty years. Having started out writing his own blog, Gunnerblog.com, he has subsequently written for *Bleacher Report* and ESPN, and is now a senior Arsenal writer at The Athletic.

SAM MEJIAS is Associate Professor of Social Justice and Community Engagement at Parsons School of Design at The New School. His academic research focuses on youth, arts and social justice. Originally from New York City, Sam has supported Arsenal since 1997, when he lived on Upper Street in London as a student.

EDDIE OTCHERE is a photographer best known for his photographs of the seminal rappers and DJs of the mid-1990s and early 2000s. His celebrated works include portraits of Biggie Smalls, Blackstar (Mos Def & Thalib Kweli), So Solid Crew, Est'elle, Goldie, Omar and many others. Since 1993 Otchere's photographs have been exhibited and published worldwide, including on the covers of major international magazines such as *Urb*, *Lodown* and *Mixmag* and on the covers of some of rap music's seminal albums.

CLIVE PALMER is the voice of the 'Arsenal Supporting Supporters' campaign and a contributor to the *Arsenal Vision* podcast, where he shares his tactical acumen and understanding of the game.

TAYO POPOOLA is an award-winning audio producer, presenter, DJ and podcaster.

He makes documentaries for the BBC on subjects ranging from music to politics, and most recently, the narrative football podcast *GIANT* for Spotify. He also co-hosts the Arsenal podcast *The Tuesday Club*.

ANAMIK SAHA is a Professor of Race and Media in the School of Media and Communication at the University of Leeds. His research is on issues of race, culture and media, with a particular focus on creative and cultural industries and issues of 'diversity'. He is the author of *Race and the Cultural Industries* (2018) and *Race, Culture and Media* (2021). His research has featured across a range of media, including BBC Radio, the *Guardian*, *TES* and *New Statesman*.

SAMIR SINGH is Diversity and Inclusion Manager at Arsenal in the Community, the community delivery arm of Arsenal Football Club.

IAN WRIGHT is the former Arsenal and England striker who joined the club in 1991 from Crystal Palace for a club record fee of £2.5 million. He would score 185 goals in 288 appearances for the club. He received an MBE in 2000 and an OBE in 2023, and is an inductee of the Premier League Hall of Fame.

BARONESS LOLA YOUNG has been an independent crossbench member of the House of Lords since 2004 and has founded and co-chaired All Party Parliamentary Groups on Ethics and Sustainability in Fashion, Sport, Modern Slavery and Human Rights. Lola is now co-chair of the Foundation for Future London, Chancellor of the University of Nottingham and a non-executive director of Bloomsbury Publishing and Futerra.

PREFACE

Arsenal's connection to Black identity is special. Its multicultural fandom reflects the changing city that surrounds the club and the unique relationship it has developed with Black British culture. From decades of fielding iconic Black players on the pitch, through the storied and diverse histories of its terraces, Arsenal has emerged as a powerful symbol of what an organic and convivial multiculture can mean for society today.

We see it on the pitch, in the stands and across everyday social experiences: in the media, music, fashion and politics, but Arsenal's connection to Black cultural identity is rarely expressed in its totality. It has emerged collectively through the club's players, supporters, and their home in North London. From fielding some of the game's most successful and charismatic Black players in Ian Wright and Thierry Henry – their legends built on the legacies of forebears like Paul Davis, David Rocastle and Brendon Batson – to the club's community work in Islington and growing impact around the world.

Black Arsenal is an exploration, rather than a celebration, of Arsenal and Black culture. It does not claim that Arsenal has a model relationship to Black identity, nor is it an exhaustive list of all things Black and Arsenal. Instead, *Black Arsenal* has been an attempt to represent and reflect upon the breadth of a delicate and complex cultural experience that has come to play a role in defining both a football club and contemporary Black identity. As such, *Black Arsenal*'s many contributions show a culture of connections and contradictions. It is the unlikely story of how one of football's grandest establishments became a remarkable manifestation of what Stuart Hall described as London's 'unplanned multicultural drift'. For many contributors in this book, Arsenal has become a palatable symbol of national identity and belonging for Black Britons, offering a profound kinship in the absence of other social institutions, rooted in a shared sense of place and understanding. *Black Arsenal* also sees how this feeling has rippled outwards, attracting broader support from other communities and fans underrepresented in the stands, as well as those who live well beyond the boundaries of North London.

As a result, *Black Arsenal* doesn't offer a single account of Arsenal and Black culture. The project has drawn upon years of thinking and lived experience: presenting contributions and accounts that frequently converge and separate, ranging from first-hand accounts of terrace culture in the 1970s and 80s, to impressionistic responses on the cultural impact of the club's Black stars, to critical interventions on Arsenal's role within place and identity. It is these points of both connection and disconnection where *Black Arsenal* contributes to Britain's wider cultural histories; providing new records of experience and critical work that traces the evolution of Arsenal's Black identity over generations of supporters and players, alongside the shifting constructions and articulations of Blackness across contemporary culture.

In general the word 'Black' takes an initial capital where it refers to Black ethnic or cultural identity, as in the phrase 'Black Arsenal'. However, this style preference is a political symbol and as such we have not imposed it on our contributors, hence the occasional occurrence of lower-case 'black'.

1

'**THESE STREETS ARE OUR OWN . . .**'

Black Arsenal, the Highbury library and the Gooner culture of conviviality

PAUL GILROY

I

attended my first, unforgettable home game at Highbury during the autumn of 1966. I was ten years old. I had been invited to the match by two season ticket holders of long standing: Boris and Jonathan Prevezer. Hardly a classic introduction, but Arsenal defeated Sheffield United by two goals to one. I was nervous walking towards the ground, but the aggressive, noisy fallout of 'Keep Britain White' was nowhere to be heard that day. This was before Enoch Powell rewrote the basic rules of England's race-talk. Looking back, my fear that Saturday afternoon serves as a reminder that we must consider the social and cultural forces that comprise black Arsenal in their entanglement with Britain's politics of immigration and the popular racism it has incubated. This means there is a value in approaching the cultural history of black Arsenal as an expression of antipathy towards racism that can acquire wider significance, meaning and applicability. It might for example, provide an opportunity to rethink and adjust our ways of understanding the political place of spectator sport in general and football in particular. Can they be significant sources of common feeling that help different people discover dimensions of mutuality and sameness? These inquiries provide a way to focus attention on the ideas of belonging, togetherness and community presupposed by the game and its fandoms (online and offline). All those possibilities should be classified as responses to the hateful summoning of race and nation that took shape in the aftermath of Powell's notorious 'rivers of blood' speech. His apocalyptic racial populism cemented foundational links between the thematics of race and those of immigration, invasion and bloody warfare. The effects of that convergence refuse to die away. Aftershocks of Powell's intervention come and go, yet they have defined the distinctiveness of British racism for more than half a century.

To those who think his remarks should be left in the past, I say that recent events demand new reflections on that dismal pattern. Events at the 2021 European championship final at Wembley underlined that it is foolish to imagine the effects of racist ultranationalism and xenophobia to be entirely residual. It seems that many

← *Previous page:* Brendon Batson.

Black Arsenal

people in our country still find the idea of being simultaneously black and British an impossible, unthinkable combination. Comparable patterns can be discerned in France, Italy, Germany, Sweden and Denmark, other countries where the boundaries of racial division and racial hierarchy are mapped neatly onto the shrinking political contours of nationality and citizenship. Things are still volatile and nothing good can be taken for granted because race-talk seems always capable of returning us to the errors, mentalities and bad habits from which we thought we had been freed. That is its unique power.

That summer of 2021, Bukayo Saka, Arsenal's latest attacking talisman, found himself freshly cast in the old English drama that assumes black players not only to be 'bottlers' but considers them to be a gang of unwelcome intruders who lack the bulldog qualities required for authentic membership of the national community. Saka's missed penalty that meant England were defeated confirmed him in the blurry roles of unwanted alien, interloper and enemy within the gates.

It bears repetition that this hostile response to black settlement emerged in the post-war era of 'Keep Britain White'. It was refined in the 1970s by groups like the National Front and the British Movement, and has lingered on guiltily in public life, intermittently fading and then flickering back into flames that have been fanned by a surprising variety of political voices, left and right, respectable and otherwise.

Xenophobic hostility was a widespread response to the black settler presence long before 1990 when another senior Conservative politician, Norman Tebbit, made an infamous attempt to harness racist sentiment politically by introducing what he called the 'cricket test'. This was an assessment of the degree of patriotic loyalty being displayed by 'new commonwealth' citizen incomers and their superfluous and deviant descendants.

Elite sport was being annexed by what we now call the hostile environment. It was positioned in the core of a vicious argument about belonging and what it might mean to be accepted in Britain as a subject or citizen. When Tebbit made that cultural barrier appear, it was answered by manifesting black Britain's rightful claims to belong and elaborating our demands for recognition, making them appear both obvious and reasonable. Those responses were fostered in large measure by the things we have come to identify today with the idea of black Arsenal.

II

Appreciating the profound significance of this unacknowledged history requires us imaginatively to grasp a combination of things that aren't usually thought to be connectable, never mind them being actually connected. The central challenge resides in how we are to understand developments on the pitch in relation to things that happen elsewhere: in the grimy

'These streets are our own . . .'

streets around the stadium; in common spaces: workplaces, school playgrounds, hospitals, dancehalls, pubs, cafes and other locations where black Arsenal fandom took shape and eventually found what we can call its characteristic Gooner swagger.

Before we can proceed, it is important to grasp that the way blackness appears in elite sport has altered markedly since the period initiated by Jesse Owens' Coca-Cola-sponsored Olympic triumph in 1936. Further important changes had followed the historic Black Power demonstration on the winners' podium at the 1968 Olympics. Tommie Smith, John Carlos and Peter Norman overthrew the pretence that sport and politics could be compartmentalised.

Today, the difference race makes infuses blackness with desire as well as loathing, anxiety and resentment. Its metaphysical subordination to whiteness is not merely a matter of appearances, biology or natural hierarchy. It is the fragile outcome of prolonged cultural and psychological relationships: phobia, distaste and resentment as well as longing

↑ A far-right/anti-immigration National Front party campaign in Islington, London.
→ Fans outside Highbury in the late nineties.

and jealousy. Those generic racial categories Blackness and Whiteness originated in the United States but they have been exported worldwide. They circulate in digital forms across the algorithmic networks of timeline media and have, as a result, become more real to many of their addicted users than actual, localised manifestations of racial injustice and inequality. And yet, in this country, football in general and the Arsenal fandom in particular have been integral to how a bleak and sometimes violent situation was improved and how new varieties of conversation were created about the dangers represented by popular racism. Once other kinds of difference become less important than what team you support, people stop seeing racialised division and inequality as either fundamental or inevitable. The crippling structural effects of the racial order are brought within the sphere of things that can be changed if there is sufficient political will to make that happen.

III

When I was putting together *Black Britain: A Photographic History*, I felt that an image of Ian Wright, captured during a game against Blackburn Rovers, could be used to underline this very point. I wanted a dramatic image to suggest that Ian had become not only an important celebrity voice and authoritative presence in the mediascape, but a symbol. His airborne body encapsulated both black

Britain's sporting prowess and the wider issues involved in the integration and mainstreaming of black culture during the 1990s in the run-up to the founding of the Premier League. That story did not begin at Arsenal, but it was shaped and amplified there.

Like Paul Ince, Linford Christie, Denise Lewis, Hope Powell and many others who combined athleticism and sporting intelligence with a measure of distinctive style, Ian Wright provided a combative rebuke to the idea that racial difference alone disqualified black people from belonging to this country or from being recognised as fully British.

That generational cohort of athletes is remembered for doing a lot of work with the Union Jack. They prised the national flag out of the hands of the white supremacists and ultranationalists who had successfully monopolised its political use. The flag was passed to adoring crowds of spectators who were hungry for more sporting victory. Many wanted to live in a normal, modern country exhibiting a less toxic brand of patriotism that revealed it to be at ease with itself and its postimperial condition. The athletes' authentic attachment, first to the Union Jack and later to the flag of St George, was so widely recorded that we know that they, and the photographers who captured their patriotic antics, realised important demands for recognition and acceptance were being made. Norman Tebbit's cricket test was surpassed, first by the athletics test and then by the football test.

Over the years, comments on the steel, strength and intelligence of George Graham's midfield identified their successes as part of a revolutionary change in the way that black footballers were viewed. Again, this is a longer story than the worthy chapters which black Arsenal contributed to it; nonetheless, Graham's midfielders made a massive impact. They destroyed the old stereotypes: the mercurial winger gloved and shivering on a wintery, windswept touchline, the beefy, herculean number 9 more suited to the boxing ring, and the dogged monstrosity of always unintelligent defenders. Graham's team shattered the racist fantasies that had persisted in football for a generation and more. The historic synergy of Michael Thomas, Paul Davis and David Rocastle (who I often saw in the long-gone Barclays Bank at Finsbury Park) was pivotal in a footballing revolution as well as to the commercial and cultural developments that were underway. Those key players in the teams that brought the title to Highbury in 1989 and 1991 detonated the racist assumptions about black physiology and temperament that governed popular sport in Britain up to that point. Of course, the Arsenal players did not overthrow the ingrained racist mentality all by themselves. Many other contributions were involved at other clubs with different circumstances, traditions and catchments, but by accident and design Arsenal led the way.

Thanks to half a century of tireless work by black communities and other opponents of racism at every level in this society, the patterns of overt discrimination, once so visible and audible along racial lines, came to be considered backward or outmoded. They had been made to look uncool as well as out of place. As a result, we have fewer Alf Garnets to deal with. Bananas are seldom thrown. The diehards are still trolling uninhibitedly online, but the NF, the BNP and their various successors are no longer peddling propaganda outside the ground. Racists and homophobes rightly pay a high price for openly expressing their grotesque opinions in the securitised environment of the stadium.

These notable changes do not mean that the hateful feelings that underpin racist attitudes have evaporated. Beyond private prejudice and personal bias, the structural, inferential and hidden mechanisms of racism and racial hierarchy continue to operate tacitly in sport and beyond. They can be hard to perceive and even harder to change.

We are not letting the perpetrators and hate-mongers off the hook if we say that people can sometimes enact those scripts without fully comprehending what they are doing. The state of social media reveals examples of how popular racism has evolved, and also how it can operate as an unthinking, default setting. Trolling and online abuse show vividly that the battle against racism remains unfinished, but the enduring patterns suggest that dealing with it requires more than general, blanket bans that shut down the symptoms but do

'These streets are our own . . .'

↑ Patrick Vieira, Ian Wright and Paul Merson celebrate after Wright's goal during a match between Arsenal and Wimbledon in November 1996.

not attempt to deal with the underlying conditions that produce them.

IV

I've already said that historians of Arsenal football club and its fans can now draw upon a huge shelf of books. With very few exceptions, those volumes exclude anything interesting, insightful or controversial with regard to the issue of racism, either on or off the pitch. I know that the Highbury library is not the main focus of this discussion, but we should acknowledge that there are also institutional issues pending in the professional and business side of the club's transition which those texts document without necessarily meaning to do so. For example, how qualified black people, mostly former players, get into high-level coaching and management positions has been a vexed topic for ages. I recall, more than twenty years ago, reading a PhD thesis written by Dr Colin King at Goldsmiths College where, aside from his academic activity, he also coached one of the football teams. It was entitled 'Play the white man: the theatre of racialised performances and narratives in soccer coaching and management'. Among other factors, King had identified the significance of using alcohol as an important gate-keeping mechanism. Paul Davis's recent book (*Arsenal and After*, 2022) provides many more insights into how the uneven development of change and equity appear

when viewed from the inside.

There must be no room for complacency about these institutional problems, not least because English football was so comprehensively made over as a global phenomenon by the economic and cultural power of the Premier League. As a result, local and provincial figurations of racial hierarchy came into contact with the projection of racialised differences on a planetary scale. This is where the Global South touches the annals of black Arsenal and alters a history that had previously been most meaningful in the fading citadels of overdevelopment.

Moving between the local runnings of North London and the extended reach of the Arsenal brand, I want to sketch components of a framework that might help us to hold together the sometimes divergent elements of black Arsenal. This attempt is strongly a matter of generational perspective. For the record, I am the same age as Laurie Cunningham and Viv Anderson. I accept that the patterns I perceive are conditioned by the historic predicament of what Linton Kwesi Johnson calls the 'rebel generation'. Things may look very different to those of you who are younger than us.

This is a provisional list of the factors that I judge to have combined to produce the things we explain as black Arsenal. First and fundamentally, we have to reckon with the uniqueness of the club's home territory: the triangle of Hackney, Islington and Haringey that converge at Finsbury Park and radiate outwards in all directions. A patchwork of

'These streets are our own . . .'

parochial forces and cultures was composed by Arsenal's gradual shift away from being classified as an Irish club and into being something else. That change was symbolised for me by the sight of Charlie Nicholas, freshly imported from Celtic, driving his expensive convertible down Stroud Green Road en route to Highbury.

During the sixties and seventies this was an area where, in local pubs, you could still find Caribbean people clustered in one bar while the Irish customers were happily congregating in the other. Those subaltern worlds overlapped and leaked, but a degree of informal segregation is part of my memory of living in Finsbury Park in the seventies and eighties.

That this special area acquired a unique character, is conveyed by the fact that it was immortalised twice in popular music. First in reggae by a local group, Paget King's Tribesman, and a second time in soul/disco style by a Zimbabwean expatriate, Fungai Malianga. These were also the streets of Brother Herman, of the Harambee Housing Association, of pioneering Caribbean restaurants, of the world-historic New Beacon bookshop, of the two Black Houses on Holloway Road, of Campbell Bunk and Little Algeria, of the Rainbow Theatre and the Mosque on St Thomas's Road.

The campaigning group Inquest, which works with the families of people who have lost their lives following contact with the police and prison authorities is, like CND and the Campaign Against Arms Trade, headquartered in the neighbourhood.

The lone-wolf terrorist Darren Osborne came into the area from Wales purposely to kill a local resident, Makram Ali, in a spectacular act of political murder which he thought would initiate a race war. This is where we live.

Local schools fostered a rich footballing culture that displaced the love of cricket among the rising generation of wannabe athletes of Caribbean heritage. *Different Class*, Dermot Kavanagh's wonderful biography of Laurie Cunningham, charts that change and rightly credits him as an epochal presence establishing a stylish black masculinity on the pitch. He raised the stakes for black belonging even if the idea that blacks played 'flashy football' was cemented in the process.

Brendon Batson signed schoolboy forms in 1966 and became the first black player to represent Arsenal in the Football League. He was Pat Rice's understudy and would leave Highbury in 1974 having overlapped with Laurie who was released by the club aged sixteen after just two years on the books in 1972. Laurie's failure to make the grade was explained by a supposed lack of stamina. This sounds like a racial trope, but it was nonetheless sufficient to prove he was not the right material for a professional career in football. Viv Anderson came to the club in the 1980s after a distinguished career elsewhere.

In their different ways, these players provided the foundations for George Graham's 1989/91 team by forcing the judgement that black players could have both an 'engine' and a 'brain'. There is insufficient space here to list all the other black English players who contributed to this history. Their overall achievement was to liberate themselves so that black players would no longer be considered a decorative and temperamental presence in teams – figures who could be defeated by wet and icy winter weather. Against that assumption, they demonstrated that 'bottle' was not lacking just at the moment the Premier League was being formed.

This brief essay cannot do justice to the expansive role of Arsène Wenger in this story. He arrived with a philosophy, an approach that tempered the appeal of victory at any cost with a number of substantial aesthetic considerations. The ball became a 'sacred' object to which a host of stylish Black European footballers came to play tribute. Their input came to embody Wenger's particular sense that the game could be beautiful as well as efficiently played. In December of 1999, my daughter and I bumped into Thierry Henry in a North London phone shop where his acquisition of vernacular English was being fostered by the friendly employees – a number of young black Londoners of his own age.

Wenger systematically acquired African footballers: Lauren, Kanu, Eboué, Kolo Touré, Adebayor. He established links enabling the scouting and professional development of African footballing talent that must be understood as part of Europe's wider postcolonial settlement with the continent. Some stereotypes of African athletic physicality did persist, but that is a complicated subject that merits an extended treatment on another occasion. We arrive now in the era of social media fandom, which was a decisive factor in Wenger's departure. Initially, virtual fan networks had been parasitic on the club and its actual fandom, but gradually the online constituency became symbiotic with them. The most successful digital fandom, AFTV, was a hybrid that successfully monetised a fan culture that nobody had previously imagined to have any value. In the process, they extended and augmented the visibility of black Arsenal by featuring commentary delivered in the vernacular speech and characteristic cultural style of the area.

Their representation of black Arsenal cannot be severed from a process of cosmopolitanisation for which Wenger, still deeply influenced by his time in Japan, supplied the figurehead. Football is not only the world's most popular sport. It's also one of the most widely shared kinds of global culture. Now the iconic figure of Spike Lee turns up, properly dressed, at the Emirates. Connections were established that would flourish further during the Covid-19 pandemic and especially in the American summer of 2020. The Black Lives Matter movement created conditions in which Premier League footballers inspired by, and working in conjunction with, US athletes 'Taking the Knee', began to kneel in silent solidarity with the African American

'These streets are our own . . .'

freedom movement and its righteous pursuit of better justice than the malign versions that routinely arrive in blatantly colour-coded form. Discussing the issue of cosmopolitanisation would not be complete without acknowledgement of the Brazilian connection that has supplied yet another shade of black to the multiplicity that is black Arsenal. How these questions of racism have been played out in the context of the women's game is another matter that merits extended discussion. We eagerly await the autobiographies of Lianne Sanderson and Anita Asante.

Lastly, the analyst of black Arsenal must bear the club itself in mind. As you might expect any socially responsible business to do these days, the football club has embraced a corporate agenda of Equality, Diversity and Inclusivity that takes on anti-racist commitment publicly as one strand among several others: disability, inequality and social injustices arising from gender. We should acknowledge and celebrate Arsenal's success in building an exemplary community programme. Perhaps it could be even more visible locally, but its depth and evident ambition speak to the evolving needs and well-being (mental as well as the physical health) of North London's culturally mixed and partly postcolonial population. There has been notable involvement in education, with primary and secondary school pupils across Islington, Camden and Hackney as well as work with victims of torture, refugees, people with disabilities and so on.

V

The appetite for exploring the theme of black Arsenal can be interpreted as a positive development that encapsulates broader issues arising from the difficult history of black settlement and the continuing struggle against racism in Britain. Interest in black

↑ Arsène Wenger with the team during a training session in 2001.

Arsenal suggests that novel ways of looking at the history of Arsenal football club are being found. They include a new reckoning with its expanded fandom and with its unique location in North London, as well as its wider significance for this country, to say nothing of its increasing planetary reach.

Thinking about black Arsenal takes conversations immediately into an embattled world that is still struggling to come to terms with the difference that racism makes. Examining black Arsenal confirms that culture – even when allied with sporting business and media commerce – can hasten the processes that reduce or mediate racism's power to intimidate, mobilise and terrify. Progress in that effort is not guaranteed. However,

'These streets are our own . . .'

analysing black Arsenal historically as a social phenomenon helps to identify some positive developments. It can gauge how our nation is being changed so that, for the most part, overt expressions of racism now appear absurd or out of date.

That important shift has been the product of a long period of historical conflict over racism, nationalism and fascism. Those battles have swirled around the stadiums and sometimes entered them. Usually, the strife has occurred away from the pitch. We must therefore resist the temptation to invent player-centred accounts of it.

Professional footballers, managers and coaches have been publishing their autobiographical writing for years. Their books present personal stories from the angles required by merching, marketing, branding and self-promotion. Even, or perhaps especially, after they have retired, that group have acquired powerful channels through which they communicate their truths to an eager public. We, on the other hand, need to be clear that they represent only one (albeit important) element in the multidimensional history of black Arsenal that unfolded in the streets, leisure spaces and airwaves of North London. The big adjustments which are now pending, await the kind of liberating impact on the club's fan culture that followed transformative publications by the likes of Tom Watt and Nick Hornby thirty-plus years ago.

Since then, Arsenal Football Club has transitioned into the symbol of diversity and plurality. But that change was not planned or organised from the boardroom. Now, at the very peak of equality and diversity management, fans are not acquainted with what the club's board, owners and managers think about that wholly unexpected development. Everything the black Arsenal initiative identifies and celebrates as precious has been dwelling quietly and symbiotically in the club's shadow for several decades. It was never amenable to being orchestrated or dictated downwards from on high. Instead, it has been an organic and often an unruly phenomenon. It expanded in its own unsteady tempo and evolved in harmony with the protean character of class and culture in North London's irreversible creolisation. On those streets, open expressions of hatred and contempt for black people are unacceptable. What counts as mere banter or righteous free speech in other locations, national and international, is not spoken out loud around here.

That fragile triumph must be unpacked very carefully. In doing so, 'Class' and 'Culture' must remain key concepts. They are not fixed or frozen. They encompass the impact of racial hierarchy and gendered inequality and help us to understand why the topic of black Arsenal has come to matter beyond the big shadow cast by the football club. If we take black Arsenal seriously, we begin to glimpse the possibility that the difficult lessons learned locally might be transposable on to bigger scales. If, for example, our divided country could opt, self-consciously, to embrace the possibility of an inevitably plural future – which has become the starting point for understanding life around here – racism might become completely unacceptable.

This essay was finished on the twenty-first anniversary of Arsenal fielding nine black outfield players in the famous defeat of David O'Leary's Leeds team in September 2002. The most interesting version of the Leeds story would not omit the extra significance that the game acquired because it followed so closely on the heels of the trial of Lee Bowyer and Jonathan Woodgate for a violent assault on a student, Sarfraz Najeib. Bowyer was later acquitted while Woodgate was convicted of affray, and you may remember that their teammate Michael Duberry was also found not guilty of perverting the course of justice.

The cultural transformation that was underway nurtured the idea of Black Arsenal. It became clearer to me watching that contest at three thousand miles distance, but it was first explained to me one afternoon in the mid-1990s when, standing outside Finsbury Park station, I bumped into Ben Bousquet, a season-ticket-holding, Arsenal-loving human rights activist who was making his way to the match.

I had been living in the US during the previous season and was a little bit out of touch. Ben tutored me astutely about the changes he had observed in the Highbury crowd. The club, he argued, was steadily becoming recognisable as a hospitable place for a rising number of black fans.

The process that began then, was not, as some unsympathetic commentators have claimed, a matter of importing essentially North American concern with the effects of racial inequality into British political life and culture where it did not belong. I prefer to see those changes as a slow process of coming to terms with the ways that racialised inequality, injustice and violence have for far too long impacted negatively upon the lives of our city and our polity. Policing is just one part of this. After all, football people know exactly how arbitrary and violent policing can get.

Facing up to these uncomfortable facts of British political life, means accepting that dealing with racism must involve both policies and politics – even though we know they won't be enough to generate the necessary cultural, psychological and emotional transformation.

During the last few years, thanks to the impact of the pandemic, some aspects of racialised inequality and injustice have become easier to understand and to condemn explicitly. For example, people were shocked when they started to grasp that our shared human vulnerability to the Covid virus was being overlaid and intensified by social and economic factors: who could work from home, who was working on the frontline and so on.

Our understanding of both class and culture has been stretched by the transformation of media technology and communication. Blackness has unexpectedly acquired a high commercial value in the mainstream. It has become possible to be a black celebrity and a black winner.

'These streets are our own . . .'

Nobody wants to be seen as a loser. Britain's black communities have been changing too. People of Caribbean descent are no longer the majority. People of direct African heritage do not share a single culture or faith. They do not always feel at home with a 1970s idea of common blackness as a public or political identity. Many prefer to present themselves in national terms as Ghanaian, Nigerian, Somali, Senegalese or South African alongside their attachments to Britain, or to affiliate with the ethnic and cultural groups of their ancestors and kin: Yoruba, Igbo, Twi.

At the same time, many anxious, insecure and fearful people try to answer the effects of austerity, impoverishment, economic crisis and political instability by returning to the certainties that racialised identity provides, seeking in that fortification ways of protecting, anchoring and orienting themselves. 'Whiteness' then composes a kind of 'tribal' association. In those circumstances, local feelings and the common culture of football fandom offer alternatives to the emotional appeal of nationalistic, racist and openly xenophobic political movements.

Of course, it may be tempting to imagine that the racial order of things has not changed in Britain's last fifty years. But that verdict is wrong. If we can cultivate the ability to think historically and politically about sporting spectatorship, we will see how things have altered over time. Contemporary arrangements might then be recognisable as a combination comprising elements that are both better and worse than the things we know from the past.

That degree of complexity requires facing up to the evolving mood of our country, confronting its class and gender inequalities, its persistent hierarchies, and behind them all, its blocked sense of who belongs here and who should be excluded from entry. All of these judgements are bound up with the way that people understand the difference that what they call 'race' does or doesn't make.

Most of the time when the idea of 'race' is invoked, users are referring to the effects of racism – on opportunity, access and economic and material well-being. Perhaps more attractive than the hard work of facing up to the difference racism still makes, is the welcome chance to enjoy black sporting excellence and style. There are things to learn from that history that extend outside AFC into people's sense of themselves, their imaginations, identities and hopes.

Of necessity, the club will always place the emphasis on looking forward: to the next game, to the rest of the season. But to make sense of Black Arsenal *we* need to combine that orientation with other perspectives. We respect the club's official history, but that respectable account has to be contextualised so that other sets of stories can be heard in a very crowded and contested media environment. They can be noisy comments shouted from the sidelines or whole narratives: life stories or partial observations delivered from angles that the club has not picked up on or been able to control. As we get into the period dominated by social media, AFC has had to compete with those commentaries in order to fix the meaning and maximise the value of its brand.

Blackness gets transmitted and cited in that circuitry, but it is not the same blackness that is manifested in the everyday cityscapes of North London, where AFTV and its various offshoots and imitators have, as I said, successfully appropriated the fan voice. The discrepant history that results from this admixture is not always heroic. It does have heroes, but they do not necessarily fit into the pantheon of Arsenal legends – either on the pitch or off.

It is easy to parrot the line that the history we need must be diverse and inclusive. Those commitments are necessary, but I will conclude by saying that they will not be enough to make sense of Black Arsenal. There is a deeper kind of kinship at stake in these unbounded commitments than locating 'people who look like you' in the club's official dreamscape, or placing an abstract commitment to multiculture at the core of the football club's professed values. Those things are necessary but they aren't sufficient. The changes that are now needed can be appreciated best when we are alert to all the layers involved – community, borough, city, region, nation and world – when we note that though they can align nicely, they may also generate conflict.

It is seldom acknowledged that sport in general and football in particular can play a role in mediating the order of human difference, illuminating which differences might be important enough to actually matter and which ones should be dismissed as minor or insignificant.

The common life of the club's fandom uncovers shared passions and fosters convergences. I end with the thought that people who live as though they are different, may actually *become* more alike when their common love of a game, a club, a team and a neighbourhood get revealed to each other, and, of course, to the whole world. ■

'These streets are our own . . .'

2

DEFINING BLACK ARSENAL

Television, national identity and
Black cultural recognition

CLIVE CHIJIOKE NWONKA

In tracing the origins of Black Arsenal as a social phenomenon, a surprisingly good place to start is with the career of a legend who never played for them. The iconography of John Barnes throughout the late 1980s had a specific resonance that, for Britain's young Black community at the time, provided an easily understandable point of racial recognition. John Barnes, who would win the PFA Footballer of the Year and Football Writers Player of the Year awards in 1988, had for many by this point been recognised as one of the best players in Europe, a visibility that brought with it the inevitable burden of racism. One photograph taken during an infamous game against Everton at Goodison Park in 1988 has become a continually referenced signpost for the racism that plagued British football in the 1980s. It sees Barnes responding to a banana thrown at him by Everton fans, who had become notorious for chanting 'Everton are white' in response to their local rivals' decision to defile the racial purity of the city's two top-flight clubs by signing Barnes in 1987. The photograph captures Barnes in full technical excellence as he nonchalantly backheels the banana onto the sideline of the pitch, a motion as synonymous with Barnes the supremely skilled footballer as the fruit was with the anti-Blackness that greeted Black footballers as they entered the football field. What interests me here is the impact of the emergence and ascent of John Barnes, in all his demonstrable sporting excellence and cultural respectability. Barnes was able to accrue a tremendous degree of Black identification and recognition, where both the Black player and the Black community are unified within English society and English football, as a space of Black alterity, invisibility and absence. In other words, the depth of Black representational identification always emerges from a place of Black representational lack.

I want to be clear that my claim that Black Arsenal is a distinctive meeting point between Black cultural memory and cultural politics of Black recognition is in no way to neglect other clubs who established, consciously or by chance, some kind of critical mass of Black players in the period or prior. We find a primary example in the 'three degrees' of Cyrille Regis, Laurie Cunningham and Brendon Batson, whose

← *Previous page:* Michael Thomas scores against Liverpool at Anfield in the final match of the 1988–89 season.

pioneering exploits and displays of Black resistance allowed West Bromwich Albion to be the first club to field three Black players in 1978. There is the Luton Town side of the mid-1980s of Mark and Brian Stein, Ricky Hill, Marvin Johnson, Emeka Nwajiobi and Mitchell Thomas, who would all become synonymous with the club's most notable moment in their League Cup final win – ironically, over Arsenal – in 1988. And by the end of the decade, Crystal Palace, QPR, Wimbledon and others would all register some kind of Black presence, although this is not to claim that this presence may not have been conditioned by racism, either

on the very terraces where they played in front of home and opposing fans, nor within the changing rooms, training pitches and organisational spaces.

So what is so particular about Arsenal and the association with Blackness? One of the ways we can think about this is through the experience of Black sporting success, and the capturing of this triumph within the medium of popular culture. It is the way in which, during the late 1980s to early 90s, a new phase of Black cultural politics and multiculture, branding and promotional culture, and the spectacle of live football combined to present a moment of Black

↑ John Barnes backheels a banana thrown onto the pitch by a racist section of the crowd during a match against Everton at Goodison Park, 1988.

Defining Black Arsenal

iconography and identification that became meaningful. I believe a defining moment is found in the game between Liverpool and Arsenal on 26 May 1989 at Anfield. This was to be the climax of the English First Division campaign of 1988–89 in which the two top teams would play each other, and Arsenal needed, and would win by, two clear goals to claim the league title for the first time in eighteen years. The game, played on a Friday evening, was watched by 12 million people on LWT's *The Match* live football programme. What is located in this game and its climax, which became central to the idea of Black Arsenal as born of a (tele) visual culture, is the way that the game can be understood not simply as a sporting spectacle, but as mass cultural theatre, and in this idea we find that, at least for myself, the central protagonists in the key moments in this theatre were Black. My argument here is that Black cultural recognition becomes particularly receptive to moments of dramatic action, accentuated by the spectacularising nature of live, televised sport.

Firstly, there is the iconic clenching of the fist by David Rocastle, having won the free kick that would lead to Arsenal's first goal. Secondly, there is John Barnes being dispossessed of the ball that would lead directly to Arsenal's second goal. And then finally, Michael Thomas's goal seconds later and notable celebration as the game's dramatic climax. What was being captured in the frames of mass television was the

↑ Liverpool v Arsenal, Anfield, 26 May 1989.

Black Arsenal

iconic image of Black people in the context of the nation. Television, so complicit in the racist characterisation, the historical reduction and erasure of Black people, was here a key to the heightening of Black Britishness as a visible presence within popular culture.

We can draw on a number of examples of how this new presence of Black identity was being felt beyond the sporting arena. Soul II Soul's landmark album *Club Classics* can be understood as the embodiment of a new vista of the cohesiveness of the terms Black *and* British, where our entry into the mainstream of British culture carried with it all the representational binds made when seeing ourselves reflected back to us on screen and throughout cultural production.

For many, the renaissance of English football in the early 1990s as a commercially lucrative *product* can be attributed to Italia 90, specifically the romance of the England v Germany World Cup semi-final that would attract a television audience of 25 million. However, the Liverpool v Arsenal league game a year before, with the capturing of its dramatic action, became the template for domestic football to be strategically packaged, placed and scheduled as compelling drama to its audience. This being so, the convergences between Black sporting iconography, popular culture and national identity are encapsulated in John Barnes's contribution to the New Order track 'World in Motion', which would come to acquire a significance far beyond its

Defining Black Arsenal

primary purpose as the official England 1990 World Cup song. Barnes's rapped line of 'I'm the England man' was not simply a claim to a previously denied nationality (Englishness) through the sporting excellence achieved by representing England, but through an association with a predominantly white English rave culture.

The creation of a breakaway English 'super league' was a threat that hovered over English football from the mid-1980s, motivated in part by the sense of urgency among elite clubs who faced both a social and economic crisis through hooliganism, racism, infrastructural problems, safety issues and decrepit stadiums. This all combined with the denigration of the national game by Thatcherism, which saw the terrain of football as a simple relocation of a hostile mainstream politics governed by social class. However, the concept of a super league was primarily motivated by commercialism, and what clubs perceived as the disproportionality of television revenue that had been equally dispersed among the Football League's ninety-two professional clubs across four divisions, despite the pre-eminence of elite top-flight clubs as English football's main attraction for audiences and sponsorship. The controversial reinvention of the English first division specifically, and the consequent reconfiguration of the entire English Football League from August 1992, was also to draw to a close an egalitarianism that had characterised the Football League from its inception, where each member was placed within a highly democratic

voting structure and an equal share of the revenue gained from broadcasters for regular live coverage of first division games from the early 1980s. In 1983, the terrestrial broadcasters paid just £5.2 million in a contractual agreement in which the Football League agreed to a trial broadcast of live games; five years later ITV would pay £44 million for the exclusive live rights to first division games, a deal that allowed the clubs to achieve economic autonomy by permitting them to retain sponsorship revenues.

The 1988 TV deal was also significant given the recommendations of the Taylor Report into the Hillsborough Disaster of April 1989, the most tangible of which was the requirement for all first and second division clubs to convert to all-seater stadiums by the mid-1990s. The hyper-commercialisation of English football that would motivate the formation of the FA Premier League in 1992 created a cascading effect across British culture. We can see this in the post-Italia 90 repopularising of football, notably in Channel 4's now cult coverage of Italy's top league Serie A through their iconic *Football Italia* programme, which the channel acquired in part in response to the sudden disappearance of terrestrial broadcasts for the nation's leading domestic league games. In securing the new Premier League's television rights, British Sky Broadcasting (BSkyB) dismantled the established duopoly of ITV/BBC and also attended to the historical paucity of live football on terrestrial television. The groundwork for Sky Sports obtaining the exclusive television rights for the new league's live matches had been laid as early as 1988 and was in many ways instigated by LWT's CEO Greg Dyke, who had been the primary factor in the new league's elitism, having identified the then-Barclays first division's reigning champions, Liverpool, Arsenal, Manchester United, Tottenham and Everton, as the league's 'big five'. They were identified not on strict terms of success (allowing for anomalies like Coventry City's FA Cup victory over Tottenham in 1987 and the League Cup triumphs for Luton Town and Nottingham Forest in 1989 and 1990). Instead, the big five were distinguished by their commercial power, financial potential and a unified modernist vision for English football that was expressed among its chairmen. This demanded an unprecedented emphasis on television and spectatorship.

The imperative to concentrate the financial potential of live televised football was not lost on Greg Dyke. Despite later agreeing to a television rights package that would include all ninety-two league clubs, Dyke's deal would also strategically privilege the leading clubs through the preferred live broadcasting of their fixtures, bringing them an increased, guaranteed fixed income stream through sponsorship, appearance fees and advertising. This agreement, which represented a 350 per cent revenue increase for the league's leading clubs and cemented the uneven redistribution of television revenue to the big five, became

the ideological impetus, structural basis and economic model for the emergence of the FA Premier League.

In all these negotiations Arsenal chairman David Dein played a key role. The initial plans for the breakaway league in the late 1980s had been orchestrated by Dein using his position on the board of the Football League, which allowed him to argue for preferential treatment for the league's superpowers, such as increased voting powers and television revenues for the leading five clubs. This helped them

↑ John Barnes and Bernard Sumner of New Order recording England's 1990 World Cup song 'World in Motion'.

Defining Black Arsenal

IT'S A WHOLE NEW BALL GAME.

F.A. PREMIER LEAGUE FOOTBALL. SKY SPORTS. LIVE ONLY ON SKY SPORTS.

achieve economic independence from the football league in the years leading up to the formation of the Premier League.

Strangely enough, BSkyB reconfigured English football as a mass cultural product by first withholding it as an exclusive televisual experience, one in which Premier League games could only be watched live on the subscription satellite channel, would equally demand a new reliance on promotional culture. The league's advertising campaign was aptly soundtracked to Simple Minds' 'Alive and Kicking': a representative player from each

of the founding twenty-two teams posed in a team photo that framed the clubs in a novel collective, just like the club chairmen who had devised it, and presented the new FA Premier League as an outcome of suppressed club rivalries that would align in a shared endeavour to elevate English football through a cultural reformation. Thus, when Sky's iconic promotional campaign for the Premier League's first season in 1992 promised a 'Whole New Ball Game', this was not simply the cosmic economic expansion of the national game through the £304 million capture of the

↑ 'A Whole New Ball Game': Sky Sports' Premier League launch in 1992. The launch not only heralded the economic expansion of the national game, but also a new era of hyper-visible Black sporting stardom.

old first division's live TV rights. It also set the economic, social, cultural and industrial conditions for the marketisation of both club and player, and with them, the emergence of a new, hyper-visible Black sporting stardom.

It might seem paradoxical to think of the development of the concept of Black Arsenal through the lens of the establishment of the Premier League. There are of course many valid criticisms that have been levelled at elite football in England, such as the pricing out of working-class supporters, the increasing gulf between club, local cultural and social identities, and the hyper-capitalism that has now permeated every sphere of global professional football. A point of differentiation and change, beyond both the FA Premier League's emphasis on club merchandise and the introduction of squad numbers and players' names on shirts, was also achieved by Sky Sports' coverage of the league through its *Super Sunday* and *Monday Night Football* programmes, which undoubtedly brought the nation into a multi-dimensional and multi-modal televisual experience in marked contrast to the previous singularity of football coverage on ITV. However, and crucial to our understanding of both the beginnings and vessels of Black Arsenal, English football and its associated marketing culture would pursue the promotion of the inaugural FA Premier League season without John Barnes as its centrifugal force. English football had entered the new decade where Barnes, whose presence filled the cultural void

created by Paul Gascoigne's post-Italia 90 move to Lazio, remained firmly placed as the first division's most valuable commodity. Barnes was afforded such a status through being a culturally transcendental figure within a lucrative promotional culture that is identified, for example, in his appearances in the now famous Lucozade Sport television advertisements. Here, and in so many other examples, Barnes provided the respectable imagery to the still socially denigrated cultures of English football as a reliable point of Black cultural identification and success built upon Liverpool's two league titles in 1988 and 1990.

If the position of John Barnes as the league's most influential player was in little doubt by the end of the 1991–92 season, the events of June 1992 would dramatically alter his position as the league's most marketable commodity. During the England v Finland friendly, the final England warm-up game before that summer's Euro 1992 tournament in Sweden, Barnes, who had struggled with injury in the latter part of the season, would sustain a ruptured Achilles tendon that would leave him unable to play for six months. Despite being in England colours in Helsinki, the image of a prone Barnes in many ways captures both Barnes and Liverpool at a shared point of decline. Just as the period had witnessed Liverpool's dominance over English football enter a gradual but no less dramatic end, with the club being eclipsed at various points by Arsenal, Leeds United and finally Manchester United, the loss of the physical

Defining Black Arsenal

dynamism and speed that had characterised Barnes at his most exciting and impactful rendered him absent at the very point of the seismic cultural change embodied in the Premier League's birth and the cultural resonance of the late 1980s and early 90s that he had accrued.

On his return from injury Barnes was devoid of all that had originally marked him as a player of both footballing and marketable distinction. The result was that the commercial viability and *visibility* of his version of Black Britishness, like the old first division football from which he had come to prominence, now appeared to belong to a different sporting, cultural and visual realm. What we see here is a transition, in my own existence, from John Barnes as the locus of Black masculine identification

that's marked by the converging of both emergence and loss. The severe physical injury that he sustained just prior to the opening of the Premier League would deny Barnes his place as the central figure of the new branded league. But it also allowed for the entry of a more dynamic and culturally segmented mode of advertising and brand culture attuned to the economic demands of the national game and with this, the marketisation of racial and cultural difference.

The idea of Black Arsenal as the contingent outcome of the conjuncture, here meaning the point at which different cultural and social trends engage in unprecedented ways and come to reconfigure social life, becomes important, and is experienced through the centrality

↑ John Barnes in television advert for Lucozade Sport in 1992, a time of transformation in the branding of Black footballers in Britain.

of Black brand culture to within English football most observed in Nike's 'Can I Kick It?' advertising campaign. For key to the agenda of presenting football as a global, transnational language is Ian Wright, the Black striker bought by Arsenal from Crystal Palace in September 1991, who becomes the ad's focal point. It uses footage from a game against Southampton at Highbury from the previous season, interspersed with images of grassroots football games among young Black children within Africa, a series of juxtapositions suggesting the global permeation of not just Wright as Arsenal's number 8, but the genesis of a new cultural identity forged in the seemingly natural union between Black player, Black music, Black people and football culture, with Nike at its centre. Released in October 1992, just two months after the start of the inaugural FA Premier League season, the TV commercial for Nike was a huge success, at a time when the UK football apparel market was dominated by Adidas and Umbro. We of course can afford to be both *scrutinising* about the orchestrating of Blackness by branded culture, while equally being *accepting* of the inevitable Black cultural associations and identifications to be drawn through the soundtrack, 'Can I Kick It?',

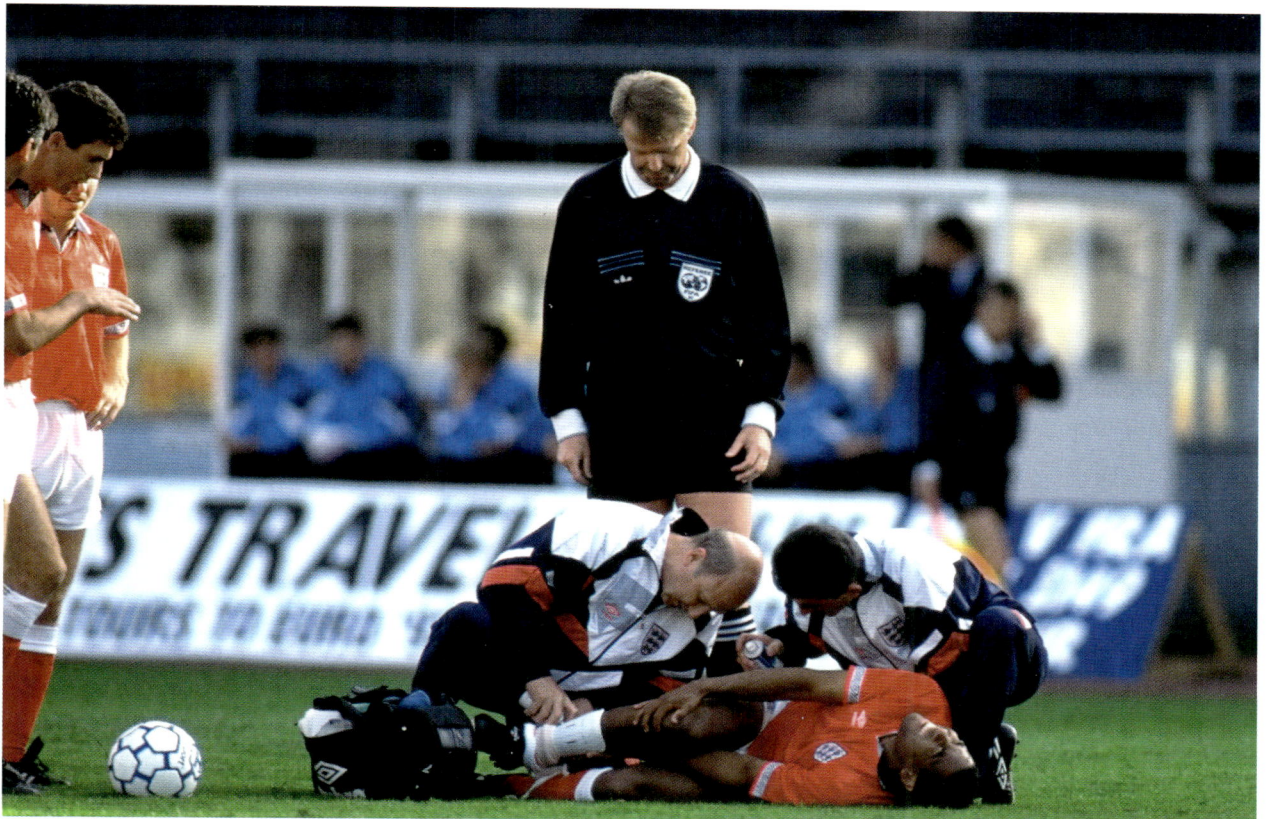

↑ Barnes lying injured during a friendly against Finland in 1992.

Defining Black Arsenal

by A Tribe Called Quest, and the equally powerful image of Ian Wright as the avatar of a Black urban masculinity and arguably, the new Premier League's most distinctive and visible cultural commodity.

What I am describing is a transition in the definition and focal point of Black footballing masculinity in the shift to a branded Black urban multiculture that accompanied the shift in British football culture. Yet the recognisability and validity of this working-class Black masculine identity was not secured solely by the singular presence of Ian Wright. It also referred to how we consumed football as a televisual experience and how the increased marketisation of football aided by the Premier League that Arsenal's brilliant yellow away shirt as a fashion subculture found a connection with emergent forms of Black urban multiculture. And we find the subtle and overt presence of all that Wright embodied in Black British music subcultures and the rise of jungle music as an instinctive Black cultural experience. In the video for the 1994 jungle track 'Incredible' by General Levy and M-Beat, the image of a young Black boy dancing while wearing the Arsenal shirt cements the idea of jungle music as an arena where Blackness as urban multiculture, and Arsenal, are further unified as synonymous concepts, but equally, as experiences made relevant and recognisable through the power of advertising. For me, the circulated image and sounds of Ian Wright, either literal, symbolic or through a cultural proxy, became the means by which

↑ 'Incredible'.

I was able to find an organic sameness between Black London and Arsenal, particularly as an expression of a multiracial, convivial culture, and within the embrace between Black music as just one of many Black cultural forms, and Black British identity as a mass promotional spectacle.

However, this is an extremely delicate and valuable *political* experience that is being tapped into by branded and commercial culture. How can Black Arsenal as an everyday Blackness and multiculture avoid being pulled into the well-intended but ultimately extractive and accumulative logic of capitalism? In October 2022, I gave a talk on this subject for some of the Arsenal club staff. One of the questions I was asked was whether Arsenal recognised this connection between the club and Blackness, and if so, how could the club best demonstrate that? It's a question that has stayed with me since then, and I believe one answer could be accommodating the identification of Black Arsenal in the personal rather than the popular, a move from the spectacular and celebratory to the unspectacular; by this, I mean understanding the expressions of Black Arsenal as a kind of *inexpression*, something that does not always require the grand demonstrations of branded content.

In making the above argument, I'm proposing that we imagine a more inexpressive mode of Black Arsenal, that being as a mode of Black cultural memory. The two illustrative examples I would like to conclude with bring us to 1993, not only because this was a period where the momentum of Black Britishness as a cohesive identity was to be contested by the political legitimisation of racism, most evident in the by-election win for the BNP in an East London council ward that September, but also because, at the personal level, there was a powerful association between Arsenal, television as a social practice, and the iconographies of Black identity.

I grew up in St Raphael's, Brent, the area of north-west London that was engulfed by the North Circular, where team coaches would often attempt to negotiate the sharp U-turn in order to shortcut through the estate towards Wembley. This allowed for a moment where those who noticed could observe the phenomenon of a team bus passing through the humdrum streets of our inner-city existence. The 1993 FA Cup final between Arsenal and Sheffield Wednesday was a particular point of cultural memory and reference. I had spent that Saturday morning at Latti and Son, an Afro Caribbean barber shop on the Harrow Road that became the site for the adolescent encounters with numerous modes of Black urban masculinity. Latti and Son was an arena of cross-generational 'Black talk', and to partake in Black talk was also inevitably to be involved in discussions of Arsenal and its Black icons, who through the imaginaries and optics of youth, displayed no significant difference or departure from the Black men who populated both the barber shop and its immediate Black environments.

Defining Black Arsenal

I would return home to be engrossed in the FA Cup coverage on the BBC that for children of the 1990s was a four-hour continuous televisual extravaganza in which the audience was given a certain proximity to both teams and their players. In a particular segment of the BBC's FA Cup *Grandstand*, Ian Wright and Kevin Campbell, a Black forward from Brixton, South London, who had emerged from the Arsenal youth team in the early 1990s to establish himself as Wright's understudy, are filmed at the breakfast table among the rest of the Arsenal squad. At one point Campbell points to Ian Wright and warns him that he is due a haircut that morning. Black hair, so central in Black people's expressions of culture and identity and resultantly, our experiences of racism, othering, and alterity, also functions as a conduit of Black commonality through which the young come into the powerful processes of Black

↑ Kevin Campbell's 1993 FA Cup final haircut.

identification, development, community and pride, developed primarily within the physical and cultural spaces of the Black barbershop. Thus, there was always a sense of cultural recognition to be enjoyed in even the most fleeting images and representations of the Black barbers and Afro hair care as a shared Black cultural practice that remained so obscure within the frames of mainstream television. Campbell is later filmed in his hotel bedroom with his back to the camera as he sits, Black barber over him and Ian Wright in tow, while he has his haircut in preparation for the final. He turns to the camera to reveal the finished fade, with all its recognisable designs, and BBC reporter Barry Davies comments on the moment as a departure from what he describes as the 'short back and sides brigade' of a previous, white, FA Cup final generation. This in turn draws our attention and an inadvertent significance to a moment of cultural transition in the traditions of not just the Cup final, but its very players and their appearance. The politics of Black recognition here is how the replication of the everyday and the commonplace experiences of Black masculine identity become accentuated by the power of television as a medium where cultural identities are shaped, negotiated, and reflected back to us.

Much of what I argue informs Black Arsenal as a concept and experience is built up by the interconnected and relevant fragments of Black cultural memory. That year's FA Cup final would occur less than a month after the racist murder of eighteen-

Black Arsenal

year-old Stephen Lawrence in Eltham on the evening of 22 April. And for those who are able and willing to recall, Stephen's image was a continuous televisual and media image across those weeks and months. So, my own encounters with the Black image in the week leading up to the game were shared between the images of Ian Wright as Arsenal's focal point, and the image of Stephen. I am unsure if Stephen was part of South East London's Black Arsenal supporters, and despite the Lawrence household being located between the borough of Greenwich's Plumstead and Woolwich districts, which in turn enjoy a close proximity to Charlton Athletic's home at The Valley, it may be that, just as the very idea of Black Arsenal is constructed upon geographic locality, it does not determine club allegiance. Mainstream television made the seemingly disconnected images of Stephen Lawrence and Arsenal's Black players at a high point of racial debate, Black mourning and visibility, both unified and significant, at least for myself.

I accept that Black Arsenal is a concept that may evolve from its original meanings as explored here. This is both inevitable and, in many respects, should be the desire, for the idea of Black Arsenal implies experiences that begin from the personal and expand to the communal within and through the physical spaces and social interactions where common points of identification and recognition can be acknowledged and developed. This is now identified beyond immediate sporting spectacles, and is found in subcultural practices, fashion, music

and the everyday conviviality that attempt to make insignificant the significance of racial difference. We are already seeing the opening fissures of the expansiveness of the term in brand culture's interest in the mass reproduction of the close interiority of Black people's cultural practices, recognition and representation. Further, with this in mind, much of what has and will come to be captured under the auspices of Black Arsenal serves as a commercial pseudonym for what is already in cultural circulation in the production and distribution of online content, which inevitably carries with it the realisation that the idea of a Black Arsenal will function as an easy and culturally validating descriptor for the most cursory applications and associations with Black identity.

History reminds us how Black experiences are continuously extracted and converted

↑ Stephen Lawrence.

Defining Black Arsenal

into commercial brands, devoid of all that originally made such experiences and vernacular practices powerful sites of Black cultural significance. However, these comments display no interest in establishing a rigid concept of Black Arsenal in an attempt to assert a commanding and permanent definition of what this is and how it should be expressed, nor to create a hierarchy of value or the privileging of one manifestation of the relationship between the club and Black identity as the true experience for another. The very beauty of Black Arsenal as a potential and expanding occurrence is what is distinctive and particular to our own interpretations, internal and external experiences, which in some ways pushes back against the homogenising of Black thought or feeling, be this directed towards Arsenal or any other iteration of fandom, allegiance or belonging. However, branding and its logic of common Black experience and sameness will always be in the forefront of our minds when negotiating the flows of modernity and the new youth subcultural practices that are so natively versed in digital culture. And the expansivity of the concept may require us to provide continued perspectives on what the role is of Arsenal Football Club as a global sporting and cultural institution in the recognition of Black identity and crucially, their own forms of expression, although Blackness, an already heavily contested term, should and will remain the constant throughout such thinking.

Black Arsenal at its very genesis is found initially in the personal and the internal, and for myself, in the Cup final replay against Sheffield Wednesday that evening. For perhaps what remains as the essence of Black Arsenal is what remains when we are able to strip its more conscious and elaborate iterations of all its excess, one that presents Black Arsenal as Black cultural memory, a Black cultural value and recognition that is not necessarily identified in the actual outcome of the game (which Arsenal would of course win in extra time) but by the geographic, audial and televisual proximity to an unfolding drama and spectacle that has both national and international significance. It returns us back to the images of Ian Wright and Kevin Campbell. For many watching the game that evening either within Wembley or through the medium of television and in the official reports, narratives and imageries of the FA Cup, the defining moment of the final is somewhat owned by the defender Andy Linighan, who would go on to score the decisive goal in the closing moments of the game. However, there is an additional, perhaps unrecognised defining moment made so by the *combinational* experience of Black Arsenal that is found, like so much of what is captured in the ideas and experiences of Black Arsenal, in the direct actions of Ian Wright.

On the previous Saturday, having scored Arsenal's opening goal at Wembley, Wright would run to the corner of the field and be engulfed by teammates Ray Parlour and Jon Jensen, with Wright made barely visible to the camera within their close embrace. On this occasion however, while Wright's

↗ Ian Wright celebrates after scoring against Sheffield Wednesday in the 1993 FA Cup final. The match finished 1–1 and was replayed five days later.
→ Ian Wright scoring again in the FA Cup final replay.

Defining Black Arsenal

opening goal would again be celebrated at the corner of the Wembley field, arriving into the screen's negative space is the figure of Kevin Campbell, who would be the first to reach Wright in celebration. The image of Campbell holding Ian Wright aloft, as both men scream, not to the crowd but so it appeared to each other, is so laden with subjectivities, that we are unable to decipher what emotions are behind the expressions, what emotions are being projected back to the audience, or crucially, how these emotions engage with and latch onto other experiences and emotions felt by those watching through the medium of television.

The fleeting image of two Black men, Black Arsenal men, within a heightened moment of public Black mourning is meaningful here, not in countering anti-racist outrage with sporting excellence or replacing Black trauma with celebration, but demonstrating how, at the level of the personal, Black and Arsenal become unified within a broader moment and structure of feeling, where race, racism, Blackness and visibility combine to produce an experience of cultural recognition. ◼

↑ Ian Wright following the first goal of the 1993 FA Cup final replay.
→ Kevin Campbell and Ian Wright celebrating at Wembley.

3

'WHERE ARE MY BROTHERS?'

AMY LAWRENCE

January 1989. Goodison Park. Upper Tier of the away end. There was a sense of fury and contempt in the chants of 'Arsenal! Arsenal! Arsenal!' that were being screamed in collective retaliation against the home supporters and their repulsive abuse of the fine players running the show in Arsenal's midfield. David Rocastle, Michael Thomas and Paul Davis were integral parts of Arsenal's pride. The word shock does not begin to express the emotion when some of Everton's fans – it sounded like a strong majority – began to chant something that does not easily bear writing down. 'Shoot, shoot, shoot that n*****.' Everton, at that time, actually had a song about being white. Arsenal, conversely, were proudly multicultural, reflective of a London scene that was by nature more cosmopolitan than any city outside the capital in 1980s England.

Of course, Arsenal had their fair share of young, white male fans that were so dominant in football fandom of the era. But that was diluted by a more diverse and welcoming crowd than anywhere else. They attracted fans from the immigrant waves that had come from the Caribbean, from Greece and from Cyprus who congregated in North London,

from Ireland because of the strong Irish presence in the team in the 1970s. This was a time not long after it was a reality to see signs outside pubs with the message 'No blacks, No Irish, No dogs'. Turns the stomach to think this was relatively recent history.

They may have been in the minority, but Arsenal for decades had black fans, female fans, fans of all types and creeds. The colours that defined inclusion was red and white – nothing else. For a travelling supporter like me, it marked Arsenal out in those days to feel more progressive than anywhere we went. Arsenal looked after their own. For that reason, several thousand away fans reacted at Goodison Park by putting across our message loud and clear. Arsenal was above such hateful intolerance.

Here's the thing. At the end of the game, a few fans loitered around the players' entrance waiting for a word or an autograph. An Evertonian joked with Rocastle: 'Eh, Rocky! Why don't you sign for a big club?' Rocastle looked him straight in the eye, cool and controlled, and retorted, 'What? And get shot?' How could we not be proud of who we were, what we were, and what we represented?

← *Previous page:* Jimmy Carter, John Jensen and Kevin Campbell unveiling the North Bank mural.

↑ Construction of the North Bank in 1992.

August 1992. Highbury. The North Bank. Construction workers were in the thick of rebuilding the famous 'end' to replace the terrace with a two-tier block of seats. The vast majority of games that were to open the first FA Premier League weekend in August 1992 saw sections of stadiums that had become ghastly construction sites, as the Taylor Report into the 1989 Hillsborough Disaster had required all clubs in the top two divisions to convert to all-seater stadiums by August 1994. David Dein, the vice-chairman who was always driven by new ideas, had come up with the creation of a mural to cover the site and make Highbury feel more like a stadium during the season.

The day before the first home game against Norwich City, the team came along to get a look at it and get familiarised before training on the pitch that morning. As they took it in, Kevin Campbell went for a word. 'Mr Dein,' he said. 'Where are my brothers?' There were no black faces among the illustrated North Bank crowd. Dein was horrified and promised to rectify it immediately. It is, perhaps, a sign of the times and different expectations of what people were expected to have to put up with that Arsenal's black players did not air any offence. 'But,' Ian Wright said, 'it was a good observation because you did see black faces in the crowd at Arsenal.'

The club had appointed a design firm to create a block of roughly fifteen hundred

'Where are my brothers?'

fans in club colours which would be scanned, printed and multiplied to cover the North Bank. The illustrator later explained that what he produced was generic, not mindful of race or gender. It did not occur to anyone in the process that such a white, middle-class group was not reflective of Arsenal's support. There were also no women, and not a lot in the way of Junior Gunners or elderly fans. Painters eventually arrived to update the mural, which was readied for the home game against Norwich. It was fairly crude, but it was important that a wrong was put right. Arsenal lost their first match in front of the all-white mural, a humiliating 4–2 defeat. It took five home games until they managed to get a goal into an end that for a while felt cursed. The jokes at the time about being inspired by the energy from the North Bank sucking the ball in were entirely fair.

If the mural was not an accurate representation then, imagine it now, three decades later, for a global superclub whose fans, players, managers, executives and owners aim for a multinational sense of togetherness. The new artwork that wraps around Emirates Stadium gives a completely different impression of Arsenal, its people and its values. The image of a fan group, called *Found a Place Where We Belong*, is very mixed, carefully selected to represent Arsenal in all its diversity. Even Dainton is there – as he should be – a reminder of a different era for Black Arsenal. We have moved on to a contemporary mural for modern times. ■

→   North Bank mural, Arsenal v Sheffield Wednesday.

Black Arsenal

4

GOING
HOME
AND
AWAY

CLIVE PALMER

grew up in Luton. My first live games were at Luton Town, Kenilworth Road – standing in the Oak Road stand where the entrance cuts through the back gardens of the terraced houses. Luton had Black players like Brian Stein and the incomparable Ricky Hill: a Black player who played like a Brazilian and the best player I had ever laid eyes on. Growing up, Brazil were supported by every Black kid, they were a form of excellence we could be proud of.

At school, we played football in the playground. Part of that ritual was to choose your team and your player. My player was normally Colin Bell, the Man City legend. But this was 1971, and the FA Cup final was between Liverpool and Arsenal, so some chose Liverpool and I chose Arsenal. Then, Arsenal won – it was destiny. A young man called Charlie George scored the winner. Charlie soon replaced Colin Bell; with his long hair he just looked different to the other players, it showed he wanted to play differently. I remember when Arsenal came to visit Luton and seeing their fans: they looked like me. But their Black fans didn't just look like me, they looked how I wanted

to look: brave, stylish, and so *London*. So much swagger. All the fans at that time walked in groups, especially away from home. You would form together and look after your own.

After Arsenal visited, I noticed a difference in the atmosphere at Luton. Luton had Black players, but when other teams came to visit, the abuse was difficult to ignore. There were monkey chants by hundreds in the crowd, then the aggression and chants that followed. Witnessing this with your mates, I was suddenly made aware of something. Despite being in the same classes, studying the same subjects, wearing the same school uniform, eating the same sandwiches at lunchtime, playing football at break time – I, we, were different to them.

When the chants start, at first you pretend you don't hear it. Then it gets so loud that people start looking at you to see how you react. The feeling of being a minority in a public place of thousands as a young man, wasn't just being made to feel different, but being made to feel less of a person than the person who is abusing you.

It shapes you. You feel smaller, it draws out mistrust and anger. I never told my

← *Previous page:* Arsenal supporters on the Clock End celebrate winning the First Division title in 1991.

parents as they would have stopped me going to football and football was everything to me. Lots of Black people at that time didn't go to football. Why do that? It was a time where the National Front were taking hold, it was a time of division. When you turned on the six o'clock news, it was always the same. The violence of the Troubles, a religious war I wasn't educated in; striking miners, presented as agitators and the enemy within; Apartheid-era South Africa, where Viv Richards refused a 'blank cheque' to play. The Windies were a proud team that became the best sports team in the world. They were Black and strong. There were also the Brixton Riots: image after image of Black kids looting and burning cars. You would cross the road if you saw a Black kid and wanted to be safe – we were guilty until proven innocent. This was the backdrop to my formative years. I needed to do something positive, I needed to form an identity. I was too English to be Jamaican but too Black to be English.

Arsenal came for me when I was ready. I needed to belong and feel like I belonged without question. Going to Highbury was serene. I became a North Bank regular, hopping off at Arsenal station and straight past the 'The Home of Football' sign. Once inside, I positioned myself high at the back, looking from behind the goal. After a few years, I knew all the faces – there was the 'Black guy nod'. To get a nod back from a main face was a rare moment of street cred. There was never any racial tension. It always felt so inclusive. Elsewhere, racial tension

had entered every part of my life: when I was at work, driving, walking through a town centre, trying to buy a drink, trying to get a cab, trying to get into a nightclub. But at Arsenal there was this protective state. All that mattered was you were Arsenal.

When other fans came to Arsenal, they could not act like the away fans at Luton did. They had to behave. There were too many Black faces and no mob to conspire with, no National Front. To me this was how it should be. I was getting comfortable in London. The nightclub scene was booming, I was at the 100 Club; The Royalty; the Electric Ballroom; Dingwalls. Then, the explosion of Soul to Soul meant that North London was not just an area, but a place where young Black British kids could feel part of something. Arsenal was just an extension of this identity, and we protected it with all we had.

Eventually my Arsenal-supporting mates in Luton began to organise a carload for away games. Off we went, pooling money for petrol and the off-licence. But going to away games was a reminder of a world outside London. It was a deeper commitment, and an eye opener for me. I didn't get into trouble, but it was close. Trouble followed you if you looked a certain way and were of a certain age.

I remember going to Norwich City in the 1980s. We arrived after drinking in the car ready to enjoy a game. As we were walking to the ground, I realised there were a lot of people around us. Four Black guys, walking and talking, oblivious to the fact that we

Going Home and Away

were the only Black faces as far as the eye could see. You don't wear scarves or shirts to away matches, but when you are Black you can't hide. Then, if you were Black, you supported Arsenal. Out of nowhere, we were surrounded and rushed: at least twenty-five of them. My friend told me not to run – we would walk to the ground together. We fronted up and fought our way to the gate. Once inside, the war stories began.

When we went away, we brought the London casual look with us: Pringle jumpers, Diadora Gold trainers and a Sergio Tacchini tracksuit. We were not hard to spot. To rival fans we were mysterious, we deliberately wanted to look different to those up north. I remember a Leicester game, where walking to the ground we suddenly heard a roar, and everyone began running – and I ran with them. Police arrived and I realised I was caught in the middle of the main Arsenal faces and we had just rushed a group of Leicester fans. I was just about in there, but it was enough. Police escorted us to the ground to avoid trouble. In that group, there were so many Black faces. It's adolescent to admit, but this was a proud day. I was getting known just because I was a committed fan.

By the mid-1980s I was in my early twenties and led a dual life: City worker by day and a pretend Londoner at weekends, where it was nightclubs and Arsenal home and away. I was a casual, but I had something to protect. Unemployment was a problem for young Black men, and I had an office job and wore a white shirt on weekdays – but I was visiting Forest, Wednesday, Millwall, West Ham, QPR and Spurs in my other existence.

Then, something changed in the George Graham era. For the first time, I fell in love with the team. George had arrived and done a hatchet job on the squad. Out went the high earners and in came a group of kids that were given prominence: Tony Adams, Martin Hayes, Paul Merson and three Black players in Michael Thomas, Paul Davis, David Rocastle. Ian Wright would follow.

Oh my goodness, I had chosen my club well! A big club giving all these London Black boys a chance. Highbury was the place to be. From then on, I never felt intimidated – this was the start of football for all. Suddenly, every mile driven, every blockaded street, every police escort through a strange town, was worth it. When you looked on the pitch and saw yourself, it was life changing. I was there at Old Trafford when Rocastle chipped Schmeichel. I was there when Wright scored in the last minute at White Hart Lane. I was there at Wembley when we lost to Luton, but I was also there the year before when we beat Liverpool.

The love-in season was '89. I was able to go to over thirty games and this was a time where it felt like destiny. Arsenal were playing Newcastle at home, and I was full of joy. I was talking to Newcastle fans in the pub, the animosity was dialling back a little: 'Meet you after – win or lose,' I said to a few of the Newcastle fans. It was one big party, then a jolt. An accident had happened at Hillsborough. As we came out of the pub, rumours started about Liverpool's Cup semi versus Forest. We heard maybe five fans had been badly hurt and some dead. We thought it was strange that Liverpool had been given the smaller end. Then as more information filtered through there were ten dead, then fifteen; the numbers kept increasing.

No one met after the game. The events at Hillsborough made us all feel mortal. We all realised this could have been any of us. We went to so many games where crowd control looked made up. Fans, Black and white, were treated and corralled like cattle – football fans were bullied and marginalised and made to feel like dirt. Hillsborough was a line in the sand for me. Arsenal were fighting Liverpool for the title and that mattered – but we all needed to take a breath. After Hillsborough, fans started to align a little. For a short period, being a fan first rather than a fan of a certain team took precedence.

When our game at Anfield rolled around on 26 May, I couldn't make it. I couldn't go to the game as work didn't let me have the day off. I watched from home with friends and the tears flowed. These were our boys, and the man Michael Thomas became a hero. A Black kid from South London had just won the league for Arsenal Football Club in front of a live TV audience of millions with a minute to go.

The celebrations were epic and went on for days. For the regulars, we went up on the Saturday and gathered outside the

↑ Crowds look on during Arsenal's match against Aston Villa, 16 May 1999.

Going Home and Away

Gunners Pub and spent the evening in the Tavern. The Sunday we went back and did it all again. Back to the Gunners. What I remember was the pure joy and how good the police were. They celebrated with us.

Arsenal continued to be prominent under George and he introduced us to Ian Wright. We had just won the league and then decided to pay £2.5m for a South London version of ourselves. Ian's message was: 'I'm not shy – I'm not going to change who I am to be at an elite club.' What he did, without realising, was give us all confidence that it was OK to be *you*. Being you was enough. Much like the Windies and other Black heroes of the time – they all screamed out

to us – it is OK to be you, it is OK to be Black. You can be successful being Black. You don't have to fully conform to blend in. Ian became iconic for Arsenal fans almost instantly, particularly for Black fans. Today, he transcends cultural groups seamlessly.

The double cup win of 1993 led to the Cup Winners' Cup final in 1994 in Copenhagen. This was one of my favourite weeks as an Arsenal fan. Looking back now, in what felt like no time at all, I had gone from being a Black fan watching my back in the furthest reaches of England to a fan that was travelling across Europe. We won 1–0 and a new identity of *boring boring Arsenal* emerged. We revelled in it – George Graham revelled in it. A team built in his own image.

↑ Fans of all ages celebrating during Arsenal's 6–0 victory against West Ham, January 2024.

After George Graham left, Arsenal drifted until Arsène Wenger's arrival, when everything changed. Arsène changed Arsenal from a London-centric club to a global organisation that was revered across the world. His approach not only transformed how Arsenal were seen by British football, but how the Premier League was perceived abroad. The English game had grown out of its island mentality and old-school ways thanks to a softly spoken French scholar who opened our eyes to the art of the possible. Arsenal was international: Wenger didn't care what you looked like or where you came from. In 2002, he fielded the first team to include nine Black players, and in 2005 the first entirely foreign starting eleven. These changes ushered in a new kind of football and a new way of experiencing the game. The transition from being a fan to a customer was tough and the old grounds made way for modern all-seater stadiums. Who would have thought that back in the day when you were jumping trains to get home from Leicester in the 1980s?

When I look around the Emirates today it's so reflective of society as I know it. There was a moment for me that reminded me how far, from a diversity of fans perspective, we have come. It was an Emirates Cup game pre-season v Seville in 2022. I travelled in on my usual route from Hitchin to Finsbury Park, and when I arrived on the overground platform ready to join the crowded walk to the ground, my eyes were drawn to a group of eight women in full burqas with their young kids dressed in the latest Arsenal kits. I smiled and thought, We have gone from running the gauntlet up north because of your skin colour, to embracing cultures beyond my own.

I owe Arsenal so much. The strength of the group, the sense of belonging: Arsenal gave me the confidence a young adult thrives upon. Arsenal came along when I needed it, and today I experience it in a different way with my son, who at twenty-two simply enjoys the environment in a relaxed way. Those early days formed me, but I prefer today – the game should belong to all of us. ▨

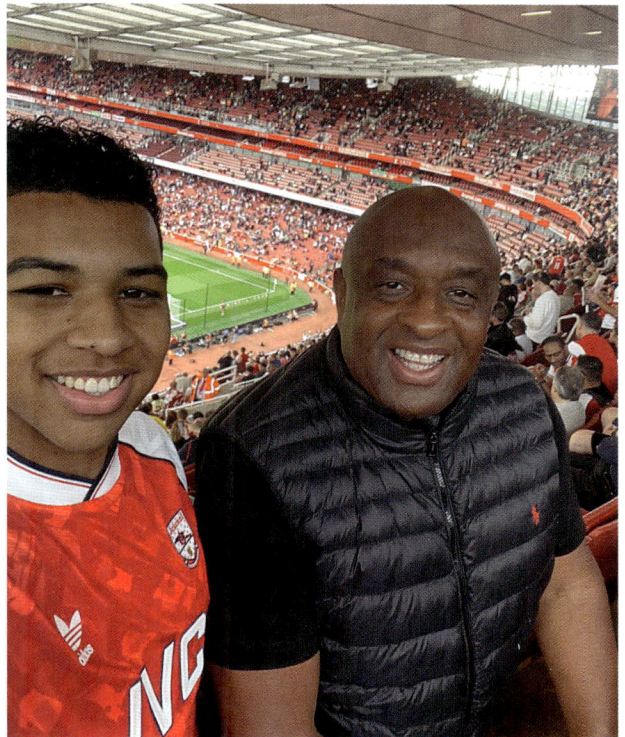

↑ Clive Palmer and son.

Going Home and Away

5

BLACK ARSENAL IN THREE ACTS

PAUL DAVIS

Paul Davis joined Arsenal in 1977 as a schoolboy. He made his debut against Tottenham Hotspur in 1980 and would go on to make 447 appearances for Arsenal across fifteen years, winning the League Championship title in 1989 and 1991, the League Cup in 1987 and 1993, the FA Cup in 1993, and the European Cup Winners' Cup in 1994. Upon retiring, he worked as a coach at the Arsenal Academy, later joining the PFA and the Football Association as a senior coach and educator.

ACT I: COMING THROUGH WITH CHRIS WHYTE AND RAPHAEL MEADE

My relationship with Arsenal began in 1971 when Arsenal won the FA Cup beating Liverpool 2–1, which was on TV. I was nine years of age. Seeing the game on TV, I just fell in love with Arsenal. It was the first FA Cup final I saw on TV. Charlie George scoring the winner was a big thing for me. It was such a dramatic goal, in the last ten minutes of the game. And he did this iconic celebration when he scored where he just fell to the floor with his arms and legs spread out, and then all the players jumped on top of him. That picture is still with me now. So that was it, even though I was a South London boy and my closest clubs was Chelsea, Fulham and Crystal Palace. It was that moment that captured me for Arsenal. I was playing football for my local football club at thirteen when I was scouted by Arsenal. Because I was really, really small

← *Previous page:* Paul Davis against Tottenham Hotspur in 1980.

as a kid, and back then it was all about pace and physicality more than skill, and I wasn't particularly quick or strong. So, I wasn't being looked at by a lot of clubs back then, and thought I was not going to be picked up by any clubs. So, it wasn't until I was thirteen that Arsenal picked me up, but I was actually training with Fulham at the time. But as soon as Arsenal were interested, I told Fulham that I had to leave. At that time, I wasn't actually signed up for them, so you could just walk away. Fulham was the club I was most connected to before

joining Arsenal; no one else was offering me trials or watching me. So, when Arsenal came in, it was a dream. I start to come up from Lewisham to train after school. And it's funny because now when I come off at the Arsenal Tube station, the inside hasn't changed at all. The metal bars are new but other than that, it's the same. It always brings back memories. Even now with me coming to games and coming off at the station, it reminds me of when I was a kid walking up from the Tube to the ground.

It was difficult being one of the only

↑ Arsenal's youth team at Highbury in 1978.

Black Arsenal in Three Acts

Black players in the team and on the pitch. Around the club in the 1970s, coming through in the youth team from my age group was Chris Whyte, who was Black. But after that there was nobody else of our age group that was from our culture. I don't feel that we had any real kind of issues within the club itself; it was probably just realising that some of the humour and some cultural things were different – that's when it really hit home. You know, these things are not really particularly funny to me, but to the rest of the group it is. So yeah, it was difficult, but not in a way that I used to go home and really worry about it. My drive was to get into the first team. And that was what took me forward at all times. How

can I play professional football? How can I get a contract? All these other things, like if someone cracked a joke, I just blocked it out. Nobody really confronted me one-on-one with racism. I don't remember as a youth player getting that sort of abuse. There's nothing I could say that any of those guys was giving me a hard time, you know, or anybody was in the club at that time. Not overtly. Maybe subconsciously they might. It's a very difficult thing, but obviously I realise that was different. The texture of our hair was different, so we used to have different combs, like Afro picks. And some of those guys in the changing room probably have never seen a comb like that before. Also music; I loved soul and reggae music. Those would be the two things that I remember were different.

Breaking into the first team was a little bit different because you're now around older, professional players who've been through some stuff themselves. And then I think that's when I started to get some things, banter, jokes in the changing rooms. I suppose that back then it was just common behaviour because you had programmes like *Love Thy Neighbour* on TV, and millions of people were watching it. There were some really racist themes within those programmes about Black people. There were several programmes on TV like that being watched by 50 per cent of the population regurgitating stuff when they go to work the next day. So, people would come into me and make a couple of jokes. And that was the first time I thought, Well, I don't really

↑ Paul Davis and Raphael Meade.

Black Arsenal

like this, so I'm going to challenge this. And that was quite scary. I do remember on a couple of occasions things being said about my race, and me going up to the person and telling them I don't appreciate what you said there, then being told I've got a chip on my shoulder, what's your problem? This was the late seventies, when the National Front was at a high point, so challenging that was quite difficult for a young person. It was a challenging situation that I was in and to challenge it in that way because you don't know what's going to happen from that. You could be ostracised, pushed to one side. Maybe I was a little bit, but I was so determined to get to where I wanted to get to. This other stuff that was going on wasn't going to stop me, even though it was difficult to challenge this kind of behaviour I got.

When I first got into the team, Arsenal weren't doing well. We were finishing tenth and thirteenth and not really pushing for anything, apart from in the first couple of years we've got to a couple of FA Cup finals. So, it was a tough time to actually break into the team because the team wasn't doing well, and I was part of a struggling team. I don't remember seeing too many Black fans at Highbury, if any. But I did have a tough time winning over the fans. I don't know whether it's because of my style or that the team wasn't playing well, or a combination of both, so it's really hard to decipher but I do remember thinking, wow, these guys are not on my side, because I'd give a ball away and there's always that growling from the crowd. And you're young as well, and there are all those comments that you can hear on the pitch. So, I think I had about eighteen months of really struggling to find my game. In the seventies and eighties there were stereotypes associated with Black footballers in the UK, which was that you were either a winger or striker, and my style was definitely not one of those players. I also didn't run around the pitch charging into challenges. I wasn't particularly quick, I was not aggressively strong, even though I could look after myself physically. My main game was a technical game. I wanted the ball; I was always looking for forward passes. The fans were maybe expecting or wanting something different from me at the time than I was giving them. It's hard to say for certain whether it's why it took me a while to win the fans over, but I'm pretty sure that would have been part of it. I suppose I was lucky. I had a manager in Terry Neill who kind of persisted with me because that could have easily gone another way.

It was so hard seeing Chris Whyte and Raphael Meade leave in the mid-eighties. Raphael was a little bit younger than Chris and me, who were the same age and came from the same youth team group. Raphael came a little bit after us. We probably played a few games in the first team together, but not too many. I definitely played with Chris in the first team. It would be interesting to see if there was a game where all three of us played together in the early eighties because that would have been the first time that Arsenal would have fielded three

Black players. Also, Viv Anderson was there, who came from Nottingham Forest. But he was also an England player, and already quite established, whereas Chris and Raphael weren't. So them leaving was a tough one because Chris and I kind of knew each other from our schoolboy days and would play against each other for our district teams. We got on so well. And he was such a good player. I loved watching him play. I think about Chris a lot as when we were coming through, we were very similar. He was similar to David O'Leary.

He was so comfortable on the ball, and he could defend. There is such a fine line, because he so easily could have been at Arsenal for his whole career. Tony Adams was coming through and there were others in that position. When I think of Chris' style I always think of John Stones. He didn't stay here despite all his talent. Whereas I managed somehow to kind of get through and make a career at the club. These things are so fine. I know he went on to win the league with Leeds in 1992. But for me, he had the ability to make a career at Arsenal.

↑ Chris Whyte.

↑ Paul Davis.

Raphael was quick and could score goals. And was a local boy as well – Chris and Raphael were both from Islington. They went to school nearby and they lived walking distance from the old ground. I was the furthest out, from South London. But we all kind of connected because we, you know, our parents were West Indian, so we kind of just gravitated. I don't think it was overt, but we kind of knew there was a connection between us. And we were able to integrate with the rest of the group. I don't remember there being any kind of difficulties between us and the other players in the squad. Raphael would have been against some stiff competition, as we had some decent strikers. Charlie Nicholas came a little bit later and left. Niall Quinn was coming through at this time. But we had some established players. I think he was up against Tony Woodcock and Paul Mariner; these were international players who were playing for England. So, it was tough for him to break into the first team. I think with making it, all these things have got to fall in line for you. I suppose he did

↑ Raphael Meade.

↑ Gus Caesar.

Black Arsenal in Three Acts

get opportunities, but perhaps the manager didn't feel like he grabbed his chances well. So, Don Howe reverted back to his tried and tested. I do feel that when I look back, if I had my opportunities, I had to just make an impression, to make sure that I played well or did something that made Don think that there's something in there for the future. And that's something that I felt I did. And even if I had a bad game, I just told myself to make the next one go well. If you don't do that it can take you longer to get over a bad performance and then you have another bad game.

ACT II: THE CLASS OF 1986: DAVID 'ROCKY' ROCASTLE AND MICHAEL THOMAS

By the mid-eighties, we'd lost Raphael and Chris, and in come these youth team players from South London, six or seven years younger than me, in Michael Thomas and David Rocastle. Gus Caesar was coming through as well. Seeing these young Black players, particularly South London ones like me coming through at Arsenal, was so important for me. I didn't actually know that they were coming through until later on as there was no real connection between the first team squad and the youth team. We're training in different places and times, so you wouldn't really know who is in the youth team until they started actually coming into the reserves. So, they were probably at the club three or so years before I even knew who they were, because I was trying to forge my own career in the first team, and I wasn't looking back. I wasn't hearing anything particularly about what's going on with the youth team. So, it's only when they were quite close to getting into the reserves that I noticed who these players were, and then recognising that some of them were coming from the same place I was coming from. I realised that they are having the same journey that I had, and I want to support them. And so I began to talk to them to make sure that they were OK, both on the pitch and off the pitch – particularly with Michael and Dave because they were from South London. It wasn't the same with Gus; he seemed to be able to look after himself, I think. But with David and Michael, I felt more protective towards them. But then I realised that these guys had been following me in my career and I was an inspiration for them to break into the team and push on. We just kind of connected and supported each other. Without it being 'them' and 'us',

we just moved into a deeper connection between us.

It was great to have three or four Black players in the same team, which would still have been rare in the Football League – definitely in the first division. When Mickey and David broke into the team, we were regulars, playing almost every game together. Whereas before it was Chris and myself and Raphael was not always playing. Me, Michael and David were regulars in the team and people were seeing us. We were regular fixtures in the team and George

↑ Michael Thomas.

↑ David Rocastle.

Black Arsenal in Three Acts

Graham came in and just gave opportunities to the young players coming through. We didn't realise again the effects that we were having being in the team, that people were coming to watch us from that point. I don't think many teams had Black players playing in their teams on a regular basis. Prior to us there were of course the 'three degrees' at West Brom in the early eighties, Regis, Cunningham and Batson, who were regulars. I would say they were the first ones and then after that it was ourselves.

I would sometimes talk to Black players from other teams in London, because obviously I knew of those guys as I was playing against them and connected to them so would be following their careers, but I didn't know them very well; we were not meeting up after games or anything. It's an interesting one because we're watching them from afar, knowing the difficulties that they are having. Because remember, back then when we played away, we got racial abuse. At most grounds it was the same. Leeds was always really tough. It felt like the whole of the stadium was on top of you. They would be racially abusing you when you're on the ball and making monkey noises. Everton would have been another. It's like they couldn't get their heads around Black players being on the pitch and just made the racial abuse well known. In terms of London clubs, Chelsea was tough, as was Millwall and West Ham. I mean, we'd get it at most grounds, but the ones I've just mentioned were really bad. I don't remember anything at Tottenham, perhaps because they had one or two Black players. I suppose once it started getting to the point where those clubs have their own Black players it wasn't so bad. But in the eighties, most of the clubs in the first division didn't have their own Black players and so it was tough. I would say the late seventies to early eighties was the worst for me personally as a Black player, playing away at those clubs. Sunderland and Newcastle were particularly bad; it was like the whole stadium was against you. I had to find out how to deal with it. Remember at this time they used to pack in 60,000 fans into the old stadiums in the terraces, all standing. It was really horrific at times.

I definitely felt a solidarity and connection with the other Black players at other clubs even though I didn't know them or speak regularly because obviously we didn't have mobile phones or social media as we do now. So, trying to connect to other Black players was not as easy as it is now. I think the only kind of connections that we forged was after the game in the players' lounges where we would just go in and meet our families and would spend maybe half an hour and then everybody's leaving. So, I think there was sometimes a connection with those players. But we didn't have any discussions around the racist abuse. We just kind of acknowledged that we knew we were all going through a similar experience, but in different parts of the country. The closest people I got to were actually the Spurs Black players – Chris Hughton and Garth Crooks – and forged a connection with them, maybe because it was that they were living in North

London, they were close to me. There were times when we connected up and did things away from football.

I do remember in the late eighties there was a Black journalist called Al Hamilton who was writing stuff around this area of the game and tried to bring us together and established the Commonwealth Sports Awards in 1980. What he was doing was trying to bring Black players together, to celebrate what we've done in the game and recognise our contribution. It was a good thing he was trying to do to bring some sort of joy within the Black community, given what was going on. He was up against all kinds of barriers because people were against that at that time. He'd put on these events in and around London that brought Black sports people together. In 1987 he organised a Black team from England of West Indian heritage to go across to Jamaica and play against the Jamaica national team. And it was something I wanted to be part of when he told me what he was planning to do, and asked if I thought Arsenal would let me go. I wanted to be part of it because I'd never been to Jamaica at that point. My parents visited Jamaica, but I'd never been back, so it was an opportunity for me to come and see where my parents were born. But it was also an opportunity to meet up with all these other Black players; Garth Crooks, John Barnes was at Watford at the time, and we could see that this guy was

↑ Michael Thomas, David Rocastle and Paul Davis lining up against Tottenham Hotspur in 1988.

Black Arsenal in Three Acts

going to be an outstanding player, Luther Bissett, Ricky Hill – he managed to get about fourteen of us, and he managed to pull it off and got us over there. It took a bit of work to get the OK with the various first division clubs. I remember Arsenal initially being reluctant because I was under contract and they didn't want me to go to Jamaica and potentially get injured, so they needed some convincing. I said to Arsenal that I really wanted to go on this and in the end, they allowed it to happen. But you have to remember back then, players had very little power, not like now. Players now can basically say, 'I'm going.' Back then, clubs had all the power. So that was the only time really that we were able to kind of get together as a group of Black players over seven days and just share some experiences.

From that group of players that came through from the 1986 youth team, Gus was actually the first one to actually make the breakthrough into the first team for a period of time, covering for David O'Leary, who was injured during 1987–88. But we only think about the mistake in the 1988 League

↑ Michael Thomas and David Rocastle together in the late eighties.

Cup final against Luton at Wembley. I do remember Gus getting a lot of criticism from the rest of the players. Not just for the Luton game, but in other situations that happened in other games. You had to have the mindset that you were not going to be affected if you made mistakes, and just somehow get over it quickly. But people didn't make it easy. If you made mistakes then, you didn't have that kind of wraparound support from people at the club, you had to kind of just deal with it. I do remember that people seemed to jump on the bandwagon and give him a hard time, even before the Luton game. I don't really know how he handled it, and if it affected him. But there was a lot of focus over his mistakes and a lot of jokes. I had this feeling that Gus wanted to deal with stuff himself. Whereas the other guys, like Michael and David, I always felt they wanted help. But that must have affected him at the time. Now, we have a completely different approach how we handle young players, particularly after they have made a mistake and how you can guide that person through it. It is so different to back then. You were you on your own, and just had to deal with it. That's how it was.

Even after winning the league in 1989 at Anfield and in 1991, I felt that the squad was not being remunerated enough for what we were doing for the club in terms of contracts. I do feel that Michael Thomas hasn't really been recognised for that achievement in 1989. I don't feel that that's come out enough. Michael had some issues with George Graham – we all had difficulty with George at some stage. If you had a little bit about you, you would have difficulties as he was very dictatorial and if you felt something was not right and needed to say something, you were going to have an issue with him. Michael had those conversations, I had those conversations, and we had some difficult times. So, when Michael left, it was so disappointing. Then Rocky left at the same time, essentially. So again, you've got a situation where you're kind of there for a long, long time and then there is a batch of Black players you are so connected to that kind of leave rapidly. I was disappointed when those guys left and went to Liverpool [Michael Thomas] and Leeds [David Rocastle]. David didn't want to go, and we didn't want him to go. It was all kind of surprising, and that was disappointing. We didn't really know the reasons why. We heard afterwards that the club found that he had a knee injury that was not getting better, and he wasn't playing every game, so they wanted to sell him. They thought they had seen the best of him. With Michael, I think it was more a personality clash with George, but yeah, it's always disappointing when players leave, especially when they're home-grown and it's under a cloud of uncertainty. Nobody really knows what happened apart from the players themselves. And they still had a lot to offer, so I was disappointed when they left, as I felt that I had been part of their journey. They called me Pops – Kevin Campbell was the one that gave me that name when he was coming through.

Black Arsenal in Three Acts

ACT III: TRIUMPH AND TOUGH TIMES

We signed Ian Wright in 1991, and Rocky and Michael had left by 1992. At the same time, there is the transition from the old first division to the Premier League. Ian was a fantastic goalscorer, but we found the transition hard in terms of being competitive in the league. You know, it was also a difficult time for me. I'd fallen out of favour with George. We had some arguments with him over how he wanted me to play, and he left me out of the team for eighteenth months. I look back on it and I don't know how I got through those eighteenth months. You know, being cast aside, literally just put to one side and forgotten about. It was tough then and it's still tough now thinking about it. I look back and I think that in those eighteen months I should have been playing; there's no doubt I was good enough. It felt like a vendetta. Eighteen months is equivalent to well over sixty games. And that would have taken me to 500 games for Arsenal, and I think that's where I should have been in terms of appearances for Arsenal. I made 447, which is good and I'm happy with, but 500 is at another level. So, I kind of look back in those terms. George could have dealt with that situation a lot better. I missed the whole of the 1991–92 season and most of '92–93. And what's interesting was that we had won the league the season before in 1991 with just one league defeat in the whole season.

I was vice-captain and captained the team for a lot of the season, and missed only one game. I've talked about this period in my autobiography, and I didn't want it to be seen as criticism of George. It's just my experience of what happened at that time. If it read like it was criticism, then it wasn't mean to be. This is what happened, and this is how I felt. I was not playing, and I felt I should have been playing.

The football industry then was very different to now. So, the fans only knew that I wasn't playing and did not understand why. The fans were being told I was injured or for other reasons, and not being told that the actual reason was that George didn't want to play me because we'd fallen out. That was a tough time trying to get through that eighteen months being fit, being ready to play but not being selected. And it still happens. But players now have a lot more power and they can speak out through their social media. They can tell their story, whereas back then we couldn't, and it was a really difficult situation for me being out of the team for eighteen months. I was in the prime of my career, I was about twenty-nine. That was a tough time.

There was no feeling of redemption when I was let back into the team in 1993 and played in the three cup finals, the League Cup against Sheffield Wednesday and the two FA Cup final games against them. I just wanted to get back and play. But there was no communication at all from George as to what happened. And I played against Parma in the 1994 Cup Winners' Cup final as well.

I knew what I could offer. And the team needed somebody like me in the side and I felt that, I kind of just did what I knew I could do, put aside what had happened and just played the game – that was my mindset. It's interesting because the relationship with George Graham started off really, really well, and then it went really, really bad. And I've always wanted to have a conversation with him about it, and ask why, but never really got around to it until recently. Arsenal had the launch of the mural artworks around the [Emirates] stadium, and George was there. I thought to myself, This is the opportunity to speak with him and ask him the question. So I said, 'You know when you left me out for eighteen months, you don't know the effect it had on me. I couldn't understand why you did that. What was the reason?' He said, 'No, there's no reason.' And I've kind of said to myself that he obviously didn't understand what I said, or he can't remember. So, I asked the question but I didn't push any further, that was as far as it got. But given all that time, I felt happy to have asked the question.

BLACK ARSENAL AND ME

Looking at Arsenal now, it's much more diverse in terms of players and the fanbase, and it's so different from when I first came to the club in 1977, and throughout the eighties and nineties when I was playing.

But I think about issues of diversity and the representation of Black people, across all levels of football from coaching, management and to the boardroom, because they're so important. I believe that if you really value people, then you show that. The next step for Arsenal is to diversify the club. To make sure it's truly diverse not just on the playing side, but off the pitch, in the boardroom and on the coaching staff. And I don't feel that the club at present can say that off the pitch as yet. It's not just Arsenal, it's across all of British football. But specifically, I want to see Arsenal move forward in this area and go to another level from the time when I started. To look at what's happening on our coaching staff or look at what's happening in the boardroom – is there diversity? I'm asking the same not just of Arsenal but of football. Because I've been in the game for such a long time at the senior level, I've seen it change and I've seen what's not changed. I feel as though I am in a good place to make a fair assessment through what I've seen and have experienced, and to share that so people can perhaps have a little think about where we are with diversity in the game at senior management, on the board, the women's game and across senior coaching positions. When we look at it, it really looks terrible. For somebody like myself, who is part of it and follows it quite closely it's quite painful to look at it and to see what's happened to all these Black superstar players who I've spoken to over the years and still speak to. I know from finishing their playing days they would have loved to have gone into management and coaching and very, very few of them managed this, if any at all. It's a badly lost generation. I feel that we need to have these conversations, because there's a lot of people that are not really wanting to discuss it, or even thinking about it. But it's such an important part of the game, and part of society that we need to talk about, to address it, and make some changes. It's something that, as you get older, you see things clearer. You have to decide how you're gonna deal with certain things that you see or hear. And we all have to make those decisions. So I think it's right to discuss these things and to try and change it or to help change it.

I was invited to the Black Arsenal Barbican Centre talk by Clive Nwonka in October 2022, and it was really interesting to me to know that there are people out there that are thinking about this area of the game and the club's history. During that event, I was asked by Clive Nwonka to say a few words to the audience. And I said that I had not recognised when I was playing for Arsenal that the work I've done on the pitch and off the pitch meant so much to Black people, and knowing this is worth more than my two league title medals. I truly mean this. Because it's the Arsenal. I'm part of this club, and the club is part of me. ■

↑ David Seaman and Paul Davis, European Cup Winner Cup final, 1994.

↑ Bukayo Saka receiving the men's Player of the Month award from Paul Davis in October 2023.
↗ Paul Davis at Highbury in 1990.

I HAD NOT RECOG
PLAYING FOR AR
WORK I'VE DONE
OFF THE PITCH
TO BLACK PEOPL
THIS IS WORTH M
LEAGUE TITLE
MEAN THIS. BE
ARSENAL. I'M PA
AND THE CLUE

...IISED WHEN I WAS
...SENAL THAT THE
...N THE PITCH AND
...IEANT SO MUCH
...E, AND KNOWING
...RE THAN MY TWO
...EDALS. I TRULY
...CAUSE IT'S THE
...T OF THIS CLUB,
...S PART OF ME.

OBSERVER

28 NOVEMBER 1971/CONTENTS PAGE 8

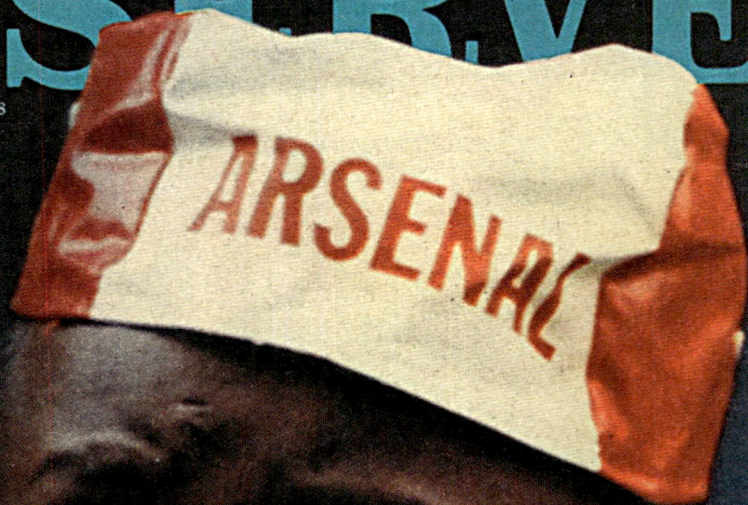

ARSENAL

BLACK BRITONS

Picture report,
page 17

Darts is the name of the game—
Paul Vaessen and Paul Davis

Opposite: Black Britons: the front page of the *Observer Magazine* in 1971.

ABOVE LEFT: Arsenal players at the Whittington Hospital in 1982.

ABOVE RIGHT: Paul Vassen and Paul Davis, 1981.

BELOW: Arsenal Schoolboys open the JVC centre with England Manager Bobby Robson in 1982.

By Fiona Cohn

Paul Davis

REACTIONS AND MORE REACTIONS . . .

When Paul Davis broke into the first team, he was one of three black youngsters who were just starting out, (the other two were Raphael Meade and Chris Whyte). At first he was well received by the crowd. They saw he had a lot of skill and thought maybe he was the player to fill the gap left by Liam Brady. But during the next couple of seasons, he didn't fulfil his potential. The fans became disillusioned, and started to give him some rough treatment.

He knows he was fortunate that the fans reacted to him because of his poor form rather than because he was black.

"If I had been getting stick because of my colour it would have made life a lot harder — because I wouldn't have expected that kind of treatment from the home fans", he admits.

Even at away grounds, Paul thinks he has been treated fairly (on the whole). All the same, he half expects to get abuse from certain groups of fans.

"If they didn't give you stick because you are black, they would find another reason," he says: "You have to toughen yourself against it. Otherwise you only get hurt when it does happen — as it inevitably does. There is prejudice of all kinds in everyday life. So it would be naive to think that it wouldn't spread to football."

Paul has never been attacked physically but one incident will always stick in his mind. It happened a few years ago, here at Highbury. He was doing some warming up exercises, running up and down the side of the pitch waiting to go on as substitute: when he heard a load of abuse being hurled at him from the terraces. He glanced around to see who was shouting at him — to discover it was coming from a black girl.

"I couldn't believe it, I think I was more shocked than anything else," he shakes his head.

Paul has strong views on that sort of behaviour: "I think I dislike the fighting and foul language even more than the average supporter does — because football is my profession and I want the game to be seen in a good light," he says.

Opposite: Paul Davis featured in the Arsenal matchday programme in 1985.

ABOVE: Viv Anderson after signing for Arsenal in 1984.
BELOW: The Arsenal youth team in 1984.

RESERVES AND Youths

By KEVIN CONNOLLY

CHRIS GRABS SIX . . . CHARLTON COP TWELVE

Chris Whyte revelled in his new forward role last Saturday. He banged in six goals in our 12-0 win over Charlton!

Chris cracked a first half hat-trick in ten minutes, and added three more in a second half romp.

Said Reserve boss Terry Burton: "Chris showed excellent skills and good finishing. He won a lot of balls in the air, too."

"We're going to have a good look at him in this forward position."

Chris Whyte . . . blasted Charlton with six goals last Saturday.

"Chris is a player who would shine in almost any position in a Combination game. What we need to assess now is whether he can do the job at a higher level."

Terry was delighted with the Gunners' super finishing. Niall Quinn bagged a hat-trick and Martin Hayes scored twice.

But the best goal came from full-back Michael Thomas, who swerved home a 20-yard bender.

"Charlton were as good as most of the sides we've met this season — but our finishing was clinical," said Terry: "We were hungry for goals throughout the team. Our defenders were all battling to win the ball back and get us moving again even when we'd reached double figures."

Arsenal: Wilmot, Caesar, Thomas, Turner, Adams, Hill, Hayes, Rocastle, Quinn, Whyte, Allen.

Two first half corners set up the Reserves for a comfortable 3-0 win at Brighton on September 14.

Roger Stanislaus and Martin Hayes netted from flicks at the near post.

Niall Quinn hit the Gunners' third in the second half. Quinn also had a penalty brilliantly saved by 'keeper Graham Moseley.

Terry Burton praised his defenders for a tight display.

"They shut down Brighton very smartly and Rhys Wilmot had only one shot to save," he said.

Welsh midfielder Jason Ball made his Reserve debut because David Rocastle was with the First team squad, and apprentice Stanislaus started in place of Greg Allen who'd had his tonsils out earlier in the week.

Arsenal: Wilmot, Caesar, Thomas, Turner, Adams, Hill, Hayes, Ball (Merson), Quinn, Whyte, Stanislaus.

BIG TEST TODAY

Today's the day when our all-conquering Reserves face their biggest test so far — away to one of the other runaway Combination leaders — Chelsea.

"I'm looking forward to us facing one of the top five for the first time this season," says Terry Burton: "It will be a good measure for us after the big wins we've had recently."

Michael Thomas . . . on England Youth duty again last week.

MICHAEL CALLED UP

Full-back Michael Thomas was on England Youth team duty again last week, in England's 3-1 win in Iceland.

Michael also won two 'Man of the Match' awards for England in last month's F.I.F.A. World Youth tournament in the Soviet Union.

Youth team in action . . .
Southern Junior Floodlit Cup
First Round
Tuesday, October 1
ARSENAL v A.F.C. BOURNEMOUTH
at Highbury
Kick-off 7.00 p.m.
Come and spot our stars of tomorrow!

SUB SCORES WINNER

Kevin Campbell came off the substitute's bench to earn our Youth team a 2-1 win over Gillingham in the South East Counties clash on September 14.

Gillingham held the score to 1-1 at half time. Pat Dolan scored our opening goal after a neat one-two.

Arsenal: Hammond, Russo, Sykes, Rivero, Dolan, McGregor, Birch, Osborne, Rebuck (Campbell), Milton, Lambert.

The Youth team went down 0-1 at Ipswich last Saturday — in a game Youth boss Pat Rice thought we should at least have drawn.

"The result was an injustice to the lads," said Pat: "We made a lot of chances and we could have been two or three up before they scored. Credit to the Ipswich 'keeper who made some fine saves, but it was one of those days when the ball just wouldn't go in."

Arsenal: Hammond, Russo, Sykes, J. Ball, Dolan, Pennington, Rivero, Milton, Merson, Solomon, Lambert.

Subs: Birch, Rivero.

● The young Gunners are away to Cambridge United in the first round of the South East Counties League Cup today.

No. 5.

YOUNG GUNNERS

David Rocastle

Finding his feet in midfield . . .

AT the tender age of 18, David Rocastle is already hoping to break into the First team this season, David has already been included in the First team squad, for our last home game, against Sheffield Wednesday.

Youth officer Terry Murphy saw him playing in a school game, and, impressed by the young man's display, invited him to come to Highbury to train. That was four years ago. When David came to Arsenal, he was playing in a right-wing position. But coach Tommy Coleman already had enough cover on the right — and suggested he switch to midfield. It's a change that's worked out well for David, who's quickly established himself as a reserve regular.

His most memorable achievement, so far, was winning the Southern Junior Floodlit Cup with our Youth team in 1983. "That win gave me a great deal of satisfaction," he smiles.

David says, he's "pleased with his progess." He averaged a goal every four games last season — and he's keen to keep up that kind of form to add weight to his challenge for a First team place.

Says David . . . "I want to see what it's like playing in the First Division." He's not quite sure how near he is to that. "One week you're training with the First team, then the next week you're not."

At the moment, football takes up all of his time. He does not have any real hobbies outside the game — because when he's finished training and playing, all he wants to do is go home and relax. He realises what a precarious career football can be . . . "One day you could go out, break a leg and you're finished," he says. All the same he's being encouraged by his family — especially his brother.

Sometimes he thinks about going to evening classes to gain some qualifications to add to his 'O' Level English and CSE's. But right now he finds this too difficult to fit in. He has to concentrate on his football career.

1985 Arsenal matchday programme.

Overleaf:
David Rocastle at Islington Town Hall during the 1989 title victory parade.

6

COOKING UP THE ARSENAL

STARDIOUS CHRISTIE

started selling food outside the ground in 2016. First, I started doing hotdogs and burgers using one small round barbecue given to me by neighbours downstairs. My friend Desmond Reilly gave me a spot outside on Hornsey Road on matchdays. I moved on to Jerk and Caribbean food because it was different, no one was doing it then and I knew the crowd would want it.

My connection to Arsenal was originally through my sister – my sister was born in Jamaica but grew up here. We used to see Arsenal everywhere, all around, and picked it up from there. I liked Bob McNab, Charlie George, John Radford, Alan Ball.

I went to Tollington Park School in Finsbury Park and used to play for the school team – Raphael Meade played with us, then Islington Borough, then got scouted for Arsenal. Coaches from the club would come in and train us. I started going to games around this time, around 1973–4. In the third year we started bunking off on Tuesdays. At first, there was just a wall to jump over to escape from the playground, then they put up a fence and hired a Jamaican tea lady to watch over us. Mrs Burdett, God rest her soul. She knew all our parents, so we had to find other ways.

When we got to the ground it felt nice because we'd bunked into the schoolboys' end. It used to be sixpence to get in, but we managed to climb over the garden walls of the houses around Highbury. The police used to come in and take the laces out of our Dr Martens, sometimes outside the ground before we'd get in. Then, after the match was over, the police used to dump them all out together so there'd be a million of us searching for our laces out on the street! The police also used to have a little pen they'd lock you in if you made too much trouble so you couldn't watch the match – you could see the sky.

Being at the game created a feeling of ecstasy; seeing what I'd seen on television live was mind-blowing. It made an impression on the whole of my life. The match, the comradery, the laughing and joking, especially from the older men who were there, who used to see us boys and give us change for Coca-Colas. From the schoolboys' end, I graduated to Little Highbury. That was a step away from being a Clock End boy. I went through the ranks of Little Highbury, where I was third in command, then I went up to the big boys with Dainton [Dainton Connell, a leading face of the Clock End in the seventies and eighties] and them lot and I quickly rose up the ladder.

Being Jamaican in the crowd never came into my mind. Football was never about politics – it was a game to enjoy. We'd go watch the match and have a fight after, but we'd never bring what was happening elsewhere into Arsenal. We never looked at colour – the only time we did was when we saw a Black Arsenal player playing for Arsenal, like Brendon Batson and Clyde Best for West Ham. You had the Black community at that time, but then you had Arsenal. Arsenal was an entity on its own. Some of us travelled between both and the ones who did, because of Arsenal, saw the world. Because I wouldn't know about Aston Villa, Leeds, Newcastle, Liverpool – but I'm going to those places when I'm eleven or twelve years old because I supported Arsenal Football Club. They took us on an adventure – a life journey.

So, I started to go to aways. One of the reasons I could go away was because my dad worked on British Rail, so we never had to pay to go on the trains. We mostly went on the specials [football specials – trains chartered for football supporters]. From the train station to the ground, it was like a parade in each town we visited because Arsenal stood out – we felt like we were on show. The Clock End crew was different to lots of others. It had Blacks, Irish, Greeks and mixed-race. Those were the four identities that made it up. It was more multicultural. When we went to Leeds for instance, who would be all-white when they came to Highbury, and came out of the station, it was like a carnival to them! Then they would see a Black guy standing at the front of over a thousand men. For the Leeds number one, that did their head in, but they still cracked on.

Clothes had to be top of the range: I was about snakeskin boots and silk shirts from Cecil Gee down Bond Street or Chevaliers. Also, Lacoste, Farah trousers and slacks. And that's how we're dressing going to football – in cashmere jumpers. Those northern crews used to follow us if anything because we looked smart. I was listening to a lot of music at the time – everyone followed a sound system, mine was Sir Biggs – some of us would go from there over to Arsenal.

Funny, we never paid too much attention to who was in Spurs' crew – we just went there to fight and mash up the High Street, because we used to march on Seven Sisters to White Hart Lane and everything would go along the way. We weren't concerned with their identity – we just went there to beat them up. The hardcore Tottenham fans were mostly white guys, but they had a few Black guys too – but we didn't have any alliance with them or anything.

Maybe there were differences: Tottenham Black guys were different to Arsenal Black guys because of the way they grew up in Tottenham and the way we grew up in Finsbury Park. Tottenham Black guys at that time, that young, weren't really worldly.

Cooking up The Arsenal

They'd never get the money to travel to away matches, they lived off mummy's pocket money. They were different from us – they were less integrated.

We had Black guys up front and up top. I used to like going to Chelsea. The only thing between us and them was a white and yellow line and a horse or two. We'd come out at Sloane Square, say three, four hundred of us; about a hundred would mess about with the shops and the rest of us would march down the King's Road. You could feel the racism at Chelsea – that's why we loved going there. When we went there, it wasn't for a feeling of football, we just wanted to beat them up because of what they stood for. The National Front were openly giving out leaflets to the crowd. I remember one time, when the NF were waiting for us at the top of the King's Road and began trying to give out magazines to our guys. Unbelievable. But the thing is, we actually wanted them there. They started to issue out their magazines to us and we dragged them in, starting an open brawl and gave them all a good hiding.

The NF dared to put a small contingent outside the Clock End in a match against Leeds in the late seventies. But they never came back after what we did to them. Ambulances and everything. I took their leaflets and burnt them. When Millwall came in '88 they gave it, but we gave them the kicking of their lives because of what they stood for. We had every route from Avenell Road blocked. The second time Millwall came in '95 it was all right – they still made their noises and that, but we never had to show them what we were about ever again. The biggest clashes for me were ones like those, sort of making a point – it meant more – but you would never say it out loud like that, because it was Black guys and white guys fighting together.

When Paul Davis came through, they made a big fanfare about it like it was a big time of change, but I'd already seen Brendon Batson play. By the time of Rocastle, Thomas, Campbell, and Davis though, they were the glory days. Everything was football. That was when I took more interest. They were not only signing Black players, but they were doing stuff in the community as well, towards Black people. That's the Arsenal World of Sports Days. But it's all down to the place, Islington and Highbury.

We opened the gate for young Black Arsenal fans. Dainton, our firm, we opened the gate for them. It's a joy to see now. They'll come to football, and it wouldn't enter their mind that there will be violence. They come to the game now, have something to eat and go home and have a family day. It was never like that before! They got it easy now compared to what it was then. We broke a lot of barriers, we broke a lot of, let's say, illiterate thinking. Today, on a matchday, Arsenal has a lot of Black workers – which is good – it entwines the community between players and spectators. Remember the days of the North Bank mural? When they literally put the paint on their faces! ◼

Cooking up The Arsenal

7

'WRIGHT, WRIGHT, WRIGHT...'

Arsenal v Millwall, 1995 and the politics of racism in London

LES BACK

an Wright has always been 'on loan' to the Arsenal and North London. Born in the Royal Military Hospital in Woolwich, south-east London, on 11 November 1963, he grew up in Brockley on the Honor Oak Estate, just streets away from another Black Arsenal legend, David 'Rocky' Rocastle. As boys, Rocky and Wrighty played football together at Honor Oak Recreation ground. Being four years younger, 'Rocky' was often put in goal by the older boys who ran the game. He didn't stay there for long because Rocky's talent was uncontainable. David Dein, co-owner and vice-chairman of Arsenal Football Club, once said of Rocastle's talent: 'I've seen the nearest thing to a Brazilian footballer you'll ever see, and he's from Lewisham.' He was scouted by the Arsenal youth programme and, ultimately, he showed the way north for his older friend.

The two Lewisham boys were united for one golden season in 1991–92 after Wright had signed for a record £2.5 million. He won the 'golden boot' that year for Arsenal. At the core of that team were two other Black South Londoners, Paul 'Pops' Davis and Michael Thomas. The story of these four Black footballers tells us something very profound about both the bravery and talent of that generation of Black Londoners and the complex nature of the legacy of racism in football and in British society.

It is telling that the footballing talents of both Rocky and Wrighty were both turned down and passed over by their local football club, Millwall FC. In his autobiography *Mr Wright*, Ian commented:

The only sniff I ever had [from professional clubs] was with Millwall. I was 14 at the time and they were the local team to me and the side I used to worship. A mate and I would bunk in at the old Den at the Coldblow Lane End to watch the Lions, so it was a dream come true when they invited me to the Crofton Leisure Centre for a six-week trial. I know I showed enough in skill and ability in that time to warrant something from it; instead, I got nothing, and that began a love-hate affair with Millwall that lasts even to this day.

Growing up just a mile from Millwall's ground, Wrighty remembered:

← *Previous page:* Tony Witter and Ian Wright in 1995.

I loved those Saturday afternoons. Any opposition player will tell you that Millwall is the worst place in the world to go because the old Den you were so close to the fans and you could hear every spit and snarl … They would give the opposing black players real violent racist abuse and then turn around to me and say 'Nothing personal, mate, it's because he's one of their black bastards.' I couldn't figure it out, but in those days I just accepted it.

It was north of the river where Ian Wright's joyful flair and hard determination made him a world-class footballer. A succession of Arsenal teams became emblematic of London's multiracial future and its Black players were the tribunes of that promise. Every game was not only a struggle to win, but also a struggle for belonging and against racism.

In an FA Cup tie against Millwall in 1995, Wrighty returned to his old stomping ground. This time it was 'The New Den' (Millwall had in 1993 relocated from their stadium in New Cross to a new all-seater stadium on Zen Road in Bermondsey) and in the lead-up to the fixture Wrighty had done an interview with Arsenal ClubCall where he had criticised the racism he'd witnessed there. The newspapers ran headlines proclaiming: 'Wright wants to

↑ Kevin Campbell is challenged by Keith Stevens of Millwall during their FA Cup third round tie in 1994.

'Wright, Wright, Wright . . .'

stuff it up racist Millwall fans.' 'Ian Wright v Millwall' was a well-established storyline throughout the nineties. Arsenal had played Millwall on three occasions in the previous two seasons, all in the two domestic cup competitions given that Millwall were in what had now become, in the post-1992 reconstruction of the football league, the new first division. Two of these meetings, in the League Cup in October 1992 and the FA Cup third round in January 1994, would take place at The Den and established a charged backdrop to the 1995 tie. Throughout both games, Ian Wright (and his Black strike partner Kevin Campbell) would be subjected to racist chanting and monkey noises from the home fans. Clearly affected by the continuous racist abuse, Wright would be booked in the first half of the 1994 game for a late challenge, and would be substituted by George Graham early in the second half, seemingly to prevent him from being sent off. In reaction, Wright would charge straight down the tunnel without acknowledging the Arsenal bench. There is also an important wider political context in terms of the politics of race and heightened popular racism. On 22 April 1993, Black teenager Stephen Lawrence was murdered at a bus stop on Well Hall Road in nearby Eltham. Five months later on 16 September 1993, across the river on the Isle of Dogs

↑ Ian Wright is substituted by George Graham during Arsenal and Millwall's 1994 FA Cup encounter.

in Tower Hamlets, Derek Beackon won a council by-election in the Millwall ward for the British National Party, becoming the first elected representative for the party. All this would provide a racially charged and heightened prelude to the public's understanding of the game.

The tie took place in South London on 7 January 1995. Marking Wrighty that night was a Black Millwall centre-half called Tony Witter. Compared to Wright, who at this point was one of the most prominent Black English footballers, Witter was little more than a journeyman player although he was beloved by the Millwall fraternity for the lionhearted way he played the game. In this bad-tempered contest, two Black players – both South Londoners – were pitted against each other: one loved and venerated, the other loathed and abused. I interviewed Tony for a book I wrote called *The Changing Face of Football* in the late nineties. Tony recalled an incident during that game which laid bare these tensions:

Nigel Winterburn played a ball down the line and Ian Wright who was just over the halfway line tried to turn against me and I tackled him and put the ball out of play. He's gone to get the ball, it's just rolling on the track and he's gone to pick it up. The amount of racist abuse that came from the Millwall fans in the lower stand was incredible: 'black this, black that,' monkey chants and the rest. Basically, I am standing not more than 5 feet away from Ian. I sort of looked at them, looked at

Ian and Ian shrugged his shoulders. Then I hear this voice from the crowd – 'Not you Tone, you're all right – it's Wrighty.' I think they just see a blue shirt when they look at me. But with Ian Wright they see a red shirt, then they see a black face. But do they not see my colour? Do I wear this shirt over my head?

In his blue shirt Tony's racial difference was somehow dissolved or seen to be irrelevant. The notion of 'wearing the shirt' summons in football vernacular the deepest levels of symbolic identity and commitment. It captures how Black players can be assimilated and become an emblem of locality and identity within football clubs while at the same time racism is licensed against opposing Black players. Racism in football works through both *some* Black players who become contingent 'insiders' while vilifying others as total outsiders.

After the game, a 0–0 draw, Witter and Wright were in the bar. 'Ian says to me: "Witts, man, how can you play here, man?" I said to him: "Ian, they're as good as gold *to me*." That's the whole thing, I am playing *for them*.'

There's lots going on here, highly localised values expressed in rabid support, social class, toxic masculinity and, of course, racism. How can a stadium full of fans love Tony Witter and – without any necessary contradiction – unleash a full hateful load of white racism against Ian Wright?

One lesson that this football fable offers is just how contingent and fragile these inclusions are within football culture. The love and worship of one Black player can go hand in hand with hating and abusing another: it just depends which shirt they are wearing. It tells us something about the complexity of racism within football culture but also why Black players have been at the forefront for the struggle for a more racially just city. In 1992, at the beginning of the first Premier League season there were 218 British players across all starting line-ups, 36 of whom were from Black and ethnic minority backgrounds, 16.5 per cent of the total. By 2022 this figure had more than doubled with Black players making up 43 per cent of the players in the English Premier League.

Tragically, David Rocastle was diagnosed with non-Hodgkin's lymphoma in October 2000. The cancer ravaged his Dionysian physique and within less than a year he was gone at the young age of thirty-three. His friends and Arsenal teammates were devastated, none more than Ian Wright. After leaving Arsenal in 1998, Wrighty had two years of moving from club to club. He played for West Ham United before brief spells at Nottingham Forest, Celtic and finally Burnley, who he helped get promoted to the first division. He hung up his striker's boots with a career haul of 313 goals in all competitions. Ian Wright retired in 2000 and began his new career as a broadcaster and pundit, often alongside his England teammate and fellow striker Alan Shearer.

As a pundit and commentator Ian Wright has remained critical of and outspoken against racism, whether it be Raheem Sterling being racially abused in Budapest during England's win over Hungary in 2021 or being targeted himself by racists on social media. Ian Wright has also been critical of the way 'anti-racist campaigns' within the football industry result in a little more than decorative gestures. He has made a passionate appeal for the need to embolden white people to find an anti-racist voice. In a moving filmed discussion with fellow football legend Alan Shearer recorded in the summer of 2021, the two friends talked about the double

↑ Tony Witter and Ian Wright at the Den, FA Cup third round, 1995.

standard applied to black and white people in the public eye. Shearer admitted as a white person to the trepidation he feels of 'making a mistake' in talking about racism. Steven Gerrard's open solidarity as the Rangers manager when his player Glen Kamara, who was born in Tampere, Finland, to Sierra Leonean parents, was racially abused during their Europa League defeat to Slavia Prague in 2021, is a hopeful sign. Wright's calls for white players to speak out, like Burnley captain Ben Mee who criticised his own fans that booed when players 'took the knee' before a Premier League fixture against Brighton, were similarly encouraging.

Wrighty transcends any claim that might be placed on him, and perhaps he's 'on loan' to everyone. During the high point of his days at Arsenal he lived in the south of the city on a 1.3-acre plot located in Bishop's Walk, Shirley, Croydon. He sold up in 2010 and moved to Kensal Rise, in the north-west of the capital. He told the *Daily Express* newspaper in 2023 that he might be best described as: 'A mix of south and north London; that's me.' First and foremost he's a Black Gunner footballing legend. But the example he sets by his unwavering commitment to challenging racism in all its forms is, in the end, a gift to us all. ■

8

MAINTAINING HIGHBURY

STEVEN DAVIS

came from Jamaica to London in 1983. I used to support Liverpool at first when I lived in Jamaica. In Jamaica, there were only two teams. Liverpool and Everton. And when I came to England in 1983, my sister said, 'Oh, they got a nice club going now, you know, they have one or two Black players playing, doing well, you should watch them.' I've been an Arsenal fan ever since.

I got my job at Highbury in 1999 because a friend's boyfriend worked in the catering department and heard they were looking for a general maintenance worker, painter and decorator. I went for an interview, and Albert Slyman showed me around. I went on the pitch and rubbed my hand on the grass. He said, 'Hey, you're not supposed to go on the pitch!' But this is the very first time I'm at Highbury, and it could be my last, so I took a risk knowing that at least I got to walk on the pitch. I went outside and sat in the benches of the ground's little car park. Albert came out with his son Steve and said, 'You might as well come up and finish the interview because the other guy didn't turn up – so you got the job. When can you start?' And I said Monday. They gave me a contract for three years, the best three years in my life, other than having kids.

There was a lot of painting: red and white, everywhere. I'd go home and see Red and White in my dreams! I did all the seat numbers, from one to 38,000. Using the stencils, I'd paint the steps of the seats, replace ceiling tiles, bulbs, door handles and things like that. The away fans would mash up the seats in almost all home games! So, after every match, the away section had to get replaced, the buggers.

There were one or two other Black employees working at the ground at the time, along with a few Black women working in the offices, and I was treated well. After a while, I became known affectionately as Yardie Man. The first guy who called me it was Steve Braddock, the groundsman. We used to play darts together after work. Before I knew it, everyone was calling me that: *Yardie Man*. It was natural. Even when David Dein said, 'Oh, Yardie Man!' I was like, what? Even Arsène Wenger called me it! I thought they were taking the piss at first, but I felt it was genuine. It was endearing – and a mad life that moved fast.

← *Previous page:* Steven Davis at Highbury.

I loved that stadium. I worked there from 1999–2001. It was like a dream. There was a feeling of being home there. I wanted to stay beyond the three-year contract, and I was given hope that I would. But because they built the new stadium, my boss said they won't renew it as they'd have their own maintenance team. The end of an era. ▪

Maintaining Highbury

9

'NEARLY THEIR WHOLE TEAM IS BLACK!'

Leeds v Arsenal, 2002

RODNEY HINDS

When Arsenal became the first club to field nine Black players in a Premier League game against Leeds in the 2002–03 season, I had a feeling something special was taking place.

Sitting in the Elland Road stand, I did detect some sort of feeling towards the Arsenal team sheet that was being read out over the Tannoy: Seaman, Lauren, Campbell, Cygan, Cole, Touré, Vieira, Gilberto, Wiltord, Henry, Kanu. Whether that was nerves by the Leeds fans, whether that was respect, disrespect, or a combination of all three I couldn't be quite sure. Put it this way, I did detect some vibes and mutterings from the home support, as if to say, 'Something's happening here today.' Some ninety minutes later, the vibes were correct as the Gunners played some of the most sublime football the famous Yorkshire pitch has ever witnessed as they ran out 4–1 victors. They should have doubled that score in truth, such was their dominance.

We often talk about diversity now, but it wasn't always the watchword back then. History was being made. There were some great names in that line-up. That

Arsenal team at Elland Road that day was something special – and not just in terms of the performance. Elland Road has always been seen as a difficult place to go to play football, the crowd get involved and make a hell of a noise, so I was also intrigued as to how this very good Arsenal side would deal with that. No problem. It was a positive advert for diversity that had never been seen before. Visionary Arsenal boss Arsène Wenger had changed English football with his unique emphasis on diet and sleep. But this fixture and subsequent line-up took things to another level. He had assembled a squad that was predominantly Black. Not only were their skins different but so too was the way they played the game; pace, movement and efficiency were noteworthy.

If Wenger's men had just been run of the mill, the powerful story would not be what it is. They were hugely successful as a collective and some of them would later be part of the legendary 'Invincibles'.* They changed the narrative for Black players due to their class. In many ways, this Arsenal squad reminded not just me of the all-conquering West Indies cricket team that

← *Previous page:* Leeds v Arsenal at Elland Road, 28 September 2002.

* The Invincibles were so-called for their unbeaten record in the 2003–04 Premier League season. Remarkably their undefeated run spanned forty-nine league matches between 7 May 2003 and 16 October 2004.

gave so much pride to the community – and that included those that didn't know, or care, about the difference between a googly or a maiden over. Like that stand-out West Indies, the Arsenal team at Elland Road in particular (and global football in general) gave a huge percentage of diverse football fans at home and abroad the opportunity to puff out their chests. They weren't just making up the numbers. They were Invincible.

We talk today about generational managers such as Pep Guardiola and Sir Alex Ferguson and they deserve their place in history. I just think that the real difference between that esteemed duo and Wenger was not so much about trophy hauls as that the Frenchman was responsible for making the talented Black footballer vogue en masse. Wenger's team came to glorious life as his team cut Leeds to shreds. Bringing a predominantly Black team to one of the most notorious stadiums in the north of England was fitting. On that day the way they played, the goals they scored, just said everything about Wenger's vision. During the course of the match, the aforementioned vibes and mutterings turned to faint praise initially and smatterings of applause thereafter. I could sense that the home support, however grudgingly in some quarters, recognised what they were witnessing and by whom. Without Wenger and his diversity of player, I don't think the Premier League goes to where it does – the most competitive and watched league on the planet.

Wenger made Black players key at one of the biggest clubs in the world. In September 2002, when they tormented Leeds in their own back yard, the Arsenal supremo more than likely made Black players even more acceptable to other clubs. Having interviewed the likes of Garth Crooks, Cyrille Regis, Viv Anderson, John Barnes et al. over the decades, the feeling I got from those conversations was that Black players were not trusted back in the day. They were given their playing opportunities one at a time; Wenger changed that mindset. Having been sports editor at *The Voice* for two decades, when I go about my professional business, I am surprised if I don't see Black players in a certain team now.

With the Premier League a global business, I am convinced that managers and coaches around the world witnessed the football carnage at Elland Road and followed Wenger's lead in allowing Black players to express themselves. There was a time when the likes of Sunderland and Burnley were topics of conversation due to a lack of Black players in those teams. The irony now is that in 2023 Burnley have been promoted to the Premier League under a Black coach and have several Black players among their number. Wenger saw the future before anybody else and had great connections in Africa and around Europe. The success of his team was made that much more powerful when it succeeded the way it did against Leeds and subsequently went on to claim silverware. If there's no success, not as many people take notice. Those crammed

'Nearly their whole team is Black!'

into the stadium as Leeds were undone had no choice but to take note. This traditional club was taken apart in a manner to which they were not accustomed.

I support Arsenal essentially because it was the first football ground I was taken to by a friend. My first visit to Highbury was an exciting occasion, made even more so because I saw the likes of Paul Davis, David Rocastle and Michael Thomas in action. To witness nine players in one team at Elland Road that I could relate to took things to another level. To watch them every week in North London was special but to see them dismantle Leeds in the way in which they did was something else. I identified with the players as they were the conduit to the club as a whole. They are, quite rightly, seen as one as the most multicultural, diverse clubs, and they are leading the way. I and many other fans from a diverse background feel that we belong, that we matter.

Wenger created a bit of a template with his line-up against Leeds. I think we always remember really exciting teams, don't we? That day in Leeds will never be forgotten, for several reasons. The style of play was sensational. The scoreline was emphatic. A starting eleven with nine Black players in it seemed unreal. However, it was real and the Beautiful Game is better off with the change of thinking that subsequently followed. ■

→ Arsenal went on to win the match 4–1 against Leeds United.

Black Arsenal

10

THE GODMOTHER OF THE ELTHORNE ESTATE

Celia Facey, Islington and Arsenal in the Community

CELIA FACEY

BEGINNING WITH ARSENAL IN THE COMMUNITY

I moved onto the Elthorne Estate on Hornsey Rise in 1978. I had just had a little baby, and started going to a drop-in centre on the Elthorne where we would meet with other mothers and kids. It was at the drop-in centre that I met this girl named Bernadette, a local mother, who initially asked me to help out at the centre. However, she later asked if I would be interested in volunteering at the after-school club on the estate, and I just thought, Oh, why not? So that's really where I began; volunteering at the after-school club and then a couple of years after I just found myself running it and becoming a staff member there, where I remained for about fifteen years. And it was through the after-school club that I got involved with other projects on the estate as I now knew all the parents and all the children who came to the club from the toddlers upwards. It was then that I met someone who got me involved in youth work on the Elthorne within the St John's Community Centre, which I combined with childminding and fostering. It was through taking a group of kids to the park and the after-school clubs on the estate that I met Jamie Wood from Arsenal in the Community at Elthorne Park in the mid-2000s, who asked if the kids would like to join a football session he was running that day. From there, I started regularly taking a group from the youth club to his sessions, and he later asked me to volunteer to run the Premier League Kicks sessions with him with Arsenal in the Community. I've been here ever since. That's how long I've been with the Arsenal.

THE ARSENAL IN THE COMMUNITY PROGRAMME

We run sessions twice a week for about fifty kids in total. The young kids start at 4.30 till 5.45. Then we finish with the younger ones and the fourteen-year-olds come in and stay until 6.30. That older generation,

← *Previous page:* Celia Facey.

we want them to stay just a little longer to keep them off the streets, you know. At least they're all with us before they're going home. It keeps them safe until their parents pick them up. But the work involves a lot beyond just facilitating football, such as education projects like taking BTECs as well as the Prince's Trust programmes and the FA Level 1 coaching badges to allow the kids to join in with organising the session to become coaches themselves; quite a lot of our kids end up doing that and moving into coaching. Every now and then, some of them who have become coaches come back and see me and say, 'Wow, are you still here?' They come back and become role models within the community for young people. Occasionally, one or two even go on to make it as professional footballers, such as Kaylen Hinds, or 'KK' as we call him. He's from the Elthorne Estate and began playing with us through Arsenal in the Community, before joining the Arsenal Academy. He later won a professional contract at Arsenal before moving to Germany [Wolfsburg]. When he would play for the Under 18s, 23s and in the UEFA Youth League, we'd take all the kids from the Elthorne to watch him play and support him. He's from the manor. Seeing someone like KK, who is from the estate you are from, make it like he did is very, very rare. But it's also hard for kids coming from here when you become a professional footballer because you need to change and keep focused. It sometimes means spending less time with the friends you knew and focusing on what is ahead because you are on a different level with different responsibilities. It's very hard to do that when you are still living on the estate. You can get easily sucked in. It's hard because you've changed. It's different being a professional footballer than when you were a kid running around playing with your friends and being carefree. But everyone knows how precious he is and how much talent he has. And he would still come back to see us and play football in the park, even when he signed a professional contract with Arsenal. That was really important and meant something to me and the kids.

WORKING WITH YOUNG PEOPLE ON THE ELTHORNE ESTATE

I had a good relationship with the young people in and around Archway, and also their parents. And because of this relationship, the young people had a lot of respect for me – even those who unfortunately went the wrong way, which can happen sometimes. They still came to the youth club and always felt that they could talk to me about their problems and get advice, particularly young Black kids. I treated them as if they were my own children. It was difficult, some of the kids ended up in troubled circumstances. However, Arsenal had a lot to offer in terms of activities that they could get involved in, such as the chance to be ball boys/girls, or referee small-sided games that Arsenal in the Community ran for the kids on Elthorne Park. But Arsenal still did a lot to bring some of the young people into the community. It was important to have that kind of involvement with the club.

I helped so many kids over the years from the estate. Given the difficulties they may have in the household, in the playground, with friends around the local area, positive role models are what you need. A little bit of discipline sometimes as well. The work Arsenal in the Community have done on the Elthorne gives at least some kind of hope that there's a pathway for them that's connected to their appreciation for the club. It helps that when they come to these community programmes at Arsenal they see other Black kids, other Black women and they feel a bit more recognised. Because Arsenal's always had this thing where you've had Black players come through, who are either from the local area or from South London. And then you've had the fanbase which is really multicultural and has been important I think for generations of Black people. They recognise that they're people on the pitch like them and are role models.

I get a massive sense of pride in being, you know, a Black woman from the community doing this kind of work. Its lovely. They call me mummy now, though. They don't argue with me! It's important having, you know, really strong Black women as role models, so having that

here in Arsenal in the Community on the Elthorne, particularly for young, Black boys and girls who are from the community, really helps. I remember a couple of years ago I was walking past the City Academy [formerly called Mount Carmel School], which is the main school everyone went to from the Elthorne Estate. A group of my kids were there – I could not see them, but I recognised them from their voices. And I heard one of them say that they wanted to do some silliness. And I just called out to them, 'You better go home now!' They then all shouted, 'Celia is coming!' and ran home. Sometimes if I'm coming back late through the park I'll see a group of them, and they'll say to me, 'What are you doing in the park at this time of night?' But I feel perfectly fine because I've known these kids since they were young playing video games at the youth club and I know the parents really well. They have that respect. They are lovely kids, but every now and then they need pulling up. But things do change and there is a different generation of parent now, so that takes more time and work to build those relationships as they are younger. I could write a book about the Elthorne.

→   Kaylen Hinds, who grew up on the Elthorne Estate, playing in the UEFA Youth League in 2016.

THE FUTURE

There is such a wide range of responsibilities in the work I do with Arsenal in the Community in terms of supporting young people, through football, mentoring, food banks, mental health issues, you know, but also there is some fun as well because you see people doing well when they come through with the programmes in the community, even just through playing football with them. And that makes a difference. They go on to get jobs or enter into further or higher education. That's amazing. But if I was to ask myself what's the most enjoyable aspect of the work I do with Arsenal in the Community, it's working in the Elthorne. It's an amazing job, and I've come to know everyone on my estate over the years. Even the kids say when I'm walking with them, 'You know everybody here!' Even now I'm looking after kids in the youth club football sessions whose parents I looked after years ago – now I'm looking after their kids. They don't believe me when I tell them, 'I looked after your dad many years ago.' That new, younger generation is who we are encouraging to help out and continue what we're doing, through helping out at the sessions we do, even if it's just to carry the bags out to the pitches or organise the bibs for the sessions. You know, some of my kids in my day and people I know are now working in that kind of field now: social work and community work with young people. Now we've got young people here helping out and taking responsibility for their own.

There are a lot of challenges and social problems that some of the kids face on the Elthorne. We have economic troubles, youth crime and knife violence – I've seen the worst side. But we encourage them not to give up. We really push them to get them to get them going. And it's not just about football. If Arsenal in the Community can't help directly, we try and get them into a different direction to get help, like assistance with job interviews or going to college. There is so much talent here and possible opportunities for young Black people from the community who could make something of themselves, be it professional footballers or lawyers. They are all intelligent Black kids.

Every year for years I say to everyone that I'm going to retire. But the response is always 'No, no, no, you can't leave!' And I'll always say, 'All right, I'll stay for another year.' And that's why I'm still here. I love working with the kids and now we've got these little new generations coming through who want me to stay around. These are nice gestures. ◼

← Children participating in one of Arsenal in the Community's programmes.

The Godmother of the Elthorne Estate

Andrew Cole in 1991. He would make one league appearance for Arsenal.

A young Ashley Cole posing with the League Title trophy.

Opposite:
ABOVE: David Rocastle, Kevin Campbell, Michael Thomas and Paul Davis.
BELOW: Arsenal fans during the title parade, Islington, 1991.

Thierry Henry after joining Arsenal from Juventus in 1999.

Patrick Vieira on the steps of the East Stand, Highbury.

Opposite:
ABOVE LEFT: Ian Wright and Kevin Campbell at Stansted Airport in 1993.
ABOVE RIGHT: Dainton 'The Bear' Connell.
BELOW: Ian Wright celebrates equalising Cliff Bastin's record with Lee Dixon in 1997.

11

MICHAEL WATSON: A LIFE FOUGHT IN RED

CLIVE CHIJIOKE NWONKA

The De Beauvoir Estate that borders Canonbury and Dalston is one of a number of housing developments that make up De Beauvoir Town. The estate itself, built by Hackney Council in the late 1960s, is a combination of several high tower blocks and a series of adjoined low rise blocks and maisonettes. In the 1970s, Hackney Council would introduce the principle of 'filtered permeability', a central pillar of the New Urbanism design movement that sought to privilege the needs of pedestrians over private vehicles by discouraging dangerous commuter traffic from passing through residential areas. For the De Beauvoir residents, filtered permeability resulted in the opening up of new play amenities and spaces that allowed for recreational activities for the young, such as street football, to be enjoyed free from the hazards of road traffic. However, the by-product was a spatial enclosure and separation, a socially contained neighbourhood.

It is this aligning of location, locality and sport that informs this chapter's interest in the symbiosis between football and boxing, for it would be football that would entice a then fourteen-year-old De Beauvoir Estate resident called Michael Watson to take up boxing, having been attacked, not for the first time, by a local bully after Watson and his friends beat a group of older boys in an impromptu football game on the estate. Black Arsenal, as both an intellectual concept and socio-cultural feeling, is something that is also bound in the practice, or necessity if you will, of watching and witnessing. This witnessing of Blackness within a space of Black absence, which produces its own practice of racial recognition, is a lifelong, recurring experience located in the depths of Black cultural memories formed in our nascent years, made all the more vivid and evocative through the influential medium of television. One of those, for me, was the boxer Michael 'the Force' Watson. Watson, of Jamaican heritage, who had moved with his family to the De Beauvoir from Stoke Newington in the early seventies, was Black, a Londoner, working class, and centrally placed in the period's most spectacular moments of televisual Black imagery on a national scale. And in these televisual moments, Arsenal seemed to be present as both the preface and coda to the Watson story.

← *Previous page:* Michael Watson defeats Nigel Benn for the British/Commonwealth middleweight title in 1989.

To be a boxing spectator in the early 1990s, either amongst the rapturous energy of the live boxing arena or from the comfort of a living room armchair, was to enjoy what many describe as a golden age of British boxing with the middleweight and super-middleweight classes at its very forefront. Having previously been in the shadow of heavyweight boxing, this was a weight division that was to be popularised by the era's eminent British promoters, Frank Warren and Barry Hearn, who by the early 1990s would bring a much needed credibility, legitimacy and prestige to the newly established but generally disregarded World Boxing Organisation – from its inception in 1988, the organisation and its champions would be treated with derision amongst the more preeminent boxing sanctioning bodies, the WBC, WBA and IBF.

This was a popularising that, like much of what has been explored in this book's defining of Black Arsenal, was brought into being as a result of the serendipitous alignment between television and a moment of social and cultural change. Before the late 1990s, the British terrestrial television landscape comprised of just four channels (the others being BBC One, BBC Two and Channel 4), and ITV Sport's investment in the sport and the subsequent terrestrial broadcasting of domestic and international title fights through contracts with both Warren and Hearn's promotional outfits in

↑   The De Beauvoir Estate in North London.

Michael Watson

the mid to late 1980s cemented the position of ITV as the primary vector of live boxing to the nation.

More than any visual medium, television is a powerful sphere where cultural identities and iconographies are made and reflected back to us, and whilst we should rightly acknowledge the often forgotten ring efforts of Nottingham's talented Herol Graham, it is Ilford's Nigel Benn, Brighton's Chris Eubank and North London's Watson who would between 1988 and 1994 contest for the Commonwealth middleweight title and various iterations of the middleweight and super-middleweight world championship, and become synonymous with the period's hailing of British boxing as a televised spectacle before the decision by Hearn and Warren in the mid-1990s to move their fighters away from ITV's terrestrial broadcasting to the more economically lucrative but now publicly restricted subscription based Sky Sports platform.

Prior to the dominating triopoly of Benn, Eubank and Watson being dismantled in parts by Dublin's Steve Collins's defeat of both Benn (twice) and Eubank (twice) the idiomatic maxim that 'styles make fights', a boxing proverb that describes the set of conditions and contingencies involved in the making of classic boxing encounters, where the boxing fight as an entertaining spectacle is made so not simply through the coming together of highly marketised, championship prize-fighters of elite ability, but their specific pugilistic approaches was the underpinning principle to their

rivalry. For those less attuned to the arcane nomenclatures of boxing theory, an easy analogy can be drawn from the intransitive nature of the hand game Rock, Paper, Scissors; the rock may well indeed blunt the scissors, but the paper will always wrap the rock, and the paper will always succumb to shredding by the scissors. In other words, boxing is governed by an absence of universalism and predictability that makes the sport, like no other, a non-linear spectacle of screened dramatic action.

However, like all variants of capitalism, the boxing *business* has always been able, to some degree, to manage and mitigate for these uncertainties through the applying of a range of industrial imperatives that collectively came to be understood pejoratively over time as boxing politics. Seemingly obvious fights go unmade, fights between leading boxers of a generation or era are delayed at all costs until the 'B' fighter is all but exhausted of all the skills or stylistic feats that would pose a threat to the A-side marquee opponent, lucrative 'cash cow' fighters are protected from dangerous challengers who may dismantle a promoter's economic model by one knockout punch, deserving contenders are denied opportunities, broadcaster-backed home fighters are awarded wins their performances in no way warranted and controversial decisions are made in the ring to preserve more lucrative future fights already in the making. Paradoxically, such boxing politics maintain the sport as a highly debatable and entertaining live phenomena, and it is the often contrasting, but at times complementary, styles that each boxer carries into the ring that will create either classic fights that increase the market value of a fighter, or diminish their economic stock through lacklustre performances where the two fighters' styles are unable to 'gel', cancel each other out, and are unable to conjure up the spectacle of blooded sporting warfare. But this cultivating of the spectacular is not something that is observed solely at the point of physical engagement in the ring.

For the very *raison d'être* of boxing promotion, like the marketing of any product, is to continuously convince its consumer or audience that what they are to encounter, despite what they have seen previously or what logic suggests, is something new and unmissable. With a heavy reliance on the pre-fight enlivened actions and words of the opposing boxers, it is the creation of (and our investment in) excessive promotion through extravagant claims and the stimulating of unwarranted excitement – in other words, the creation of 'hype', that make us believe that *this* fight will be different. Thus, boxing as the spectacular is determined not just by the boxers' stylistic predilections and techniques, but the collision of their respective personalities and public personas.

In Benn, his status as the era's most dangerous practitioner of licensed hyper-violence was somewhat reflected in the very nickname the 'Dark Destroyer', whose time spent serving in the British Army in Northern Ireland in the 1980s underpinned a fearless, menacing nature further propelled by a youth spent fighting against racist National Front gangs in London's East End. In the ring, Benn possessed an intentionally crude and homespun boxing style that was somewhat compensated for (or complemented by) his almost unparalleled knockout power and an aggressiveness and relentless, attritional in-fighting style of an exciting crowd-pleasing pressure fighter who combined elements of a high-guard European trained boxer with the all-action, come-forward pursuit of a Philadelphian slugger.

In Eubank, a Dulwich born, Brighton based fighter who had spent the early part of his career training and fighting in New York's South Bronx, revelled in a deliberate, caricatured aristocratic posture and demeanour that bellied his impoverished and troubled upbringing in Peckham. In many ways, it was this extroverted choreography and his embracing of his pantomime villain public image that firmly established Eubank as the era's box office draw, and was assisted by his unashamed displays of vanity and material extravagance; an excessive, regal satirical presence adorned with expensive jewellery, sunglasses, a trademark cane, top hat and monocle. However, it was his commitment to the relentless public denigration of his opponents, delivered in a received pronunciation that produced, before his opponent had even entered the ring, an air of superiority and social dominion that in evoking amongst the public and spectator alike an insatiable desire to see Eubank

Michael Watson

boxer that emerged as antithetical to both Benn and Eubank in both fighting style and crucially, attitude, public image and relatability. Softly spoken, respectful but quietly determined and confident, Watson, a devout Christian, was a patient, skilled, well rounded and perfectly balanced boxer, and of the three possessed the superior technical skills and boxing fundamentals that had been developed through the UK amateur system that brought him to within one win of qualifying for the 1984 Olympic Games in Los Angeles. For so many, both within the boxing fraternity and the local area, Watson, who supplemented his still extremely modest boxing earnings with plastering and mini cab driving, retained an attachment to his North London community through his love of Arsenal and the Black Christian church that only cemented the perception of him as an accessible everyman within a field of arrogance, brashness and a status driven separation between sporting superstar and the public that made them so. With Eubank in possession of the WBO middleweight belt, and Benn as the Commonwealth title holder, Watson, understandably, commendably, but ultimately (for the fighter) unsatisfactorily, became firmly fixed in the nation's imagination as the era's people's champion.

The synergetic iconography of the Eubank/Benn/Watson triopoly can undoubtedly be identified in their differing responses to the orthodoxy of boxing as business before boxing as sport, a set of contrasts most observed during

defeated in the most brutal fashion, would subsequently encourage his opponents to forgo all sensible game plan and attack with a reckless abandon that would simply play into Eubank's hands. In the ring, Eubank displayed an unpredictable and eccentric boxing style that would frustrate opponents, coupled with a seemingly impenetrable chin that was built into the mental makeup of a fighter who possessed an iron will to survive.

Whilst both Benn and Eubank, in their firm understanding and adherence to the basic economic decrees of boxing in how their attention-grabbing antics participated in the generating of anticipation and hype, displayed a number of commonalities, in Watson, however, we were confronted by a

↑ Michael Watson in January 1991.

the fight between Watson and Benn in a £40,000 purpose-built 'supertent' in Finsbury Park on 14 May 1989 for the British and Commonwealth middleweight championships. The binary between Benn's wealthy extravagance and ferocity and Watson's quiet affability simply accentuated the common-sense belief that Watson would be quickly destroyed by Benn's destructive knockout power, and Watson would enter the ring as the overwhelming underdog despite enjoying the home advantage of being just across the road from Finsbury Park station and minutes to Arsenal's stadium. That evening, Watson would knock out the Dark Destroyer in round 6 in one of the biggest upsets in British boxing.

However, despite Watson's continued success, there was a tremendous economic disparity that remained between him and the two other leading fighters in the period. This would lead him to successfully sue his manager/promoter Mickey Duff in a landmark ruling that which would effectively bar individuals from acting as both boxing manager and promoter, allowing for greater financial returns for future fighters. It was the promise of the world title, popular recognition and overdue financial reward that would await Watson in June 1991 at Earls Court, where he would enter into a highly controversial and contested bout against Chris Eubank for the WBO's middleweight world championship title.

↑ Michael Watson promoting his next fight at Highbury.

Michael Watson

Such was the strength of Watson's support for Arsenal as part of his regional and personal identity that, as he approached the ring, the ITV Sport anchor Jim Rosenthal would repeat Watson's pre-fight claim that 'the Gunners won the title, Spurs won the cup' (the 1991 FA Cup) and in winning the world championship 'He's gonna bring about a treble for North London,' and would comment on stories that had propagated in the media in the build-up that Watson would actually be carrying Arsenal's recently won league title trophy into the ring during his walk. However, without the trophy in hand, but with his boxing shorts bearing the Arsenal colours, Watson would dominate the bout over twelve rounds only for the judges to award the fight to Eubank by majority decision. Watson, who had ended the fight hands aloft to the piercing arena-wide chants of 'Arsenal' that when coupled with the commentators' declaration that 'it's been a very good night for the Watson family of North London', was placed at the centre of a televised sphere unified in the inconceivability of anything other than a wide points win. Seconds later, Watson would be left distraught at the victory that had been denied to him, and the controversial conclusion would lead ITV's own commentary team to describe the decision as a 'robbery', and further implant in Watson's mind the idea that he was in an endless fight against not just his opponents, but the boxing establishment and its economic interests.

However, the public condemnation of the decision, which was augmented by a journalistic outrage that combined vitriolic written columns with Watson's Arsenal-draped image across various national newspapers' front and back pages, coupled with the renewed adulation for Watson, would create a powerful public fervour for a rematch, undoubtedly assisted by the instinctive sense of indignity and disrespect expressed by Eubank at the very thought that his victory was a decision of anything other than his boxing superiority. Like the most classic forms of narrative drama, of which televised boxing of that era or any other performs as a simple variant, the degree to which a story's audience is drawn and retained is through the strength of its presenting of easily identifiable binary characterisations of positive and negative, good and bad, likable and unlikable, hero and villain.

To this end, there is a highly significant subplot that emerges to become one of the defining features of not only the events of the fight, but the much broader narrative of Watson and what came to be one of the defining features in the relationship between Watson and Arsenal. Watson would wear the Arsenal colours once again during the 21 September 1991 rematch with Eubank, which was to be fought at the still nascent but increasingly competitive super-middleweight division. More significantly, the fight was to be held at Tottenham Hotspur's White Hart Lane.

Watched by 22,000 within the stadium and a 13 million television audience on ITV, the event would be telegraphed through *The Big*

→ A poster for Chris Eubank and Michael Watson's rematch at White Hart Lane for the super-middleweight title in 1991. The choice of location brought the North London footballing rivalry into the boxing ring:

Watson opted to wear the red and white of his beloved Arsenal, while Eubank wore the Tottenham Hotspur home kit shorts of that season as a direct challenge to Watson.

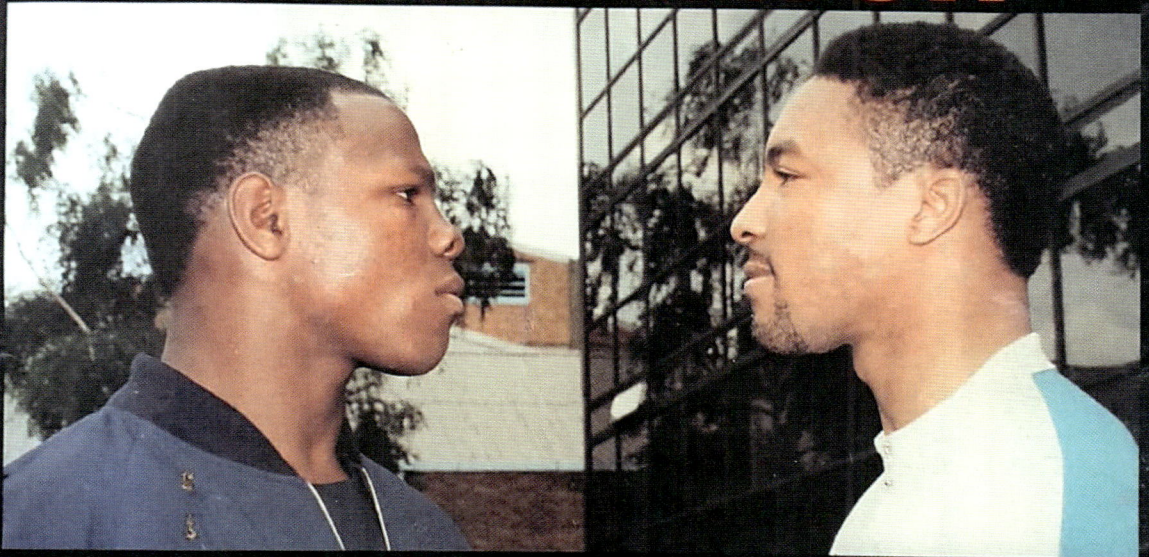

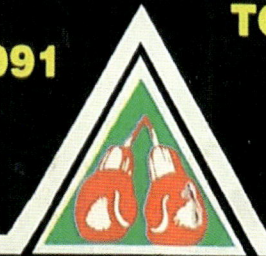

Fight Live, the London Weekend Television-produced programming for ITV's live boxing coverage that would place particular interest in the significance of both Watson's lifelong support of Arsenal and the location of the fight, all of which was captured in the live build-up to the rematch. Watson is framed against the backdrop of the White Hart Lane pitch whilst being interviewed by ITV, having just witnessed Eubank storm out of a pre-fight press conference that had taken place some weeks prior at the stadium. Here, Watson reiterated his intention for the fight to be seen not only as his securing of the world title, but as the defence of the very respectability of British boxing.

Later, Watson would enter the ring wearing a red and white robe with the Arsenal cannon logo embroidered on its back above his name, where Jim Rosenthal would comment on the overwhelmingly positive reception Watson would enjoy despite being within enemy territory. Watson was of course not oblivious to the meaning of the fight being staged at White Hart Lane as no different to any other version, be it as football fan or fighter of the Tottenham v Arsenal rivalry, and would insist on occupying the away changing room. As Watson was pictured waiting in the ring in red and white, ITV's commentators would make frequent reference to Watson's devotion to Arsenal, reminding the audience that Arsenal had won earlier that afternoon (they had beaten Sheffield United 5–2 at Highbury, and many of the team's players had made the twenty-minute trip up Seven Sisters Road to the fight) and one would comment that Watson's entry into the ring must surely have been the first time that someone covered head to toe in the colours of Arsenal would receive such a positive reception within White Hart Lane.

With few exceptions, such as Glasgow's Old Firm of Rangers and Celtic or to a lesser extent Edinburgh's Hearts and Hibernian, the UK's two-team footballing cities generally eschew any strict adherence to inherited political, ethnic and religious allegiances. Indeed, despite the faint associations with Catholicism and Protestantism that was said to have informed Liverpool and Everton up to the mid-to-late 1970s, there is no clear social division organising the club's city-based support. Liverpool is a city where both red and blue can be found in the same neighbourhoods, streets and families, reflective of a unity between the two clubs that serve as a collective identity, one that was made all the more significant by Thatcherism's concerted attempts at the political, social and economic destruction of the city throughout the 1980s.

In London the picture is even more complex. Given the vast number of professional clubs that are scattered across the capital, the doctrine of support for a club via geographical proximity is undermined by the natural spaces of cross-cultural, regional and spatial interaction in schooling, and the even tighter-knit spaces of the home, where the density of both post-war and modern housing estates shape the convivial conditions of life within the metropolis. Thus, despite a general understanding that the bulk of the match-attending support for Arsenal is sourced from Islington, Camden, Brent, Barnet and Hackney, with Tottenham from the boroughs of north-east London, Essex and Hertfordshire, the four miles that separate Highbury and White Hart Lane are laden with non-linearities and cross-pollinations that spill into the everyday flows and locations of human engagement.

The potential for the already highly anticipated bout between Eubank and Watson to be presented as a crystallisation of Tottenham v Arsenal, and in turn provide a compelling and extremely marketable under-narrative to the fight, was of course also not lost on the ever-performative Eubank. Emerging from the changing rooms to his trademark theme, Tina Turner's 'Simply the Best', Eubank wore the Tottenham Hotspur home kit shorts of that season (1991–92) as a direct challenge to Watson. In effect, both by serendipity and strategy, the bout became a site where the histories and colours of an eighty-two-year-old local footballing rivalry were to be superimposed onto the boxing ring and contested over thirty-six minutes. Fighters, promoters and broadcasters alike were unified in the endeavour to relocate a virulent footballing rivalry from the pitches, pubs, and playgrounds of North London to the ring. Eubank had never previously expressed any particular interest in football. His donning of the Spurs shorts served as yet another iteration of the mind games that

were the defining feature of his performative oeuvre, though they had so far been unable to unnerve the focus of the Arsenal-inspired Watson.

The fight itself can be understood as commencing not at round 1 but round 13, picking up just where the first bout left off. Watson would again dominate Eubank with a combination of subtle but effective movements, front footed punching and strength and fitness. By the tenth of the twelve scheduled rounds, Eubank was behind on all the judges' scorecards. Further, Eubank would be knocked down by Watson with eighteen seconds of the penultimate round remaining, and despite Eubank rising from the canvas and receiving only a standing four count instead of the required eight, there was a permeating feeling of *fait accompli*. Eubank would need to knock Watson out, which at this as any other stage of the twenty-three rounds they had fought in total, seemed a chimeric impossibility. However, at the very conclusion of the round, Eubank suddenly landed a powerful uppercut that sent Watson to the canvas, falling prone with the back of his head and neck landing heavily on the ring's bottom ropes, creating a whiplashing effect. Displaying the kind of inner strength and tenacity when most hurt that would come to define him, Watson also got up immediately and was able to make it back to his corner, albeit with the assistance of his trainer Jimmy Tibbs. To the unaccustomed and casual boxing spectator, Watson's unsteadiness and look of disorientation

Michael Watson

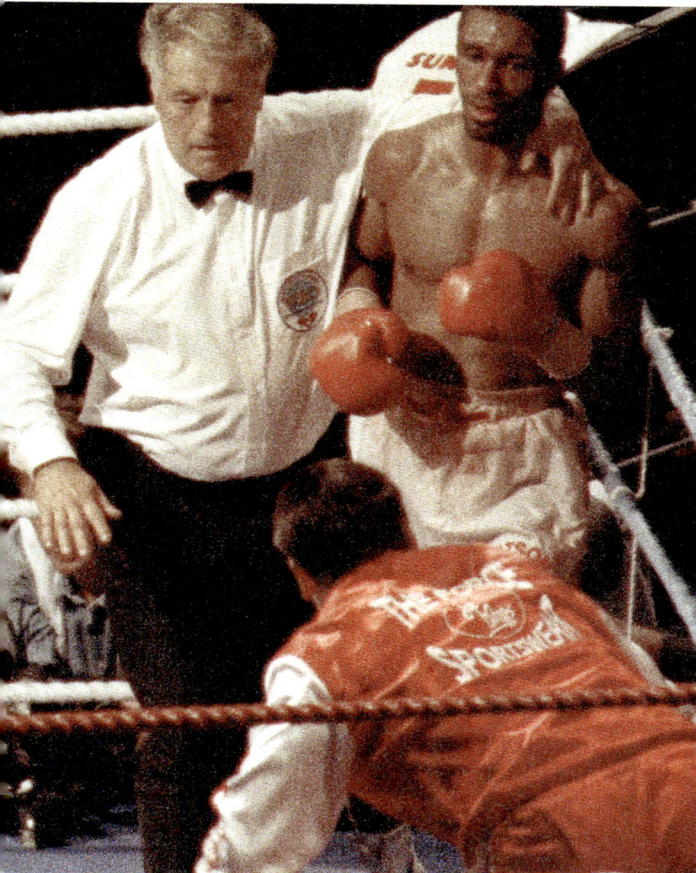

displayed as he rose for the twelfth and final round may have appeared as the simple bodily after-effects of a knockdown that would perhaps take a few moments to shake off. But for those more knowledgeable of the physiological effects of boxing and the specific mannerisms of the boxer himself, as Watson emerged from his corner needing to be physically pulled to the centre of the ring to perform the conventional touching of gloves as a mark of mutual sportsmanship and respect towards the shared display of stamina to have survived to the fight's final three minutes, it was clear that something was dramatically wrong.

Watson, having been on the front foot for the vast majority of the fight, immediately retreated to a corner and recoiled against the ropes as Eubank threw a barrage of unanswered punches, convincing the referee to stop the fight. Watson was again guided to his corner by a combination of the referee and his trainer, and as Tibbs and the official engaged in heated debate over the legitimacy of his intervention, Watson was now in the throes of a new battle. Unbeknown at the time to Gary Newbon, the ITV presenter interviewing the victorious Eubank live on air, the spectators at home and at ringside who could see nothing beyond the sea of bodies packed in the ring that traditionally greets the conclusion of a major boxing match, Watson had collapsed in his corner of the ring, slumping into the arms of Tibbs. Shockingly, there were no equipped ringside doctors, ambulance or paramedics present at the event, and it would take nearly

eight minutes before any kind of medical assistance would arrive. The stricken Watson would later have to be carried out of the ring by Tibbs and his two assistants in the absence of a stretcher, the index of an entire culture of institutional negligence that is undoubtedly captured in the now famous but no less heartbreaking image of Watson, still draped in Arsenal's red and white, lying unconscious and starved of oxygen on the canvas, his head resting on a briefcase.

A total of thirty minutes elapsed before Watson received oxygen treatment at North Middlesex Hospital's neurosurgical unit. It would be two hours from the conclusion of the fight before he entered the operating theatre to undergo lifesaving surgery, having been transferred to St Bartholomew's Hospital because North Middlesex did not have the required neurological facilities. Watson had sustained a severe subdural brain haemorrhage, much exacerbated by the absence of oxygen, of which the saucer-sized blood clot had starved his brain. He would spend forty days in a coma. Doctors advised his family that he would never emerge.

Watson would confound the medical experts. He regained consciousness and survived several brain operations, spending the next seven years battling to regain his hearing, his speech, his mobility and the use of his limbs.

Despite an outpouring of support from throughout the boxing world, the financial dictates of boxing politics meant that the televised pursuit of super-middleweight supremacy simply proceeded with the era's

← *Previous page:* Eubank defeats Watson. Watson collapses in the ring after a 12th round knockout which leaves him with irreparable brain damage.

remaining protagonists. Eubank would continue his reign as the WBO super-middleweight world champion, albeit with a marked change in his boxing style. He failed (or refused) to knock out all but two of his next fifteen opponents before suffering the first of two defeats to Steve Collins in 1995. Nigel Benn, who sat ringside in support of Watson during his last fight and would become extremely close to Watson in the ensuing years, would win the WBC super-middleweight title the following year, now under the guidance of Tibbs.

In watching again the fight in its entirety from the vantage point of the present day, with the benefit of all that is now already known or learnt about the aftermath of the bout, what becomes valuable to us is found not primarily in the memories that are recruited in the revisiting of a historic and tragic event, but the images, words and gestures that were missed, went unseen, unheard or unremembered, that take on newfound significance. Here, it is the comments of *Big Fight Live*'s anchor Rosenthal, who would in the closing words of ITV's live coverage turn to his co-commentator, the former Scottish lightweight world champion Jim Watt and ask, having now seen Watson end two failed world title challenges prone and badly hurt on the canvas, 'Is he [Watson] one of those fighters that we'll remember in future years as a nearly man?' Watt, who like Rosenthal, those in attendance and the viewing public, had believed that the prone Watson had been overcome by exhaustion, would make

reference to both his damaging eleventh-round knockout loss to the Jamaican WBA middleweight champion Mike McCallum the previous year at the Royal Albert Hall in his first world title attempt alongside his current condition in the ring to preface his own question of 'can he recover from that?' with the speculative answer of 'I don't think so.' It is through the revisiting and freezing of time that is permitted to us in the archive of television that allows us to see how these questions, that would surely have served as a deeply chilling epilogue had the incident ended in fatal tragedy, have now, for those who remember, become a question that would come to be answered repeatedly and emphatically by Watson himself in the ensuing years. It is significant in the context of Black Arsenal as a (tele)visual culture that Watson's first public appearance after his injury would be in front of 18,000 at Highbury in 1993.

He had spent nearly two years away from the public eye, firstly within the walls of Hackney's Homerton Hospital, where his recovery was so remarkable that he convinced his dumbfounded doctors to let him continue his rehabilitation at his home in Islington. He would still require expensive twenty-four-hour care. On 28 March of that year, a fundraising benefit match for the Michael Watson Trust Fund set up to support his rehabilitation was organised jointly by the club and Benn's former manager, Ambrose Mendy. Watson, who had played in an Arsenal celebrity side prior to his injury, would be in the

Michael Watson

stadium to see a celebrity Arsenal XI for his benefit. In not too dissimilar fashion to the subplot of Eubank v Watson II, there would be another, more benevolent iteration of the North London derby, where a veteran Tottenham side would play an Arsenal XI that would feature the recently transferred Arsenal midfielder David Rocastle, and former players John Lukic, Alan Ball, Chris Whyte, Liam Brady and Charlie George. Such was the global permeation of the Watson struggle, Highbury would be graced by the presence of the legendary American middleweight champion 'Marvelous' Marvin Hagler, and live performances from the Pretenders' Chrissie Hynde, the reggae band Aswad and the London Community Gospel Choir. The event's programme served as a visual document of Watson prior to his injury, and he is pictured posing at Highbury with Arsenal's 1991 League Championship trophy. You could easily mistake Watson for an Arsenal player of the period. Later that day, Watson would finally emerge in a wheelchair from a large crowd of protective aides and members of the Arsenal Ladies squad onto the Highbury pitch to a rendition of Bob Marley and the Wailers' 'One Love', eventually reaching the centre circle, guided by Arsenal forward Kevin Campbell.

What is being explored here is the connection between football and boxing that is tied to a social milieu where both sports enjoy a particular synonymity as a distinctively working-class sporting and cultural activity, made in part by the realities for young people who are born and raised within a social and physical landscape where football playing is an instinctive and inexpensive feature of low to no-income inner-city living, and fighting, be it through the body, spirit or in the combination of both, is not simply an anti-social class-based posture but often an instinctive mode of spatial, economic, physical and personal survival. Television, with its finite capacity to craft its own realities, can often present the most inaccurate picture of the economic truths of elite sport, and despite the alluring glamour of professional boxers on primetime television, only an extremely small number of the boxers who emerge from Britain's housing estates and working-class environs will ever be able to sustain a

↑ Michael Watson on the Highbury pitch in 1993.

living through boxing alone, yet alone earn the kind of money from the sport that will allow them to live in relative comfort once their careers are over.

It is possible that this is unreality, that the televised boxer and the televised football player, emerging from the very same lower-socio economic backgrounds and physical sites, share only a visual presence across event-led sporting broadcast that offers the audience the perception of wealth and financial security, but conceals the more austere economic precarity that essentially tell us why fighters 'fight', means that boxers can often see an attachment to the nearest major football club as equally a point of attachment to regionality and locality *as* personal identity. But I am offering a particularly romantic idea of how a boxer's footballing allegiances flow naturally from one's birth and upbringings in the sporting city, and there is the potential to nuance this argument.

We seldom hear of professional boxers professing a love for their local rugby club, be they from the historically elitist Rugby Union cultures of the south or the northern coal mines and textile mill towns that line the M62 corridor and adjoin the Rugby League clubs of Huddersfield, Bradford, Wigan, Warrington, St Helens, Leeds and beyond. On the other hand, while the publicly expressed support for one's local football club was previously a novel and generally benign occurrence, what boxing has now produced is the *expectation* of televised interviews with an up-and-coming boxer expressing their ambition to fight at their hometown football stadium. Like all things dependent on the attention economy, boxing, on either side of the fighter/spectator divide, is now more than ever a heavily saturated and competitive marketplace. Given the importance placed in the fighter-as-commodity, such football club associations can be viewed as part of a cynical promotional culture of self-branding through the easily acquired support from a ready-made fanbase. The professional fighter as a representation of a geographic, cultural and social specificity can at its most strategic allow the individual to present themselves as the public embodiment of the distinctive identities, conventions and idiosyncrasies of a city or region that are held within a club's terrace culture, while maintaining one eye on its large-capacity stadium as a lucrative income-generating venue. This claim to a club allegiance as promotional culture finds various manifestations: the sporting of their club shirts in press shoots, the club crest emblazoned on their boxing apparel, ring walks that are made to the club theme or the invitation to parade their newly acquired titles to a crowd of unquestioning supporters on matchday.

A prime example is found in Ricky Hatton, the Stockport-born light welterweight/welterweight champion and lifelong supporter of Manchester City, most evident by Hatton's ring entrances made to the thunderous soundtrack of the terrace anthem 'Blue Moon'. Hatton's devotion to Manchester City would bring a decidedly working-class British footballing

Michael Watson

atmosphere to the otherwise glamorous and exclusive sporting arena of the MGM Grand Garden in Las Vegas, most notable in the build-up to Hatton's 2007 world title unification fight against Floyd Mayweather Jnr, where the Michigan-born American world champion would goad both Hatton and his 30,000 travelling supporters by wearing a Manchester United shirt during the press tour. In the fifteen years since, the replication of Hatton's mass support through appeals to his local football club's fanbase has become the strategic model for much of British boxing's promotional endeavours. There is Josh Warrington, the Leeds-born two-time featherweight world champion who, in his first world title attempt against Wales's Lee Selby in 2018 at Elland Road, would be accompanied into the ring by former Leeds United player and cult icon Lucas Radebe. Kell Brook, Sheffield's Winkobank Gym-trained former IBF welterweight world champion who would regularly adorn the red, white and black colours of Sheffield United in the ring and would eventually fight at Bramall Lane, became an embodiment of the distinctively multicultural part of the steel city.

There are also a host of British boxers who during their careers would reference their support for local football clubs as a conduit for the affirming of the connection between fighter and place, such as Hammersmith's ex WBA super-middleweight world champion George Groves (Chelsea), former WBO heavyweight champion Herbie Hide (Norwich City), the former unified super-middleweight champion Carl Froch (Nottingham Forest), Barnet's former IBF middleweight champion Darren Barker (Chelsea), Islington's middleweight/super-middleweight world title contender John Ryder (Arsenal), Kevin Mitchell (West Ham), the Dagenham lightweight world title challenger who would fight at his beloved Boleyn Ground, Liverpool's four Smith brothers and unified world champion Natasha Jonas (Liverpool), and Harlesden's Olympic gold medallist and former IBF super-middleweight world champion James DeGale (Arsenal). Hackney's light-heavyweight world title contender Anthony Yarde's sponsorship by Adidas has brought with it the opportunity to establish a more strategic connection with Arsenal that was further cemented by the club's kit manufacturing deal with Adidas in 2019, and he would train in the new Arsenal 2019–20 shirt for his world title bout against Sergey Kovalev in August of that year. Toxteth's Tony Bellew also offers a novel example of a more sincere unity between fighter and football and who throughout his career would enter the ring to Everton's Z-Cars theme, and Bellew's own relationship to the city of Liverpool expressed in his still passionately demonstrated devotion to Everton leaves us in little doubt that had he not become an elite boxer, he would still be firmly placed among fans within Goodison Park's Gwladys Street End.

Watson, however, possesses a different kind of synonymity with Arsenal. He continues to be bestowed with the kind of cross-generational support from the fanbase and a recognition from within the club's culture that in no way can be categorised as a branded adulation. For as we find in some of the examples above, the strategic and marketed associations claimed between local boxer and the local football club rapidly evaporate as their careers end (or once they lose), indicative of how the mutual genuineness of the boxer-as-community representative through elite football clubs can only truly be assessed at the point of the decreased visibility of the boxers themselves as commodified prize-fighters. Watson, however, who would never win a world title and whose final fight was on that fateful evening in 1991 at Tottenham Hotspur's White Hart Lane stadium, retains an indelible connection with Arsenal that is unaffected by the cruel but inevitable logic of the boxing business.

In 1998, Watson would be awarded £1 million in damages after successfully suing the British Boxing Board of Control (BBBofC) at the High Court for negligence. The court ruled that the BBBofC failed in their responsibility to ensure that there was sufficient medical provision at a fight and that the provision and administering of medical equipment such as oxygen and resuscitation devices at the fight undoubtedly would have significantly altered the outcomes for Watson after the incident. The medical and safety requirements and procedures that are now in place to ensure the health of boxers before, during and after bouts are in no doubt a result of the near decade-long legal fight that Watson fought and won.

Watson was twenty-six when he last entered the ring against Eubank that fateful evening, an age where both boxer and footballer, barring injury or other anomalies and unforeseeables, will begin to come into their physical, performative and cumulative prime. Watson took to the Highbury pitch in 1993 under the medical judgement that he had suffered irreparable paralysis. But Watson believed not only that he would walk again, but that he could compete, that he could apply his competitive spirit to a seemingly impossible sporting challenge, just as he had done previously against business and Eubank.

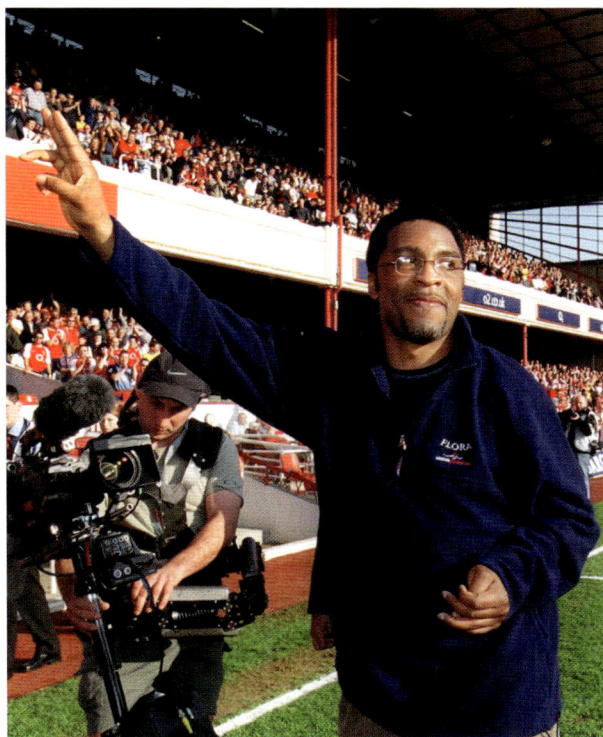

↑ Michael Watson celebrates completing the London Marathon at Highbury, 2003.

Michael Watson

Nearly twelve years after his final fight, and alongside his neurosurgeon and Eubank, Watson would over six days complete the 2003 London Marathon, an unbelievable feat given his prognosis in the weeks and months after the Eubank bout. In doing so, he raised £150,000 for the Brain and Spine Foundation. It is significant that at the point of this personal triumph, he would again return to a sold-out Highbury, ten years after his first appearance following the tragedy, this time not bound by the wheelchair to which the medical experts had insisted he would spend his life confined, but on his feet. Again he received a standing ovation from the Arsenal crowd, the kind of hero's adulation reserved only for the celebratory fanfare of testimonials or for the very greatest of Arsenal players bowing out of Highbury or the Emirates for the final time. It is with some looseness that I describe his presence at Highbury that day as a 'return'. Many would argue that he had never left, and it feels more than appropriate for him to be described as 'Arsenal's Michael Watson'.

The legitimacy of the cultural recognition of Watson *as* Arsenal, a figure who is able to transcend and unify both sports, would be further affirmed in the unveiling of the Arsenal crowd mural installed on Emirates Stadium in May 2023. Here, the illustration reproduces an iconic picture where Watson is captured in the spectacular triumphant pose of a prize-fighter, arms aloft after his victory by first-round knockout over Anthony Brown at Bethnal

Green's legendary York Hall on 1 May 1991, a triumph that came just five days before Arsenal captured their second league title in three years, defeating Manchester United at Highbury. There is a particular poignancy that is contained in the illustration of Watson, quietly placed among the other supporters. Only those with the most limited awareness of Arsenal's cultural history would fail to notice the bare bodied silhouette of a boxer, whose classic red gloves point to a fighter of a different age. Yet he is also inconspicuous, lost in a sea of cheering fans in Arsenal shirts holding banners. In many respects, this evokes the very essence of Black Arsenal: how the club has become an expansive space of Black identification and the recognition of integrated difference, while remaining, in many ways, *indifferent* to this difference. The paradox here is that Black Arsenal flourishes most, is most experienced and most identifiable, in the inelaborate, the unexpressed and the undeliberate, a set of tenets that mirrors the characteristics that made Watson such a relatable figure. It is echoed in the very title of the mural artwork: *Found a Place Where We Belong*. We should draw particular attention to the word belonging, a term that implies, among other things, a mutuality between person and place, a place of unconditional acceptance and recognition, where the club becomes a space of affinity among peers, where social, racial and economic hierarchies can *potentially* be flattened, reconciled and made unimportant, where cultural and spiritual bridges are formed and maintained in ways that would be unattainable in other spheres of life, but are latent within the stands.

Unlike Tony Bellew, who live on Sky Sports would capture the WBC cruiserweight world title among 15,000 Evertonians under the lights of an erected boxing ring in the middle of Everton's Goodison Park, Michael Watson would never have the chance to step into the boxing ring within the ticketed and televised parameters of his beloved Arsenal Stadium. However, while it is indeed the case that Watson served as a loyal representative of Arsenal, it is also true that at each juncture in his life, Arsenal has been in Watson's corner. Any exploration of his trajectory will reveal a fighter whose battles, be they against his rivals in the ring, or the physiological, mental and neurological struggles of surviving a coma, life-threatening brain operations and the subsequent long rehabilitation, or in his successful challenge to the BBBofC that would usher in legislation that would change the sport for all professional fighters, or spiritual, in the resilience and fortitude displayed in completing the London Marathon – all these were fought for, with, through, alongside and within Highbury, and with this, all that unfolds on its turf and contained within its terraces. ■

↑ Michael Watson and his image on the Arsenal mural.

Michael Watson

12

EZRA COLLECTIVE

The Arsenal, the Black diaspora and making connections through music

CLIVE CHIJIOKE NWONKA

Brothers Femi (drummer) and TJ Koleoso (bassist) make up two of the Mercury Music Prize-winning jazz quintet Ezra Collective. Alongside keyboardist Joe Armon-Jones, trumpeter Ife Ogunjobi and tenor saxophonist James Mollison, the London-based group, who fuse Afrobeat, jazz, hip-hop, reggae and soul, have released two studio albums, *You Can't Steal My Joy* and *Where I'm Meant to Be* that has seen them collaborate with artists such as Loyle Carner, Nubya Garcia, Moses Boyd, Jorja Smith and the Oscar-winning filmmaker Steve McQueen.

Femi and TJ were born in North London and are both lifelong Arsenal supporters.

CLIVE: The best place to begin is by asking how it all began for you as Arsenal fans? Because the whole idea of Black Arsenal as a project is exploring the organic connection that Arsenal has made across the Black diaspora, be it in London, be it in Manchester, be it in New York, Accra or Nairobi. And in bringing those people together for conversation, they all have different narratives around what the starting point was. For some it was a connection to Ian Wright. Some was going to the Notting Hill Carnival as kids and seeing Arsenal shirts and making the connection there. Others were through parents or grandparents. So, every story is different. What was yours?

FEMI: We're the product of what you're talking about. My uncle migrated to the UK from Nigeria, and Arsenal was the first and only team he supported on arrival. His first game at Highbury was in 1994, and he's had a season ticket for over twenty years. When I was born, one of the first things my uncle said to my mum was that he's going to be an Arsenal fan, to which my mum said, 'Well, I'm not funding it.' And so he signed me up to Junior Gunners not long after. So, I've been a Junior Gunner the same amount of time I've been alive; we inherited his connection to Arsenal. And in the same way, I think why I'm so passionately such a massive Arsenal fan is that I don't have any connection to the word 'English', or to the word 'British'. I have a connection to the word 'London'. But we don't necessarily have a flag that represents that. For me, Arsenal became that flag. It's my identity. This is why I love that I'm a North Londoner. I love that I'm an Arsenal fan. It's like my identity. So, in the same way I was taught from birth that I was Nigerian, I was also taught that I was a Gooner. That's basically what happened. TJ was born sixteen months later.

TJ: And I just followed suit. But I think one of the things for me was it wasn't difficult to engage with Arsenal. Looking back, obviously at the time you don't realise you don't even know what the game of football really is, but it wasn't difficult to engage with Arsenal as a club. My first memory of watching the Arsenal must have been on a highlights programme or something like that. But it's Sylvain Wiltord scoring against Man United in 2002 to win the league at Old Trafford and Kanu jumping over Wiltord's head in the celebration. Kanu, that guy! We were taught that Kanu was our hero.

FEMI: And then he played in the 2002 World Cup. I think your first World Cup always changes your life. Like everyone's got a 'this was my first World Cup' connection, memory or story. I would have been about eight years old. And Nigeria qualified. Who was the one person that I recognised? It was Kanu. He was there, and Freddie Ljungberg was playing for Sweden, who were in the same group as Nigeria, but I knew I couldn't support Sweden. That didn't make any sense to me. Weirdly, I don't know why Ashley Cole didn't have that effect on me with England. They were in the same group and

same club team. Maybe it was just being a Junior Gunner and getting the birthday card with Kanu's picture on. Having Kanu at the World Cup playing for Nigeria and being an Arsenal player was a big deal. I guess we just saw ourselves in who and what he was and what we were told to be. Do you know what I'm saying?

CLIVE: You're from an area [Enfield] with a huge Spurs fanbase. When you're in school, was there ever any of the kind of pressure you get when you are really young from friends to support their team, i.e. Spurs? We have a lot of historically dense Black community areas such as Edmonton, Wood Green, Tottenham, Bruce Grove, Broadwater Farm that are all within the vicinity of the old White Hart Lane stadium, but it seems like a lot of Black people who live in those areas still support Arsenal.

FEMI: You know, it's really interesting though. The Tottenham Stadium is just over there. It's literally fifteen minutes away from where we are right now. But it was always Arsenal. Our primary school was very Black and I don't actually think I remember anyone that supported anyone other than Arsenal. But I remember the Tottenham pressure happened when we went to secondary school in Enfield and joined a local football team called Percival. At the time it was a very white working-class club within a very white working-class area of Enfield. They were all Spurs fans – all of them – which definitely wobbled my vibe, but my uncle's influence was much more important to me than what anyone there had to say.

TJ: But I think also around that time, in the early 2000s, we're really getting into football and there was a clear pull towards Arsenal. We talk a lot about the 'Arsenal way', like there's an Arsenal way of doing things. It's maybe the subconscious, underlying way that Arsenal operates and conducts itself. I remember growing up watching the 2002–03 season where nine out of the eleven players against Leeds were Black. And that for me felt very much normal. There was a complete normality to me to watch nine Black players play for Arsenal and identify with that which would have been different to if we were watching Tottenham or any other club. So what for us seemed normal in the early 2000s would have been the same for my uncle when he was watching Rocky, Paul Davis, Michael Thomas, Kevin Campbell and Ian Wright playing. Of course, Black people will have an affinity for Arsenal, and I think there's a kind of underlying multiculturalism that was running through Arsenal from the very, very early days. We were never scared to sign African players, for example, whereas other clubs seem to avoid them because of the African Cup of Nations – a 'we're gonna lose them for a couple of weeks' response was what you would hear. That just never seems to be a conversation with the Arsenal. I think that's why there's so many Black people living in London that just have an affinity for Arsenal.

FEMI: Ian Wright. He surpasses Arsenal. He's a Black figurehead for the country. He is so popular beyond team allegiances. Yeah, I imagine he couldn't walk into the Spurs pub and people be like, 'hi', but know what I mean? His cultural impact is so powerful and I think that effect really filtered out from football and I think everyone kind of sees something in Ian. And his story of how he came into football late is so Black. I remember a few years ago Ian Wright did an '80s v '90s radio clash on No Signal Radio against Julie Adenuga. And he did like a 10 versus 10 clash. And it just felt like you were listening to one of your uncles who's had a good drink and got on the decks kind of thing. And I think that that effect was so serious upon a lot of Black people.

CLIVE: You mentioned the multicultural experience at Arsenal. There's something about the connection between Arsenal, Black identity and music subcultures that was emerging in the late 1990s. I remember going to garage and jungle events in the early 2000s and seeing different kinds of people all wearing the Arsenal 1992 banana shirt, which is insane thinking about it, but it became so normalised. So, when you mentioned about multiculture, often a lot of people I went to the games with who were white, Irish or white English got their sense of interraciality and appreciation of Black culture and Black identity through the club and through a shared appreciation with Arsenal, its Black players and Black fanbase, which speaks about the power of the Arsenal culture to connect different races.

FEMI: Yeah, I mean, we are avid attenders of Arsenal pubs across London. Be it the Twelve Pins, be it the Tollington Arms, be it the Old Triangle, all of them, we're regulars and I have never felt intimidated or othered by those places. But if you were to ask me, do I generally feel confident and comfortable walking into pubs? The answer actually is no. Like I wouldn't walk into a pub near Spurs, ever, but I don't think that's because I'm an Arsenal fan. I think it's because there's an inclusivity that Arsenal as a club has had for such a long time. It has always felt like an inclusive space for Black people, which is why, you know, why so many Arsenal fans are Black people. If you look at the blackest area of

the UK, it's London. And then you have Tottenham, which is to me a Black area. Until you put 'Hotspurs' on and then I see something different. It's a really interesting thing that happens. To me Arsenal felt like the immigrant home beyond Black people. All the Turkish people we grew up with are Gooners, all the Greek kids are Gooners. It's like it felt like it was a bit of a safe haven for that multicultural expression.

TJ: I think Arsenal fans are exposed to Black greatness a lot earlier than most other fans, and I think because it was really early and really evident and concentrated in the early nineties. It was like, oh yeah, there's a group of them. There's like this faction of Black fans and they worshipped Ian Wright very much. They got Wright on the back of the shirt, and it was like, 'this is our guy' and I think there was like a kind of racial barrier that was being dissolved. Because they were seeing Black excellence so vividly and then you teach your kids that, as young Black fans, you go to an Arsenal match. And it's not like they're seeing Ian Wright in you, but they understand that there's a bit of you in Ian Wright, and I think that's what you're feeling as an Arsenal fan. So, for us it was Thierry Henry.

CLIVE: There is something that is very, very indescribable about the Black Arsenal that you're mentioning, specifically the idea that there is a sense of a safe haven when you go there, you know their fanbase is extremely multicultural and accepting that the actual

Ezra Collective

local areas many not be the same as well, but people who are Black just simply go because they recognise themselves being recognised on the pitch as well as off it.

FEMI: I imagine it's like that. I remember I had a drum teacher at university who was a big Chelsea fan. And he's a white guy, and someone that is heartbroken by racism, like it breaks him and he really takes the baggage on. And every time he'd watch Chelsea, there'd be something – he basically had to stop going to the stadium because he hated being around it so much and I can imagine when a club's fanbase gets accused of racism, as a non-racist football fan, it must be like so embarrassing because they know it's true, and it's probably someone I sit right near. Whereas I feel if an allegation was made that an Arsenal fan was racist, I'd be so confident in knowing it was the *extreme* minority. It was just that one. It's not a racist fanbase. I'd be the first to flag it if it was, but it isn't. You know what I'm saying? I'm sure people have

stories of incidents that have happened, but once you create a place or a haven where everyone feels safe you end up seeing it all around the ground. I think Gay Gooners is quite interesting. Because they had to endure for so long the songs that people were singing in the football stands that were extremely homophobic. But it felt like Gay Gooners was one of the first to stand up and say, 'We are not tolerating this, we're going to be here, the banners will be right up there and remain visible.' Essentially, the point I'm making is the moment someone or a group feels accepted and safe, it will breed among those people within the stadium and fanbase. I'd love to know the statistics on female Arsenal fans in comparison to other clubs. It's hard for me to judge because I don't go to away matches as often as I do home games. But I'd not be surprised if there were more women watching Arsenal. I mean, we sold out 60,000 at the Emirates for the women's game. Do you know what I mean?

TJ: Even from before, like if you look at what Arsenal Women was, back in 2004–05, where basically the whole England team played for Arsenal, we won the UEFA Women's Cup with Faye White, Rachel Yankey, Alex Scott. Alex Scott is a Black woman, and one of the most abused presenters online. And she's adored by Arsenal. Male Arsenal supporters as well, we'd watch the Women's FA Cup with her playing for Arsenal. It's going back to us saying about there's an Arsenal way of doing

↑ TJ Koleoso on bass.

things. For Black people, you can definitely see it. But also for women, Gay Gooners, international Gooners. It's amazing what we seem to be able to do.

FEMI: Everywhere where I am on tour, I can always find this. The one that shocked me was when I was in a remote place in Denmark. And I typed into my phone Arsenal FC. And five minutes' walk from my hotel is a massive Arsenal fanbase. Arsenal banners everywhere. Everyone was like, 'Oh my God, you've got the [London] accent!' You know what I mean? For a team that's never won the Champions League to be that big in the middle of Denmark? And it's the same all over, from Lagos to Tokyo, Sydney, I've had mad nights in New York watching Arsenal at 11 a.m. and it's already all kicking off. The Kenyan Gooners. Do you know what I mean?

CLIVE: There is so much of Arsenal that we find is embedded in elements of Black culture, music, fashion, visual media. The connections we made as young Black people going to the carnival and seeing Arsenal shirts, even more so now with the Jamaica shirts Arsenal released in 2022.

FEMI: I think it's pop culture. My uncle always used to say to me growing up that the thing he loves about Arsenal is that everyone else's names, they are all areas. Chelsea, Manchester, but we're just the Arsenal. The only Tube station – Arsenal Tube station – got changed because of Herbert Chapman

and all of that. You go back into the past and you see all of this kind of stuff that makes Arsenal distinct. And there is the cannon, our badge. We don't even need to see the whole badge; you just need the cannon to know it's Arsenal.

TJ: I mean, it's all kinds of stuff. There's so many statement pieces about Arsenal, the red shirt and white sleeves, you know? And yeah, Arsenal is also about pop culture; all the elements of what makes things classic and make things pop culture, we seem to have them all. The name, the station, the vibe, even just being from N5, you know? All of these little things, these little pieces that you associate with Arsenal. Then when you look through all of our history and the affinity Black people have for Arsenal – the only thing you can really say is that it just makes sense.

CLIVE: Thinking about music, you know more than I do about Wengerball and what

↑ Femi Koleoso on drums.

Ezra Collective

that means. And for me from the outside, I thought about a certain rhythm that one observes while watching that football. The movement of the ball, the two touches, the tempo, the intonations. You know that I'm an Ezra Collective superfan. And the genealogies of your music, which goes back to Afrobeat and jazz fusion as well, there's a certain intonation there that I feel. Maybe through being Nigerian and recognising the ways your music makes connections with other forms of music expressions or Afro-Diasporic practices. I do make connections between what I hear in your sounds and certain forms of Wengerball in terms of the intention there, which is about a certain rhythm that one uses that also makes connections. I'm also thinking about Nigeria, Nigerian culture and football in the 1990s and the way Nigerians played the game. There's a lot of connections there between the Nigerian style that we know, what I saw in Wengerball, and what I listen to and think and feel when I listen to Ezra Collective. I'm really thinking about timing.

FEMI: Timing, absolutely. But it's also about the expression of yourself, and loving how our differences can contribute to one beautiful thing. And one of the things I always find so fascinating about Arsène Wenger is how the players would say that he didn't really say anything to them at half time. Like they'll go in for the half-time team talk and he would just basically not really say anything. A lot of the times the players, when they were getting prepared, he

wasn't like, 'You do this and you do that.' It was like, 'Go out there and play.' One of the biggest criticisms of Wenger when it started to get a bit sour was he wasn't up on the sidelines coaching players, he would just sit there and watch the game, almost like I as a fan would. But I feel like Wenger understood the beauty and the value of individualism – working out where the collective space can be found. And I think that's so similar to music, especially in music like Afrobeat, because it's like, we all have an individual, specific part to play. It will only sound good if we're together, but you have to do your part on your own. And I think there's a real similarity to the creativity required to score a goal against a good defence as there is to the creativity of getting a dance floor to go to the next level. Because it's like, I can't do TJ's job for him – I have to trust him to do it. But I need to be there for him, so that when he drops that bass, I'm ready with the drum beat to go with him. At the same time, it's a very soulful thing. I love football when someone does not have the ball. Because the difference between professional football players and people like us is not when they have the ball, it's when they don't have the ball, how they think. For me, if we have the ball, we all kind of know what the aim is. Shoot it in that direction. It's when you don't have the ball and you have that Thierry Henry ability to be like, 'Wait, wait, wait, wait, sprint, run, bang, pass has gone, goal. Bloody hell, everyone screaming.' And music is so similar. It's like if he is soloing on the trumpet. Wait, wait, wait, wait. It's not the time, it's not the time until he's hit that note, and then crash, bang, everyone launches into the next section of it. It's a real similarity and I definitely, definitely feel it. Those players were definitely playing with an Afrobeat, a Fela Kuti flair, and it's so exciting because it just seems like it's just come back a little bit now. I love that they're playing out from the back because there's a beauty in watching it. It goes from Ramsdale to Saliba, Saliba straight back to Ramsdale, back to Saliba. Once they get it from Partey to Ødegaard, it's on. You know what I mean? And then it's like, is it going in Saka's direction? Is it going in Martinelli's direction? Who knows? It goes to Saka. And then I don't know, Ben White overlaps. Back inside, and then Gabriel Jesus scores, and then, you know what I mean? Scream and shout, four more pints of Guinness. You know what I mean? Like, it's a perfect day.

TJ: Yeah, I think, yeah, certainly watching the great Arsenal teams, there was this freedom of expression. Kolo Touré and Sol Campbell were different players. Tony Adams was different, Lauren was different. Every single player that came in, it was like they were all allowed to have such personality. Wenger wanted them to be the best version of themselves, rather than be like, 'Touré, you're coming in to replace Tony Adams. Do this, do that. Nah, you go and be Kolo Touré. You're an athlete. Shoot from fifty yards. You're not gonna score. But still go for it. Eboué. The most African of African players. But he was allowed to

be himself. And it was about these players fitting in as individuals. Arsène Wenger picked players he thought could play in that kind of way as opposed to picking players that were just good and then trying to make them fit into a rigid model. It's almost like this audacious individual confidence in the players, but also this ability to try and prop up the other players around them. As much as Henry was a superstar, in one of his highest scoring seasons (32, 2003–04), he assisted 23 goals. So you've recorded the highest assist numbers ever in the Premier League. You've come second in the Premier League goal scoring charts behind Van Nistelrooy by one goal. There was this unbelievable selflessness. There are people like Bergkamp, who technically is one of the greatest players of all time, and Henry came in and he was happy to be the provider too. You know, could you imagine? It's just like all these players that have this unbelievable humility, but at the same time, when they got in there, there's a crazy amount of confidence. I guess the word is meekness. It's this power that was under control, you would see them passing it around, and like you're saying, it's not time. It's not time. There's this tension that's being created. It's tension. It's tension until there's a release. And when we play our music as a collective, we're all about building tension, building tension, waiting for the release, and I think that's where I draw the equivalent between what was Wengerball and Afrobeat, or whatever music we play, where there's this quiet beat, you know, but something's going

Black Arsenal

to happen but you don't know when, and then it just happens, and bang.

FEMI: I mean, even listening to this now I'm thinking like, if you could connect the West Indies cricket side from the eighties, the Chicago Bulls in the nineties, the Nigeria team from between 1994 and '98, to the Arsenal team we'll be talking about now – these are African individuals with African rhythm. And that's what kind of connects them all together. And that's why it's beautiful. That's why it's beautiful to watch. Football, in its essence, shouldn't be a beautiful thing. You know what I mean? Flat back four. Hoof it. Route one. That's what football is in most of the country's leagues. But there's a different way of playing it, and that's where it becomes the beautiful game, and it's this, the flair, it's the movement. It's just individual brilliance connecting together. ◼

13

BLACK WOMEN LOVING FOOTBALL

'Whoever heard of Gillespie Road.
It is Arsenal around here!'*

BARONESS LOLA YOUNG

There is a basic assumption that football fans are mostly white, mainly male, sometimes Black and male, but rarely Black and female. In this brief essay, I aim to give a glimpse of the football lives of three Black women – Sophia Walker (aka Queen Gooner), Lerina Bright and me – and suggest the nature of our attachment to football. Suggesting we have such affiliations can seem like a radical act in itself as we seem to be largely invisible when it comes to research on fandom.

Being a football fan doesn't come cheap – tickets, travel costs, TV subscriptions and so on, mean significant expenditure most weeks for about ten months of every year. Many women have work and domestic responsibilities, and are less likely to have spare money to spend on the cost of tickets, travel and childcare. These factors may contribute to the lack of Black and other women fans in stadiums but while the lack of research may well reflect reality, it shouldn't preclude considerations of the ways in which Black women identify as football fans.

Both Lerina and Sophia were introduced to football as young children by older male relatives or male friends, either in a stadium or watching television. This was not so in my case. I was about fifteen when I became a secret Gooner. The 'origin story' of my own relationship to Arsenal FC often elicits surprise and curiosity, so I have included a short explanation along with the extracts from the semi-structured interviews held with Sophia and Lerina.

Sophia is from Leeds, in northern England, so how did she come to support Arsenal?

I grew up in the seventies and eighties … Racists were everywhere in the country, but in Leeds it was particularly bad. I heard of friends who, older than me … were getting beaten up in stadiums. Leeds fans were handing out National Front fliers in the crowd … I always wanted to support a team. And I was like … I don't care how good they [Leeds United] are … I don't care. I'm not going to support them. Red is my favourite colour … I just saw Arsenal wore red, and I loved it. And in '79 … we won the FA Cup against Man U, that also helps … I've been an Arsenal fan ever since.

← *Previous page:* A fan at the Millennium Stadium, Cardiff, for the FA Cup final in 2002.
*   Herbert Chapman, manager of Arsenal Football Club, during talks about renaming the local Tube station. Gillespie Road station became Arsenal station in 1932.

Once she moved to London to pursue her career, Sophia started attending Arsenal matches, initially on her own. Socialising outside of matches isn't only about going to the pub, though that is a dominant feature, especially for men: it's also about feeling comfortable enough to build friendship networks having sat next to the same people every week.

I started making friends … two guys, both Black. That was the other thing I really loved about Arsenal … I'd watch other games and like, look in the crowd, and they would be predominantly white … [at Highbury] you could see there was a number of Black and Asian faces as well … for me it's the most diverse. Even now, when I go to the Emirates, I cannot get over how diverse the crowd is … I work on football a lot. So I've been to a lot of stadiums … and quite often I will look out to see how many Black people there are. Even though it's not about that, as a Black person I can't help it … you need to see it … in comparison to what I see at the Emirates, [it's] not even close … [not] even other London clubs.

Given the racism in football, it's unsurprising that Black people feel reassured by the presence of other Black people in potentially hostile spaces. This is especially important for Black women, who may feel more vulnerable to white male hostility than Black men.

↑ Arsenal fans at the Emirates Stadium in 2021.

Black Women Loving Football

I asked Sophia whether the significant numbers of Black players in the Arsenal squad had been a deciding factor for her in maintaining allegiance to the club. That led to some thoughts on the England men's team, and past, negative associations.

I remember … watching stuff with my parents, especially sport … And because they're from Jamaica, obviously they were never going to support England: they always supported Jamaica. And so … I wouldn't support England, because of the way that the Black players were treated … the racist abuse John Barnes used to get … Well, why should I support a team like that, if they're not supporting people of my colour? And so … I supported Brazil as a kid … They play gorgeous football, and they're not getting racially abused by their own fans.

Even though much has improved in terms of crowd behaviour, there are still moments where rival football banter morphs into physical confrontation. I wonder whether Sophia has felt threatened when going to matches. Neither of us has ever attended away matches. One place we both agree we won't be going to is Tottenham Hotspur. That rivalry is so intense, the atmosphere at home games can feel toxic enough to put off some Arsenal fans from attending.

Sophia hasn't felt unsafe but she has experienced discomfort at an Arsenal home match, hearing antisemitic slurs directed at Tottenham. She called the people out for their use of Y— and explained its loathsomeness to the offenders by comparing it to using n— against Black people. It might be different in other parts of the ground, and at away matches, but neither of us has heard other racial abuse, though I have seen a banana skin thrown onto the pitch.

Podcasts for football fans have proliferated and there are several entertaining and informative Arsenal pods on offer. These can help to reinforce the sense of belonging to a community, which became particularly important during the Covid lockdowns in 2020/2021.

Arseblog and *Arsenal Vision* are two of my regular listens, the former featuring questions from Sophia/Queen Gooner several times. At the end of the 2022–23 season, presenters from the two podcasts combined for a celebration at the Union Chapel on Upper Street, Islington, a short distance from the Arsenal stadium. Sophia attended the event.

It was a brilliant experience, just being surrounded by five hundred Gooners, everybody on the same page … It was a good way to unburden yourself … with friends and like-minded people, and then to top it all off, Wrighty [Ian Wright] turning up … they wouldn't let him talk … He kept trying to talk, and they just kept singing 'Ian Wright, Wright, Wright'… It was the perfect end to the season, and it was the night before the Wolves game … [I thought] even if I go to the Wolves game and it's crap, because I had that experience the night before, I won't care.

Commentators and fans alike have observed how different the atmosphere in the stadium is now from the latter days of Arsène Wenger's tenure. Then 'it was really vitriolic … It was toxic.' It was a difficult period for Arsenal fans, with the divided fanbase coming to blows on the North Bank and the banter from rival fans mocking the club, feeding the bitterness displayed in the stadium. I'm sure Sophia wasn't the only supporter who considered giving up her season ticket. The reality is though, that if you do, you're unlikely to get one again. Sophia had been on the waiting list for ten years before being allocated a seat.

Once Mikel Arteta established a cultural reset, with a strong emphasis on the importance of fans, the atmosphere in the stadium improved. It didn't happen overnight, but strategies for reigniting fans' love for the club have had an impact, helped by some excellent performances on the pitch.

Although some of the fiercest arguments take place online, Twitter and other platforms also provide a space where fans can connect. The crossover between the online and actual world happens every now and then, a matchday tweet revealing that you have been exchanging direct messages with the person sitting behind you for years. Or a song shared online develops into a stadium staple.

I love 'The Angel (North London Forever)' [Arsenal's anthem, sung before every home match]. It is absolutely perfect for that team. It's perfect. Thank you, Louis Dunford [composer] … it just feels like we're getting back to where we should be … even the murals [artwork on the stadium wrap]. It just looks amazing … Me and my mate, we did a walk around to look at it all. It just looks fantastic.

Sophia connects with Arsenal fans around the world online.

I've met so many Gooners that I chat to regularly, constantly on Twitter … a Black Gooner from Philadelphia … I reckon we've been talking to each other on Twitter for ten years. Anyway, he messages me … 'Oh, my God, I'm coming to London. I've got a ticket for a game.' We met up … We watched the game. We chatted for hours … I would never have met him in a million years, but he's part of the Arsenal family … He just told me so much about Philly. I told him about England. It was just brilliant.

The idea of football being a 'family' is often referenced but repeating it doesn't conjure it into reality. The theme has to be threaded through every aspect of the club's operations. For Sophia, it does seem to be working: 'I do feel like I'm part of the Arsenal family … That's exactly how I feel.'

Sophia mentioned Arsenal's Jamaica kit in the familiar colours of the national flag; one of the tops was gifted to her. It pays homage to all those men and women of Jamaican heritage who've played for Arsenal, a respectful gesture that resonated with the Jamaican diaspora in the UK as a whole. Of course, the tribute makes commercial sense given the extent of the Jamaican diaspora around the world, especially in the UK and the USA. It's another way of capitalising both on the global popularity of Premier League football and Jamaican culture's reputation for being cool. Nonetheless, it also carries a positive resonance for Black communities internationally.

The stadium artwork has also had an impact, the section that carries the flags of Gooners from around the world being especially striking. Again, for Sophia, the Jamaican connection is significant: 'I took a picture of the Jamaica one [Gooner flag] for the Jamaica Gooners obviously … But yeah … It just looks amazing. So good.'

There's been a significant shift in the perception of the women's game, and although I'm clearly biased, it's fair to say that Arsenal Women have been at the forefront of that shift. The club has demonstrated a commitment to supporting and promoting the women's game for decades, having won sixty trophies during their history, and they remain the only British women's football team to have won a European club competition.

The stadium artwork emphasises the extent to which there is a 'one-club' mentality developing, and the women's team's achievements are given prominence alongside the men's: this contributes to that feeling of being attached to family. Over 60,000 fans watched Arsenal's semi-final exit against Wolfsburg in the UEFA Women's Champions League in May 2023.

I love the Arsenal Women as well. I know a lot of people don't watch both, but I do, and I love the fact that they've got the historical thing with the women as well … I love that [winning the forerunner of the Women's Champions League] was incorporated [in the stadium artwork] with the golden Invincibles' trophy and all the players … it just looks amazing … even now, I'm talking about it … it's giving me goosebumps. I just love the thought that's gone into that [stadium artwork] because once again we are one … And it's another reason why I just love this club … and don't get me wrong. They annoy me, I get angry … but you know I love this club … I do feel like it is an Arsenal family. It's not just a football club, and I love that about us. I love it.

We barely touched on the lack of ethnic diversity in the women's game, which is particularly noticeable on the pitch and stands in stark contrast to the men's and youth squads. This is one area where Arsenal don't seem to be making any more progress than other clubs. A concerted effort to change that picture is needed, as while both Sophia and I actively support Arsenal Women, I know of other Black female fans of the men's team who feel no affinity with Arsenal Women because of that absence. Rachel Yankey, Danielle Carter and Alex Scott are Arsenal legends, pioneers of the sport, and heroes for many because of their achievements with club and country: where are their successors?

The absence of Black first team coaches in elite level football in England is also notable and both Sophia and Lerina responded to this issue when I raised it. While Sophia pointed to the lack of opportunities, the speed with which Black managers appeared to be sacked, and the length of time taken to be appointed to a new club, Lerina suggested that a lot was to do with the strength of networks involving former England players. Recruitment processes seem stubbornly weighted towards favouring those on the inside of the football establishment.

There's so much I love about football, and Arsenal in particular, but just as I can't accept the idea of buying clothes without considering labour exploitation in the fashion industry, neither can I enjoy watching a match without trying to address some of the disturbing practices that have grown from its success. Football is one of the less well-known sectors where children, young people and adults are trafficked, abandoned and abused but I knew nothing of this until I met Lerina.

Highly profitable for the criminals involved – arrests, charges and conviction rates are pathetically low – their activities damage impoverished communities, principally in African and South American countries. Lerina is a leading figure in the development of international initiatives advocating for victims and survivors of exploitation in sport. Lerina's not an Arsenal fan but trafficking in football should concern us all.

Lerina took up her first professional role in football in Northern Ireland in 2007. I wondered what it had been like to work as a Black woman in a politically sensitive environment. For Lerina it was 'the most fulfilling sporting experience', feeling that: 'as the Black person, you have nothing to do with this … I just felt out of this equation, whatever was going on there. I'm not part of this …'

After Northern Ireland, Lerina took up roles in countries around the world, all focused on football, getting to know and understand how the institutions worked.

In 2016 Lerina read a newspaper article on football and trafficking:

I thought to myself, What is this? You know? … I thought, I've been in this space for many years, and I've never seen this … then you have an 'Aha!' moment … at that time, my first thought was it must be the agents … these bad agents … And at that time I was still madly in love with football … So I thought, Who were these bad guys, the agents trying to make the sport look bad?

This revelation led to Lerina establishing an NGO to address the problem in 2017. I met Lerina at a conference, shortly after her discovery and it's thanks to her that I learnt about the exploitation of children and young people in and through football.

Traffickers approach families, mainly in impoverished communities, claiming that there's an opportunity for their boys to play football in Europe and become rich. Some 'agents' even claim to be talent spotting on behalf of successful clubs. It's easy enough to produce fake credentials and claim to be a representative of Arsenal FC or another big, global club.

Relatives borrow money to pay the agents for their children's travel, accommodation, kit, etc. But the children can end up being dumped in a foreign country without any money, and left to beg on the streets, forced to work in mines or factories, or trafficked into the sex trade.

Another form of exploitation, less obvious to spot, occurs when a rogue agent hands a child or young person over to a club outside of Europe's top divisions. If they don't succeed in breaking into a professional team, again the children may be abandoned far from home. They may have talent and may move up the football pyramid to a respectable level, in which case the initial dubious means by which they were 'signed' is obscured, along with whatever bad experiences they've had on the way. Their status as trafficked children is erased.

Lerina realised that fake agents were only part of the problem. The success of these trafficking crimes depends on the involvement of other actors. She says '[there is] … complicity at a governmental level … complicity from the visa-issuing agencies, complete complicity from the football associations themselves.'

For those who think this couldn't happen in the Premier League or another professional league in the UK – unfortunately you're wrong because several cases have been exposed in news reports and documentaries.*

As for my story: I suppose I could claim I was led to support Arsenal Football Club by a parent – it's just that the parent in question was the London Borough of Islington, aka my corporate parent. Circumstances took me from London into a children's home in Hertfordshire but eventually, Islington social services squeezed me into an oversubscribed children's home in Highbury.

It was strange: it felt like every corner I turned, I would find reminders of my unwanted status as a care-experienced teenager. There were children's homes in Ardilaun Road, Conewood Street, Highbury New Park, and of course Elwood Street, where I lived. In all, there were about ten homes nearby – and houses in Drayton Park and Highbury Fields where I'd experienced failed attempts at foster care.

That's how Arsenal Stadium came to be so important to me. You might think that the presence of a football ground was a strange kind of salve for being in the care system. But the presence of Arsenal encouraged me to stop defining myself as the Black girl from a children's home in Highbury, a girl who lived in *an institution*, to become the Black girl who lived down the road from the famous Arsenal Football Club.

One of the high spots of the time I spent in that home was the church service attended by the Arsenal football team. That and the knowledge that the shy young man who helped deliver groceries to the home was Pat Rice, later to become an Arsenal Legend.

Loyalty to Arsenal was my secret for some time: it wasn't something girls would shout about in the sixties and seventies. Back then, I knew very little about football, apart from the fact that girls and women weren't allowed to play. Living in Arsenal's heartland gave me the vicarious experience of the excitement generated by the sight of twenty-two men kicking a ball around a field. Decades later, as a long-time season ticket holder, I understand all of the agony and ecstasy I used to see and hear played out on the streets surrounding Highbury Stadium.

These conversations have led me to think that Black women have limited visibility in academic and market research relating to football fandom. If the 'football family' is really interested in being more inclusive, it needs to dig deeper into how different communities of interest view the game.

Woven into the ninety-minute stories we watch each week are our pasts, and the preoccupations that go beyond the games themselves. As spectators, I'm sure that challenges such as racism, sexism and misogyny, homophobia and human rights inform what we see on the pitch and compel us to consider how being a fan contributes to our overall sense of belonging.

Big thanks to Lerina and Sophia for their generosity in giving their time and energy for these conversations. COYG!!! ■

↑ At the FA Cup victory parade, 2014.

Black Women Loving Football

14

KANU TO KELECHI

SEAN JACOBS

The English Premier League and British football barely featured African players before Arsène Wenger arrived as manager of Arsenal Football Club in 1996. By the time Arsenal dismissed Wenger in 2018, he and the club had earned the distinction of being primarily responsible for mainstreaming African footballers in the top flight of the English game. At one point in the mid-to-late 2000s, at least seven of Arsenal's eleven starters on any given matchday were Black, either the children of African migrants to Europe, African-descended players from the Caribbean, or – the largest category – players born in an African country. By 2023, at least twenty-two African players had played for Arsenal thanks largely to Wenger.

At least three African players – Lauren, Kolo Touré, and Nwankwo Kanu – were regular starters for the Invincibles, the legendary Arsenal team that went unbeaten for a whole season in 2003–04. The last major player signed by Wenger at Arsenal was also an African: the Gabonese Pierre-Emerick Aubameyang. In this way, Arsenal inaugurated a revolution about race in British and global football culture.

Represented by these players and their successors on the field, Arsenal came to represent London's diversity, especially its African-descended diasporas. As Arsenal legend Thierry Henry commented on the occasion of his retirement, Arsenal, by being one of the first clubs to have Black players at the heart of its team, became the club of the people and the streets. All this combined to cement Arsenal's place in African football lore and to make it the most supported football club on the continent, especially among football fans who came of age in the twenty-first century.

Like other professional clubs at the pinnacle of the English game, Arsenal had historically recruited only white players from Africa. The first was a descendant of white South African settlers, Dan le Roux. He had an unremarkable career at Highbury between 1957 and 1958, playing in only seven matches. The first Black player to sign for Arsenal was Brendon Batson, a Grenadian-born immigrant to Britain from Trinidad. Batson played ten times for the club between 1971 and 1974 before moving to West Bromwich Albion in 1978, where – together with Cyrille Regis and

← *Previous page:* Nwankwo Kanu celebrates the first of his two goals against Middlesbrough on 24 April 1999.

Laurie Cunningham – he came to be part of perhaps the most iconic trio of Black players at an English top-flight club in the seventies. Batson's signing also opened the way for a smattering of Black players whose parents were also from the Caribbean to run out for Arsenal for the first time, and the side that in 1989 won the Gunners their first title in eighteen years featured the unforgettable trio of Michael Thomas, Paul Davis and David Rocastle. When the Premier League was born in 1992, Coventry City were the first, that same season, to pick an African footballer to start a league match: Peter Ndlovu from Zimbabwe.

It was left to Wenger to sign Arsenal's first player from the African continent, Christopher Wreh, from Liberia. One of Wreh's distinctions is that he is one of only two players – the other is Thierry Henry – signed by Wenger when he was at both Monaco and Arsenal. But perhaps a more significant detail of Wreh's biography is that he is a cousin of George Weah, the future president of Liberia, who, also a footballer, won the Ballon d'Or in 1995 – the first and only player to have done so while representing an African country. It is also Wenger's relationship and success with George Weah at Monaco that explains his subsequent affinity for African players. (It bears mentioning that when Weah won the Ballon d'Or, he called Wenger on stage and handed him the trophy instead. Later, when Weah became president of Liberia in West Africa, he invited Wenger for an official visit and awarded him Liberia's highest honour:

'Knight Grand High Commander of the Humane Order of African Redemption.'

Wreh had a decent career at Arsenal; he spent four years at the club, and an additional three years loaned out. He contributed to the club's FA Cup (scoring the goal that won the semi-final) and the Premier League double in 1998. It was Kanu, however, whose 1999 arrival forever changed the perception of African players in England. Kanu had previously won the UEFA Champions League with Ajax and the Olympic Games with Nigeria. A proven winner, he was a tall, rangy player able to score goals from apparently impossible angles. Kanu was, in Wenger's words, a 'genius, creative, technical, brave, a player everyone admired'. He quickly became a cult hero at the club.

In 2000, Kanu was followed by Lauren, the son of Equatorial Guinean exiles who fled to Cameroon and then Spain, where Lauren started his football career. In 2002, after a short trial, Kolo Touré joined Arsenal from an academy in Côte d'Ivoire. In his book about his time at Arsenal, Wenger singles out Touré, along with Sol Campbell, as 'fundamentally important' to the success of the Invincibles. Bought on the cheap (he cost just £150,000), in Wenger's words, he 'became one of the best central defenders in the game'. Next came Emmanuel Eboué, who also started his career at the same academy in Abidjan, the Ivorian cpaital. These players, along with recruits from France, the Netherlands and elsewhere (at one point, controversially, Wenger fielded

KANU WAS, IN WENGER'S WORDS, 'GENIUS, CREATIVE, TECHNICAL, BRAVE, A PLAYER EVERYONE ADMIRED.'

no British-born players), would form the nucleus of Arsenal's success in the first decade of the twenty-first century.

At the beginning of the 2010s, as that first group aged and moved on, Wenger made another run with a new crop of players, with another group of African players at its core – including Alex Song, Alex Iwobi, Emmanuel Adebayor and Gervinho. Both Song and Iwobi are part of African football's familial legacies, respectively those of Cameroonian Rigobert Song and Nigerian Jay Jay Okocha. However, success became more elusive for Wenger's next generation (these teams won the FA Cup multiple times and qualified for the Champions League every season,

but never won the Premier League again), and by 2013 Arsenal fans were beginning to call for Wenger's dismissal. With Wenger's eventual departure, also went Arsenal's reliance on players who came directly from Africa, though Wenger's successors would continue that legacy in some way by relying on or signing the children of African immigrants in London – like Eddie Nketiah and Bukayo Saka – on the club's books.

When Wenger signed players like Kanu, Lauren, Touré and Eboué, English football was still distrustful of foreigners, especially players and coaches from outside Europe. African fans, watching via satellite television, recognised themselves

↑ Thierry Henry, Nwankwo Kanu and Patrick Vieira.

Kanu to Kelechi

in Wenger (he was one of the first foreign coaches in the Premier League). His players, with their accents, hairstyles, fashion and joyful football – though when they needed to, they could also play physical football – presented a stark contrast with their very stereotypically English white competitors. Wenger also seemed unfazed by African players flying off every two years for a month to play in the African Cup of Nations, further endearing him to African fans who felt disrespected by Europe's top leagues, their clubs and managers when their native sons were denied the opportunity to represent their countries.

Today, the African legacy at Arsenal is felt more off the field than on. Of the most popular 'fan TV' outlets of English Premier League teams on social media, the ones aimed at Arsenal fans are the most diverse. On YouTube, Kelechi, a Nigerian immigrant scientist and Arsenal fan, is now equally recognisable as Arsenal's Ghana international midfielder, Thomas Partey. Kelechi autotunes Afropop songs to describe his mood before he gives his match analysis on Arsenal Fan TV. That channel and its offshoots have done more to highlight African participation in the World Cup and the African Cup of Nations among British

↑ Kolo Touré and Nwankwo Kanu, 2002.

Black Arsenal

166

and American football supporters. All this has cemented a view of Arsenal as open, welcoming and diverse, and above all as representing democracy, anti-racism and forward-looking, something in short supply on the continent. There's therefore a grim irony in the fact that the same club now also (since 2018) advertises one of Africa's most efficient dictatorships. Every time Arsenal FC players run on the field with 'Visit Rwanda' on their shirt sleeves, they advertise a legacy – authoritarianism – that the new generation that found an affinity and identity with the club would like to leave behind. ◼

↑ Kolo Touré and Emmanuel Eboué after the FA Cup final between Arsenal and Manchester United in 2005.

Kanu to Kelechi

15

THE VIEW FROM THE NORTH

Yorkshire, Black Arsenal and Class Identity

DAVID FORREST

I spent the first seven years of my life in Yorkshire's largest city, Sheffield. In the 1980s the place had a proudly progressive political identity, and a strong anti-racist movement, of which my mum was a part. She was particularly active in supporting the Somalian refugee communities who moved to the city in that decade, and the families of the kids at our school and within our circle of friends came from all over the world. My parents divorced in 1992 and we moved to a village in West Yorkshire in the heart of the coalfields. For mum, this was something of a homecoming, having grown up in a mining family. We lived on a redbrick council estate that backed onto rolling fields, typical of the region, where industrial and agricultural landscapes bled into each other. The deep wounds of the miners' strike were still visible, and even as a child I recognised that the politics of this place were different from where we had come from.

The year we arrived I fell in love with Arsenal. I suppose the fact that the club played two cup finals against Sheffield Wednesday that season had something to do with it – my interest piqued by my 'hometown' pitted against an unfamiliar opponent, football matches that seemed to reflect my own displacement. In a single parent family unencumbered by football connections, I was free to pick my team, and my mum didn't stand in my way. In fact, she became an Arsenal fan with me. At my new school my classmates were either Leeds or Barnsley, the local clubs, or Manchester United and Liverpool, the glamour teams. Arsenal were different, and so was I.

By the 1993–94 season, I was obsessed with Ian Wright. His grace, swagger and fire were intoxicating. The following year, we drew Barnsley in the Coca-Cola Cup third round and Mum got us tickets. I was euphoric. I would see my hero playing at a ground just ten miles from our house. What I didn't know then was that in my moment of joy, Ian Wright was having what he would later describe as 'one of the worst nights of my life', receiving persistent, dehumanising racial abuse throughout the game. That night, Arsenal, and Ian Wright, represented difference, and difference was to be feared.

Sport is one of the central means by which Yorkshire's myths of grit and stubbornness embed themselves in the regional psyche, traits that are so easily

← *Previous page:* David Forrest, aged eleven.

→ Barnsley v Arsenal, Oakwell, 1995.

Black Arsenal

transformed into anger and fear at what is perceived as other: sport as a proxy for rigid essentialism, narrow masculinity, overbearing whiteness. I felt this acutely when the cricketer Azeem Rafiq shared his experience of racism at Yorkshire County Cricket Club. Nothing of his heartbreaking testimony surprised me. I had heard racist language disguised as banter throughout my time playing cricket, and the attempts to discredit Rafiq reminded me of the reactions when Jonathan Woodgate and Lee Bowyer were arrested for grievous bodily harm and affray after an Asian student was attacked in Leeds – sporting allegiance easily trumped social conscience. (After two trials, Bowyer was completely acquitted but Woodgate was found guilty of affray and sentenced to 100 hours of community service.)

But Yorkshire has other sporting stories to tell. When I was growing up, Sheffield's Prince Naseem was the country's most exciting boxer, Leeds's Ellery Hanley was coaching GB Rugby League, Brian Deane played across the county's best teams, and two seasons after Wright's racist abuse, Clint Marcelle would score the goal that got Barnsley promoted to the top flight, while the following season, they would sign Bruce Dyer, an elegant and cultured striker from Crystal Palace – Dyer was worshipped at Oakwell, and still lives in the town. These sporting lives were built on deep struggles for acceptance. If we speak of Black Arsenal as a way of recovering, remembering and recognising, then we must also tell the sports stories of Black Yorkshire.

The View From the North

Arsenal showed me that another England existed – another way of being, of living together, one that contrasted sharply with my everyday reality. When we won the double in 1998 Fabio and Grooverider started their Radio 1 show, and KISS 105 launched, bringing the sound of the London underground to Yorkshire. I got my first pair of decks and would catch the bus to Leeds to buy records and tape packs. The posters on my wall of Kanu, Vieira and Bergkamp sat alongside flyers for club nights and raves I was too young to get into.

When I left home for university in 2002, I realised that football had made my world bigger. In Freshers' Week, Arsenal was a bonding mechanism; it's how I met Indi, a working-class Asian kid wearing his club shirt like a beacon. He was born in London but had moved to Birmingham as a child – Ian Wright was his hero, too. Indi died suddenly in 2016, and my mum – who had laid the foundations for my footballing passions – died in 2022, after a long battle with dementia. Both lives were enriched by Arsenal. Grief helped me to make sense of football as something more than a game – as a bridge between people, a shared culture, a way of seeing and celebrating difference.

Twenty-five years after that night in Barnsley one of the fans who'd abused Ian Wright wrote to him to express his shame and to ask for forgiveness. Wrighty accepted the apology, replied with 'love', and told him that 'there is redemption for everyone'. Following Mum's death, I returned to the village. Its proximity to Leeds has turned it into a commuter haven, new housing estates have cropped up, patterns of migration have changed. There is still the air of conservatism, but the remoteness I encountered as a child is no longer there, replaced by a tentative opening up to the world. The collective feeling of holding on to *something* – closely, blindly, out of fear – is fading. ■

↖ Barnsley's Neil Redfearn and Arsenal's Glenn Helder jumping for the ball, 1995.
→ Arsenal v Aston Villa at Emirates Stadium in 2022.

16

ARSENAL AND BLACK IDENTITY

24 September 1991

IAN WRIGHT

Ian Wright joined Arsenal in September 1991 from Crystal Palace for a club record fee of £2.5 million. He would go on to score 185 goals in 288 appearances for the club, winning the Golden Boot in 1992. He would win 5 major trophies in his 7-year spell at the club, including the 1993 FA Cup and the Double in 1998. Wright would win 33 England caps in this period (9 goals). He received an MBE in 2000, an OBE in 2023, and is an inductee of the Premier League Hall of Fame.

I had a deep connection with David Rocastle before I joined Arsenal from Crystal Palace because we were from the same place in Brockley. We were so close, and I followed Arsenal because of him. Before I joined Arsenal, I was also aware that they already had this core of Black players – Paul Davis, Michael Thomas, Raphael Meade, Chrissy Whyte, Gus Caesar, and Kevin Campbell was coming through as well. There were other teams at the time that had Black players, but Luton Town and West Brom were the main ones for me when I was younger. Luton had the Stein brothers, Mitchell Thomas and Ricky Hill. Then at Crystal Palace it was myself, Andy Gray, Tony Finnigan, John Salako, Mark Bright, Richard Shaw and Henry Hughton when I first got there. So, there were a lot more Black players beyond Arsenal then.

We went to watch Palace a couple of times, but Millwall was the one we went to a lot as it was nearby. People seem to believe that I was a Millwall fan, but I just went to watch them. When David went to Arsenal as a kid, everyone on the Honor Oak Estate began supporting Arsenal, as a way of supporting him as he was one of us and we were so proud. So, it's always been Arsenal really, and then obviously once David broke into the first team, it kind of cemented it for us. But the first football kit I ever had was a West Ham one because of Clyde Best. Ade Coker was also there. With Tottenham we saw Chris Hughton playing, then Mitchell Thomas, and Garth Crooks was there. So, you kind of resonate with all those teams because of their Black players, but not with Chelsea because we knew first-hand what Paul Canoville was going through. Chelsea was the only club at the time that I just had no love for. But with Arsenal, I knew that they had a pipeline of Black players. When you looked in the reserves, you saw Black players

← *Previous page:* Ian Wright's league debut v Chelsea.

coming through like Andy Cole. It was a case of following a team you know has Black men.

Looking back, what really turned a lot of things for me was the game when West Brom beat Manchester United 5–3 at Old Trafford in 1979, and Cyrille Regis, Laurie Cunningham and Brendon Batson destroyed them. I remember it like it was yesterday. To watch them on that stage, they were amazing. Stewart Houston was assistant manager at Arsenal when I joined, and he'd played in that game for United. Watching that and watching what Laurie Cunningham did to him and seeing Stewart trying to kick him, trying everything he could to stop him and Cyrille – he just couldn't stop them. That made me say I want to be Laurie. I wanted to be Laurie Cunningham because he was closer to the way I played than Cyrille was. Cyrille was more up straight, obviously powerful. But Laurie had the skills I wanted and saw in myself.

REPRESENTING BLACKNESS

I joined Arsenal in September 1991. David was there, Paul Davis and Micky Thomas were there, and Kevin Campbell was coming through. I remember the

↑ Ian Wright and George Graham, Highbury, 23 September 1991.

Arsenal and Black Identity

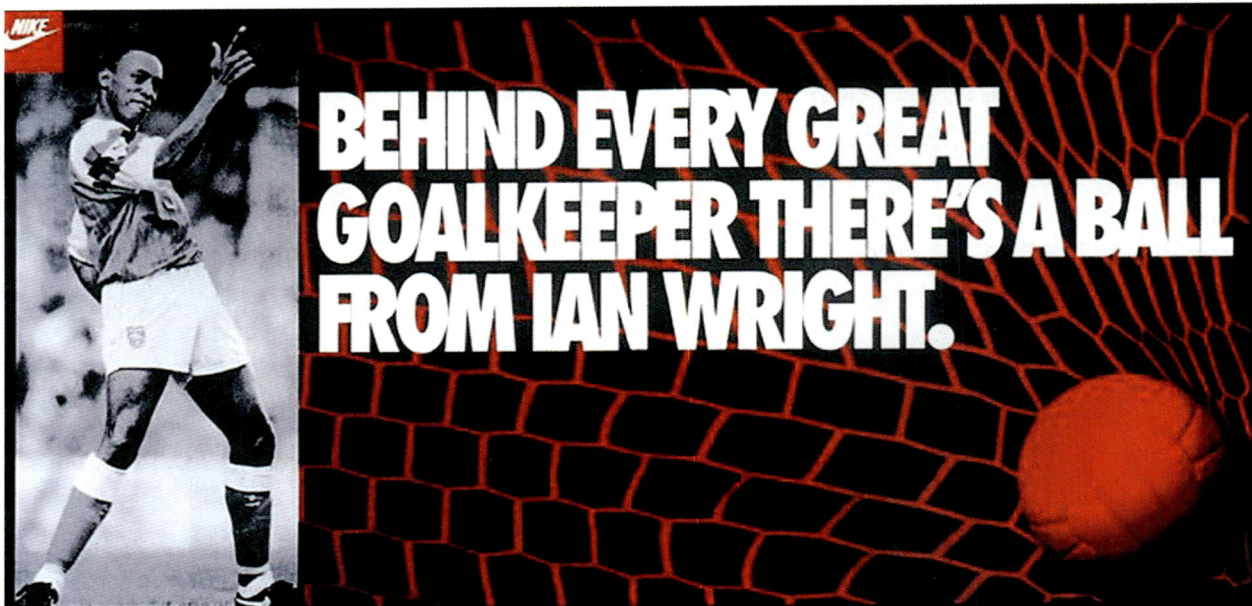

BEHIND EVERY GREAT GOALKEEPER THERE'S A BALL FROM IAN WRIGHT.

press conference so well because George Graham was vexed with me for wearing the clothes I wore. There was a lot of shit around it that day at the club simply because George Graham told me that I needed to wear a suit to training that day. And for some reason, I don't know why, but I didn't bring a suit. I was also kind of vexed with him anyway, because when I actually signed, I didn't see him – he was nowhere in sight. It was David Dein and other people from the club who did the signing. So, I never saw him because he was playing golf somewhere. So, what happened was I signed, trained, and just as I came in from training, David Dein said, 'You have to go to Highbury for the press conference, did you bring your suit?' I said no and so when I got to the ground, George Graham saw me and asked, 'Is that

what you're wearing?' and I said, 'Yeah, it is.' This is how I dress. You know, I mean, this is it. This is me. Why should I come in a suit? Me coming to the press conference in a suit is not going to give you or anyone else the true reflection or representation of me, is it? You're not gonna think the same of me.

I'm so pleased that that happened and how it happened. It just happened very naturally. I didn't wear the suit, I didn't bring the suit. And I'm wearing the clothes that I wear normally. You know, why should it be any different at a press conference? Man's wearing a leather jacket and a baseball cap. That's me.

Looking back, I'm so pleased about that moment because you don't realise at the time how much it meant to Black people. Now people come up to me and they say

↑ → Ian Wright's Nike campaigns in the 1990s epitomised the burgeoning relationship between players, clubs and commercial brands as the new Premier League transformed the footballing landscape.

what you've done in the past and how much it meant to them to see somebody that was just like them, who came off their estate. I didn't realise at the time that that was happening because I was just *being*, I was being myself. So, to know now that it was resonating so much, it means everything. I was always true to myself and real. I was never a tick-boxer, and I wasn't going to dance. But you don't realise the gravity of it at all, the amount of people that you're actually reaching by just wearing those clothes in a press conference. Just the pure celebration in saying or doing something in an interview. You might kiss your teeth. You might do something that resonates

with that culture. And then all of a sudden, everybody's just saying 'yeah, that's my guy'. And that's what they tell me now, which is really quite nice, because I think it's important to know who you are and where you came from. Because for whatever reason, I wouldn't have looked right in that suit.

That period of the early '90s when I joined was so important. All five of us ended up playing together against Leicester in the Coca-Cola Cup in 1991 when I scored on my debut. Me, David, Paul, Mickey and Kevin. I was meant to be on the bench, but Alan Smith got injured so I started. I mean, all five of us are South London boys, but it was the

Be like Ian Wright from the moment you start dribbling.

FOR YOUR INFORMATION, NIKE MAKE SHOES FOR STRIKERS AGED SIX MONTHS AND UPWARDS. ANY EARLIER AND WE'D BE KITTING OUT SPERMS.

Arsenal and Black Identity

I REMEMBER WHE
KEITH CASSELL
MILLWALL WHEN I
HE WOULD RECEIV
ABUSE AND TH
TO ME THEN, 'OH
DON'T WORRY AB
IT'S JU

I USED TO WATCH
PLAY AGAINST
AS YOUNGER AND
ALL THAT RACIST
WOULD SAY IT
OU'RE ALRIGHT.
UT IT. YOU'RE OK.
HIM.'

only time we all played together, because Mickey then left in dramatic circumstances. They wouldn't pay him properly. David and Mickey left within months of each other, then Paul is out of the team. In one season, they're gone. That was devastating for me because when I signed, I thought I was going to be here with David for a while and then in one season, bam, he's gone. I was devastated. Having five Black players from South London playing in the top flight was important. We had the Palace team, but they weren't winning titles. That's different. These boys were there when Arsenal were winning the league.

I joined Arsenal at a time when British football was changing dramatically from the old first division to the Premier League, and there was so much marketing happening. I was sponsored by a global sportswear brand and they asked me to do the 'Can I Kick It?' commercial at the start of the 1992–93 season, which used the song by A Tribe Called Quest. I remember when we were talking to the brand about the commercial and they played it and I said, 'Yeah, that's the tune.'

You know, I mean, they used an image of me doing the bogle on the pitch in another advert. But again, the thing about that is I'm quite pleased that I didn't take on the enormity of what's happening at that time and how things were changing culturally with advertising, promotional work and the Premier League. Because I'm just trying to do my thing here. So, for me, when those commercials were being played, it was all

about the attitude I was trying to put out because I was trying to *be*. I was almost feeling like, yes, I'm being accepted for who I am. But then at the same time, the mainstream press was continually trying to suppress me and to suppress my natural self like we see them doing to other young Black players now. Your natural exuberance. They tried to suppress it, but I got so much love from people, from kids who would say, 'Go on, bro, you're just representing us.' I didn't even realise. When the 'Kick It' advert came out it was like everything for me went to another level. And that's what it comes down to. Just being able to be seen for what you can do. It was everywhere. I remember driving past it and I'll be like, shit, you know, man, it's all getting a bit too much!

I remember the issue with the mural at the North Bank that same season. Me and Kevin Campbell were training with the others on the Highbury pitch and Kevin said 'how come the mural has no Black faces in it? The club has to change it.' And he went to David Dein, and they changed it and put Black faces in. We played the first game of that season against Norwich with it still not having any Black faces. It was for the next home game against Sheffield Wednesday when it was changed. It was really quite interesting because Arsenal as a club was very innovative. That was the first time you ever saw something like that. I mean, all the other grounds building new stands at the time had just nothing, they were just construction sites. And then you had this mural at Highbury that we couldn't score

in front of. I think the first game I scored in front of it would have been against Man City. I remember Sky Sports commentators making a big deal out of it when we finally scored our first goal in the mural end.

CHALLENGING RACISM

There was so much happening at that point in the nineties concerning racism in the UK. There was so much racial violence around us. Arsenal would play Millwall a lot in that period and there was an issue every single time. The Millwall fans would racially abuse me and throw coins at me. We played them in 1993 at The Den and George Graham substituted me because I was on a yellow card, and he thought I was going to get sent off. There was always this underlying thing with Millwall because of the racism. So, I remember before the FA Cup game in 1995 I came out and said, 'Listen, Millwall fans are racist thugs.' I got horrific racist abuse all game, and Tony Witter, the Black Millwall defender, was marking me and heard it all and challenged it. And they said, 'Not you, Tony, we mean him.' It was confusing because when I used to go and watch as a kid, they used

↑ Ian Wright celebrating with fans at the 1994 Cup Winners Cup Final in Copenhagen.

Arsenal and Black Identity

to say the same thing when abusing Black players, 'No, you're all right. You're one of us.' I remember when I used to watch Keith Cassells play against Millwall when I was younger and he would receive all that racist abuse and they would say it to me then, 'Oh, you're all right. Don't worry about it. You're OK. It's just him.' I'm quite pleased that people like Tony came out and challenged it. I wanted to play for Millwall when I was younger because I used to go with the fans and there were people there I knew, but then once you start to realise the racial element to it and how bad it was, that's when I stopped wanting to play for them.

I've said to people, I don't support Millwall. I've got an affinity with them because it's the first place I ever saw a football match, but I support Arsenal. I would talk to Black players at other clubs about our experiences of racism when we got together with England. As Black men, naturally I would speak to Paul Ince about what would happen to him when he went back to West Ham or Les Ferdinand when he went to Millwall. We would of course talk about the racist abuse and the stick we were receiving. It was so normalised. So that's how we would speak about it. It wasn't like, you know, something that we need to sit down over and do something about because we couldn't see any pathway where this was going to get any better for us. You couldn't see that. So, it was just pure defiance for me on the pitch. I don't think I had many good games against Millwall. I scored against them for Palace. But with

Arsenal, I didn't have good games because it went to another level of intensity and hatred, because now all of a sudden, they've seen somebody that they rejected is now back and thriving in the top team.

I had such a strong affinity with the Arsenal fans for this reason. I remember the Cup Winners' Cup final against Parma in Copenhagen in 1994. To get suspended in the semi-final and miss it was devastating because it was such a big game. Obviously, the Champions League has gone on to become what it is now. But for me, at the time, to get to the Cup Winners' Cup final and miss it was devastating. You know, if Arsenal had lost, I just felt like the blame would have been on me because I believed I would have scored in the game; I just believe I would have done something. But in the end Alan Smith scored the winner and it was brilliant because when I joined Arsenal, it all changed for Al and he actually apologised to me about how he thought of me when I signed, not realising that those changes and him losing his position had nothing to do with me. So, I was kind of pleased for Alan Smith in that way because that was almost like his farewell to Arsenal. You know, we are talking about somebody who had won two golden boots before I arrived. And so, you know, he had his moment but for me it was different. Obviously, I wished I'd played the game, but I liked being with the fans and being among it and being with the guys in the dressing room, I literally celebrated like I played. But this moment when I jump

into the crowd with the Arsenal fans at the end of the game is something that I always loved because I got booed at most of the grounds I played at. I would get booed with every touch and people wanting to have you booked and referees calling you over every minute. For certain referees, a Black man like me is kryptonite to them because they can't deal with someone like me because I'm not afraid of them. There's nothing they could do to me, beyond the authority they have over me on the pitch in that moment. And they used it, and especially when they were in their offices with their officials and they're thinking 'Don't worry, I'll make sure this Black guy knows who's boss.' That's the

vibe I got from certain referees. It was the same vibe when I received an MBE in 2000. Kate Hoey [then New Labour's Minister for Sport] publicly criticised me and tried to get it blocked because she deemed me to be unsuitable. This is someone who used to work with David Rocastle when he was in the Arsenal Youth Team [Hoey was an educational advisor at Arsenal in the 1980s]. She was a Labour politician. And I was thinking to myself at the time, how dare you? But that's what I was up against.

↑ Rocastle, Thomas and Wright celebrate as Wright scores his first goal for Arsenal against Leicester City, 25 September 1991.

Arsenal and Black Identity

'ROCKY' ROCASTLE

When I joined Arsenal, the idea was that me and David would be there together for years. It was devastating for both Mickey and Rocky to leave like they did, but obviously, it was especially hard when Rocky left. I didn't expect it. It was a real bolt out of the blue because I went to the training ground and he was outside crying, and I said, 'What's happened?' And he said he'd just been sold to Leeds, and I couldn't believe it. It got to the point where Tony Adams was trying to talk to me because I didn't want to speak to George Graham because I was like, fuck you. So, Tony spoke to me, then I had to go and see George Graham. And then he had to explain to me that 'This is football. This is professional football at this level. This is what happens. Players come and go. That's how it happens. You know that.' And you know it was hard to deal with. It was hard to take because I never saw it coming and that's why I felt as upset as I did because I never thought of it like that because my mind wasn't in that place. I didn't come from that place where football is so ruthless and cutthroat. It's why I always engaged with the players in the reserves and youth teams at Arsenal. It's because of the nature of my emergence in the game. I was like them guys, you know. I had come from non-league and then all of a sudden, I'm signing for Crystal Palace, I'm among professionals and nobody's taking any notice of you. You can't

see anybody that you can relate to. So, when I joined Arsenal and I started doing stuff with the guys in the reserves, I just spoke to them and treated them like normal. I didn't come from that place that George Graham was describing. I didn't know that suddenly somebody that's been at the club for so long could leave in such a way. It was just cold and heartless. It felt like George Graham just offloaded him the first opportunity he got, and I wasn't expecting it. I've never forgiven George Graham for that. Paul Davis had got the same treatment as well, when he was out of the team for eighteen months. It was rough and ruthless. It was really hard seeing Rocky leave because of the way it was done.

BLACK ARSENAL: GENERATION TO GENERATION

With Black Arsenal, I understand what it means now. We have the players, the fanbase, we have the history of Black players from all over the world and we have a deep connection with London. And I guess the next generation is led by Bukayo Saka. It's not about passing the baton, but connecting two very, very distinct generations. There is my generation of Black Arsenal. And here is a new one. Saka, he's now the star boy. I'm just pleased that when you go through our history, Brendon Batson, Paul Davis, Chris Whyte, Rocky, Mickey, me, Patrick Vieira, Thierry Henry, there's always somebody there who's championing us. We're very fortunate to have Saka. He's got something where people will follow him. There's a realness to him and a pureness to him. He's going to be an achiever. He's going to inspire people. Just in the way he is, the way he plays, and what he brings. Arsenal again have got somebody in their ranks who can galvanise that kind of thought from Black people. Where young Black people can look at him and say, 'Yes, that's how I want to be. That's the guy.' I'm so pleased to be close to him. He is someone that didn't just take the number 7 shirt – he knows everything about Rocky, he took the time to learn and ask about him. That makes me emotional.

It's a special shirt and a special number to all of us so to see Bukayo in Rocky's shirt knowing how great they both are as players but also as people and what Arsenal means to both of them – there isn't a better match. Hopefully he doesn't have the same experiences as many of us that came before him, but we've seen that he's had some of it as well [racism experienced after the Euro 2020 final]. We just need him. Reiss Nelson, Eddie Nketiah. I have so much love and support for these young men. 🟨

↑ Ian Wright and Bukayo Saka at Emirates Stadium, 2023.

Arsenal and Black Identity

17

FROM HIGHBURY STADIUM TO HIGHBURY STADIUM SQUARE

TARIQ JAZEEL

Turn left out of Arsenal Underground station, walk a few hundred yards along Gillespie Road, and you soon come to an innocuous looking street on your right called Stadium Mews. If you are lucky enough to have the right key fob, you can enter through the secure gates here and walk another hundred yards or so to another set. Use your key fob again and you'll soon be at what was the corner flag between the North Bank and the West Stand at Highbury Stadium. It is now, of course, a vast residential complex: Highbury Square, or Highbury Stadium Square as some call it. If you're an Arsenal supporter, if you ever watched a match at Highbury before the club moved to the Emirates in 2006, or even if you remember watching televised games at this iconic stadium, the view from here will likely evoke nostalgia, familiarity, wonder, and a smile that hints at all of this and more. You might also be forgiven for a vague feeling of loss, discomfort, even sadness.

From here, the complex is unmistakably stadium shaped. The footprint of the old pitch has been preserved, but what was once the famous turf of Highbury is now an artfully landscaped communal garden separated into mini-quads by rows of pristine boxes and tall grasses, gravel beds punctuated with carefully crafted concrete benches, and illuminated glass light wells. The neat, mowed grass carpeting each of these mini-quads is an unmistakable reference to the sporting stage that this gentle communal garden has replaced. Surrounding this echo of matches once played are four banks of sheer glass windows and sliding glass doors standing six or seven storeys high. North, South, East and West. North Bank, Clock End, West Stand, and of course East Stand. The walls of glass are punctuated by balconies, lights, curtains, blinds, the clutter of domestic possessions, and glimpses of current lives lived in this famous address, the club's home ground from 1913 to 2006. As impressive and tantalising as this view is, standing here at the corner flag there is little that would tell you exactly which stadium this vast stadium-shaped complex is. For that, head left, walk around the landscaped gardens, then turn right at what would have been the other corner flag. Halfway up

← *Previous page:* Highbury, East Stand Concierge.

↗ Top: Arsenal tube station.
→ Bottom: Highbury's East Stand.

Black Arsenal

the gardens, go left directly into the glass fronted complex. Using your key fob once again you'll enter the old East Stand, and soon enough you'll be at the concierge desk in the hallowed cream and white marble floored halls. The Deco futurist styling, large mosaic Gunners logo on the floor, and statue of Herbert Chapman will leave you in little doubt as to where you are. But if you wanted any further evidence, exit through the large doors through to Avenell Road, turn around so your back is against the low-rise terraced housing immediately opposite and the North London residential streetscape that surrounds you, and you'll see the unmistakable red and white façade of Highbury Stadium's East Stand – the Art Deco frontispiece added to Archibald Leitch's stadium design in 1936. Your smile will probably get a little bigger. This is Highbury. Now.

By the late 1990s, Arsenal Football Club knew that a move to a brand-new stadium was inevitable. Islington Council had refused planning permission to expand Highbury, so a new state-of-the-art stadium was the only viable option for a club with a 38,000 capacity and huge waiting lists for each match. As Arsène Wenger wrote in his autobiography, 'We had no choice … We were like a company that had to turn down clients.' The Emirates build cost £390 million. It started in 2004. The club was financially dependent not just on the sustained, if not emphatic, on-pitch success that Wenger delivered through the 2000s, but also on the banks. And the banks were

in part persuaded by the club's ambitious and unprecedented development plan that would turn Highbury Stadium into Highbury Stadium Square. Conversion of the site into 650 upmarket one-, two-, and three-bedroom residential flats and penthouses promised a valuable source of revenue for the club in the face of its financial commitment, and the scale of this development project saw Arsenal FC plc become the largest property company in England for a period in the early 2000s. Though the 2008 property crash placed immense pressure on the success of the project, the development and sale of the units has been a key part of Arsenal's long-term plan.

Economics aside, the quality of the build, attention to detail, and the preservation of the heritage of Highbury Stadium and its link with Arsenal FC, between place and club, have been exceptional. Highbury Stadium, now Highbury Square, remains part of the club's physical and emotional landscape; a visual and material manifestation of the club's spiritual home, and perhaps moreover of the club's deep roots in this North London residential neighbourhood. And the project has offered a select group of Arsenal supporters, as well as property speculators, the opportunity to buy a little piece of that intangible heritage. Yet, if you don't buy or rent at Highbury Square, you won't be in possession of that precious key fob that affords you access to the interior of the complex. If you're

← Highbury Square in 2009.

From Highbury Stadium to Highbury Stadium Square

nonetheless curious, you would need to walk around the complex, down Gillespie Road and right into Avenell Road, past the East Stand, stopping short of Aubert Court, the council estate that abuts the old stadium. Here you'll find the one public right of way running east–west through the complex, between the end of East Stand apartments, landscaped gardens and West Stand apartments on your right, and the Clock End apartments on your left. You can walk this pathway in daylight hours only. You will still be separated from the complex on both sides by thick, secure gates, and monitored by CCTV.

More than a decade ago, I was fortunate enough to have one of those key fobs. I rented a flat in the East Stand, and like many of my neighbours who were also Arsenal supporters, the thrill of living there never got stale. Yet the complexities and subtle forms of exclusion and surveillance that go hand-in-hand with any gated community were also difficult to reconcile with my daily postcode pride. For example, as much as I enjoyed the communal landscaped garden, it never quite felt like a socially acceptable practice to kick a ball there. Though I often hated myself for it, as much as anyone I got drawn into paranoid discussions about tailgating and the imperative to make sure security gates shut behind us. And I was always aware that omnipresent CCTV cameras serving the purpose of safety offered a substantial side dish of exclusion to the curious neighbours, the fans, the season

ticket holders, and the nostalgic majority without a key fob.

As successful as Highbury Square has been, there is no doubt that it has been part of the broader middle-class restructuring of place that has swept across London in late modernity. Though sensitivity to history and heritage has been at the centre of the Highbury Square development, regeneration projects that have property speculation at their heart do not have a principled commitment to housing for the many. Take a walk around Highbury, and the cheek-by-jowl juxtaposition of council estates and low-income housing with upper-middle class and super-rich residences soon become apparent in ways that will probably not surprise any Londoner who has seen the shape and demographic composition of their neighbourhood change over the last thirty or forty years. In a city where average house prices have risen 650 per cent since 1995 (in Highbury, the figure is 697 per cent; in Birmingham, the UK's second largest city, the figure is 352 per cent), neighbourhoods have been, and continue to be, markets where value and profit have either been extracted or are latent, awaiting the developer's Midas touch. And as the demographic composition of an area gradually changes, of course so does the neighbourhood; an artisan butcher here, an expensive cheese shop there, another greasy spoon cafe gives way to a gourmet restaurant, and so on.

We should be under no doubt that projects like the Highbury Square development have been part of this trend. Though the stadium has been a fixture in Highbury since 1913, its redevelopment and commodification as property must be seen in this context. At today's market prices, flats range in price from upwards of half a million pounds for a one-bed, to up to two million pounds for a three-bed penthouse. This is not housing for the many, and beyond its not insignificant intangible heritage value, this is not housing that has served a majority of the existing local community. In her classic 1964 book *London: Aspects of Change*, Islington-based planning theorist Ruth Glass coined a term for what she referred to as the 'upper-middle-class takeover' of the poorer enclaves of Hampstead and Chelsea, an 'invasion' that she noted had in 1964 already spread to Islington and other parts of north and north-west London: 'gentrification', she called this phenomenon. It's a word with which most Londoners today will be familiar.

In the context of the refrain 'Black Arsenal', where we rightly both celebrate and interrogate the significance of Arsenal's contribution to the representation of Black life and the club's special relationship with Black Britain, the question of gentrification begets more questions. In Highbury, Finsbury Park, Holloway and beyond, the intersection between working-class culture, race and histories of African and Caribbean migration are well known. Arsenal's umbilical and historical connection to the organic multiculture of this part of North London are explored throughout this book, but the Highbury Square development pushes us to ask about the social, economic and not least demographic effects of the club's pursuit of property-led regeneration of the area. What economic, social, and emotional effects has it had on Highbury's multi-ethnic working-class community? How does Highbury Square orient itself in a landscape where existing estates and low-income council housing sit within such close proximity? And not least, how do we reconcile these patterns of neighbourhood change with the narrative around the club's historic relationship with a Black Britain, and Black London, that historically is also working class and immigrant? There is no doubt that Highbury Square is an exclusive development, but we should also remember that that very adjective betrays a latent proclivity to *exclude*. ■

18

THE MARGINS

EDDIE OTCHERE

was a modern fan, before the modern fan existed. I had no interest in the game of football, apart from youthful exuberance and the chance to kick something hard and far. A snap of the hip, the slap of foot hitting ball, and the curving arc as it disappeared into the distance. ''Ave it!' I didn't care about accuracy or trying to score a goal, the force of hitting it, driving it far, far away, was what I was interested in. The intricate etiquette and tribalism of football moved grimily over my head. I didn't care who played where or why, or how your allegiance to a team was imparted under the skin of your being. I was not spending long summer evenings playing rush goalie or headers and volleys.

Football was something that happened over there, to other people. But Ian Wright changed that. I learnt about football and the Arsenal, because Ian Wright, with his explosions of joy every time he scored, made me. I supported him, and through him learnt the ways of football. Or, at least enough of it not to be shamed in a conversation about trophies, and formations, and who had the best sponsor's logo on their shirt, or to briefly show an interest as another

World Cup or Euros rolled round, and St George flags appeared from nowhere to be draped outside windows, bearing allegiance to a country that nurtured me but only grudgingly supported my existence.

I supported one player: Wrighty. Following his career, from the time he was underrated, to the time he was overrated, and then after, in that slow, twilight decline to being properly appreciated, with his legacy secured. The data that governs modern football can't tell you about the times that matter. These are moments where the stats make no sense – there is a sense of magic about them – and riding aloft that mystical wave is a black horse ridden by Ian Wright charging out of Brockley into the sunset, down Woolwich high street.

The Arsenal is itself a simulacrum. Hailing from the south, moving to North London and embodying the spirits of the two cities, North and South London. Its name does not preclude its village associations but, rather like some Chaucerian character, it is the Arsenal, last of the English clubs to hold the definite article in front of their name after incorporation. It is a stop on the Underground and a well-marketed construct

← *Previous page:* Scenes from 1990s London nightlife.

Black Arsenal

of the values of London and holds more than the villages of Chelsea, Brentford, West Ham, Tottenham, Millwall, Crystal Palace will ever hold.

That said … It's 1994 and that year London had its own defining sound that resounded across the planet, we called it jungle and its bass lines shook the very foundations of what London was capable of doing. That season Arsenal had finished twelfth, Chelsea eleventh … and I cared nothing for the margins. That carnival, you'd hear M-Beat and General Levi's 'Incredible' everywhere, and in their video you'll see a yout' schucking out in the 1993 Adidas Arsenal away kit. I remember myself there: the JVC logo adorning the shirt and a Sega Saturn game controller in my hand as I play J League Super soccer, the Japanese edition of Virtua Soccer. The future is being written around me as the sounds of the twenty-first century are being crafted by producers in London, north, south, east and west. I'm just about to leave the house: camera in my bag, red Ralph Lauren shirt, Moschino trousers, white Reebok workouts, green Stone Island jacket, Next pants and Arsenal socks.

Wrighty's Arsenal meant jungle, fashion and football. It was nothing for me, being a Stockwell kid, to hop on the Northern Line and travel ten stops to my job in Camden Market. In Camden, I was exposed to an aesthetic. An aesthetic which was sharp and meant there was no question what you were coming in. Woodhouse on Upper Street was the epicentre of a kind of London re-seller of anything Italian: there was Massimo Osti, Stone Island, CP company, then Camden Market for Diesel and Kung Fu slippers. The style of my times, fusing jungle and football, had transitioned off the terraces because it was situated in an area of London that held its own, gave space to the culture and was populated by the locals, fashioned in their post-work finery. Those North London lads all held themselves up with a working-class pride in Ralph Lauren and Reeboks. You can say every village in London has a look, and some villages have stronger looks than others.

↑ Ian Wright dancing on the pitch.

The Margins

Then there were the clubs: The Astoria on Sunday for Roast; The YMCA on Tottenham Court Road on Tuesday night with Thunder and Joy; Orange at The Rocket on Holloway Road and A.W.O.L. at the Paradise in Angel. Man-a-man is geared up: Versace, Moschino, Ralphie, Armani, Paul Smith, name brands, cause the yout' works hard for the money so now comes time to show and prove.

When Arsenal made Wrighty one of theirs, the south came with him. We continued to see this rude bwoy go on to prove himself for London as the greatest of all time. Nike made an advert about him out on Hackney Marshes, the surprise of seeing that celebration as he scored against everymen, on those green fields, the cheeky chirpiness of 'Parklife' encapsulating the mischief that whirled around him.

It's no surprise his prowess in the league was never matched when he played for the kingdom. England will never witness great football until England has a coach that respects us. Furthermore, England will never have the coach England deserves because she will only ever be allowed to bring science, skill and magic to the women's game. Ask Sir Alex who his greatest teacher was, and it'd be his mother. England never had the centre-forwards it held in its rank on the field. Wrighty had thirty-three caps and nine goals – so many opportunities to show that energised magic denied. So many times the scapegoat for the kingdom's failure. Never truly appreciated by the kingdom, Wrighty was always appreciated by the Arsenal, the rude bwoy hero front and centre. *179 Just Done It*. Emblazoned on his shirt and carried in our hearts.

My love of the Arsenal is entwined with my love for Ian Wright, the flash of the gold tooth in his grin, as he curls over laughing at his own joke. The unconfined joy and pain as he kicks every ball and stretches every sinew in the analyst's chair. He is South London's glory, burnished by his time with the Arsenal. ▪

19

ARSENAL IN THE COMMUNITY

SAMIR SINGH

I grew up in Newington Green, on the Islington and Hackney border, very close to Arsenal Stadium in Highbury and so I was only ever going to be a Gooner. Like many families of South Asian descent, we owned a newsagent so my earliest Arsenal memories were fans calling in to the shop to buy sweets on their way to the ground. I think that because we were local to the ground and so my mum knew and saw many Arsenal fans, she was happy for me to go to Highbury from a young age with my friends despite the general media thrust (this was the early nineties) related to hooliganism and racism. I've been going up the Arsenal since 1989 and since 1996, to this day, as a season ticket holder.

Since 2005, I have worked for Arsenal Football Club, first on setting up the new museum at Emirates Stadium and since 2007 for Arsenal in the Community whose holiday football camps I used to attend as a child in the old JVC Centre behind the Clock End. Arsenal in the Community is itself connected to (Black) British history as it was the 1981 inner city riots in Toxteth and Brixton that led to the formation of football in the community schemes. Inner cities had especially suffered with industry moving out and it was felt that football clubs were one of the few remaining institutions that could both help restore pride and provide employment. For many young people in the inner cities, it is still the football clubs which they look to as an institution they can trust. So it was with great excitement that I contacted Dr Nwonka – I was hoping that the Black influence in the community would be conveyed – people like my colleague Beverley Nicholas who has worked for Arsenal in the Community since 1987, or Celia Facey, one of the youth workers around Elthorne Estate in Archway, a matriarch-style figure who all the young people round there look up to.

If I think of Black Arsenal, I can't help but also think of our academy players who are overwhelmingly from a Black British demographic, keeping pace with those changes in London where the West African population now outnumbers the West Indian. Credit must go to our academy leadership as they are making efforts to ensure that the staff at the academy reflect the young players.

Being asked to write a piece for the *Black Arsenal* book has required me to think about my identity growing up. In the late eighties there was certainly not a separate South Asian identity; in short Black = Not White – that was it … there was no term like BAME. A very famous women's rights organisation in Southall which primarily led the Punjabi Sikh community was called the Southall Black Sisters. Why I write this here was because certainly when it came to football, I considered myself Black. Of course, I had Charlie Nic[holas] and Smudger [Smith] on my wall, but I also had Rocky, Paul Davis and later, my all-time hero, Wrighty. In the eighties there was a dearth of South Asian players – sadly, to this day, there still is – and I couldn't ever see myself being regarded as a white player. Therefore it was the Black players I wanted to be or, more importantly, who looked most like me and so who I *thought* I could be. I think ethnicity is more fluid nowadays, especially in London: I see white kids pretending to be Saka. I don't know if this would've happened in the eighties. So, back then, those Black players did not just represent Black people but also Asian people too.

Representation is clearly important – when you feel you can fit in somewhere, you find a sense of belonging. Black British influence on London culture ran deep in the nineties and alongside Ian Wright and Kevin Campbell on my walls were

↑ Arsenal in the Community.

Arsenal in the Community

flyers from the jungle and drum and bass rave scene, alongside my Arsenal heroes. Those rave crowds, as at Highbury, were similarly mixed – representative of London demographics. Black Arsenal, for me, is of more interest, importance and relevance off the pitch; many clubs across the divisions regularly field Black British players but that does not necessarily translate to the terraces even in areas where there is a large Black British population. So, when I first learnt of 'Black Arsenal' my first hope was that the focus was not too much on the pitch but on the fans – that's where Black Arsenal permeates most. When I first heard about Black Arsenal, my first thought, I'm sure like many, was of Dainton 'The Bear' but I was also thinking about a fairly sizeable group of Black Gooners, all now in their fifties and sixties who are all from South London – I know from speaking to many of them over the years that they were drawn over the river, despite being closer to other London clubs, because they felt welcome on the North Bank and the Clock End. And therefore I think our Black fans of that age group have as much to do with Black Arsenal as the Black players. When I mentioned the Black Arsenal concept to a few of my Black Spurs-supporting friends, their reaction was identical; both immediately got the concept and acknowledged that this was a uniquely Arsenal thing, which they were secretly jealous about. ■

↑ → The No More Red kit, launched in 2022 by Arsenal and Adidas to support community projects that combat knife crime.

ABOVE: Ashley Cole, Patrick Vieira and Sol Campbell celebrate winning the Premier League at Old Trafford on 8 May 2002.

BELOW: Thierry Henry celebrating against Panathinaikos at Highbury in 2004. He claimed he had been racially abused by home fans during the away leg of their Champions League tie.

Opposite:
ABOVE: The famous 'Va Va Voom' Renault television adverts starring Thierry Henry epitomised the popularity of footballers, and Arsenal players in particular, off the pitch in the early 2000s. It was the first time Renault had used a celebrity in one of its adverts.
BELOW: Sol Campbell on his first return to White Hart Lane after leaving Tottenham for Arsenal that year.

ABOVE: Gilberto Silva at Arsenal's training ground.

BELOW: Lauren with former European featherweight champion boxer, trainer and lifelong Arsenal fan Jim McDonnell.

Opposite:

ABOVE: Sol Campbell scoring against Barcelona in the Champions League final, 2006.

BELOW: Johan Djourou and Theo Walcott playing video games in their hotel room during a pre-season training camp in 2010.

Mo Farah, holding the Arsenal-inspired running spikes he wore to win the 5000m World Championship.

Opposite: Arsenal fans remember David Rocastle during their match against Reading on the twelfth anniversary of his death.

1967 - 2001

Alex Scott during a visit to the Whittington Hospital in December 2017.

Opposite:
ABOVE: Arsenal under 23s win the Premier League 2 title in 2018.
BELOW: Mo Elneny.

the Arsenal

Welcome to North London
Arsenal
Home of the Arsenal

UGLY
'COME TO SEE
THE ARSENAL'
SKETCHES

ROCASTLE
PRINT TEXT
ACTUAL
SIZE

VICTORIA
CONCORDIA
CRESCIT.

ARSENE
KNOWS

ARSENE
KNOWS

GILLESPIE

Emirates

INVINCIBLE

to Ooh to be
obe a Gooner!

WE'RE THE CLOCK END
WE'RE THE CLOCK END
WE'RE THE CLOCK END

old Arsenal
ud to bay that name
s wearing that song
win the game

14

20

DESIGNING *FOUND A PLACE WHERE WE BELONG*

REUBEN DANGOOR

← *Previous page* Arsenal mural artwork.
↑ *Found a Place Where We Belong* stadium crowd mural.

Found a Place Where We Belong is the last of eight artworks that have been designed and placed around Emirates Stadium to capture the club's heritage, culture and community. They all have different themes, but the main thing that connects all the murals is their size. The actual area that we had to present the artwork on are massive and so they have a really good capacity for detail and quite a lot of them utilise this in different ways. For the club's motto *Victoria Concordia Crescit*, which means 'Victory Through Harmony', we have these huge towering Arsenal figures and powerful and epic feats of greatness that could also be related to the Invincibles artwork. When designing these, I was referencing an old painting with a military theme completely unrelated to sport, so basically it became a collection of players as generals and soldiers, inspired by neoclassical French revolutionary paintings. But it was amazing that the people in the paintings are practically life-size and seeing that collection of people together was really powerful. So, when I began researching ideas for *Found a Place Where We Belong*, I thought it would be amazing to have this

mural presented in a similar kind of way. If you look at all of the Arsenal murals, they all have a painterly kind of quality. We didn't just want to have photographs of fans on the side of the stadium. And then obviously when you start digging into club-specific murals, the North Bank one obviously came up which was still lodged in people's heads. There were a lot of issues around race and representation with that. The club were very keen to have an accurate reflection of their fanbase, not just in London but as a global club. But also it was to reflect the kind of diverse nature of their fanbase which the 1992 mural definitely didn't do unfortunately.

This mural was an attempt to show loads of fans and try and keep them almost as you're looking at life-size people. It's almost overwhelming as you have so many people. But then if you look closely, you can see it's Ian Wright, its KSI, its Mo Farah, there are people from different generations there. There are fans from a hundred years ago and they're still in black and white. There's Dainton 'The Bear' on there who had such a cult connection to the club. We purposely kept people a little bit inconspicuous 'cause in a similar way to the way that you would describe the Arsenal fanbase, you got like a multi-millionaire director next to the tea lady who served in the director's box for fifty years. So, the mural may feel like it's all about the club, but it isn't – it's for everyone. It's *for* people as opposed to *by* someone. The process of all of the murals involved massive collaborations with fan groups to understand what people wanted to see and what was important to them about Arsenal. And the multiracial nature of Arsenal and subsequently the mural was so important.

In terms of my interest in Black Arsenal, there is a presence of a famous group of Black Arsenal players on the Highbury mural called *Remember Who You Are,* which is of the whole of the East Stand and is an interpretation of that very famous dressing room picture of Paul Davis (who's smoking a cigar), Kevin Campbell, David Rocastle and Mickey Thomas. There's a recreation of that picture at the bottom left hand of the Highbury mural; Mickey and Davis are hanging out the window, you've got Kevin Campbell holding a champagne bottle because, according to the club photographer, he then poured it over one of their heads. It captured a moment in the club's history, although they're quite small within that window because it's the building that takes precedence. Players used to lean out of the dressing room window as people would walk past the old Highbury Stadium and interact with the fans.

The interracial nature of the mural happened very naturally because Arsenal, as a fanbase, is incredibly multicultural and there have been lots of very prominent Black players who played for the club. Arsenal obviously famously fielded nine Black players, and players like Ian Wright and Thierry Henry loom large over certain generations. Wright was a London icon for a lot of people. Arsenal's got an incredibly multicultural nature, it feels very London, very representative of London's cultural mix. Arsenal feels very representative of *London –* certainly for me growing up in East London (I later moved to North London). And when I look at my friends or the area that I lived in, I also see this integration in the Arsenal fanbase. So, the mural is both naturally and purposefully diverse, and the club itself were always keen on representation; we reached out to the head of Arsenal Kenya, Arsenal Egypt – they wanted to be able to call out as many fans from all over the world and as many important people to the club as possible. As obviously there's only a limited amount of space there had to be an element of selection, but the actual response that the club got when they put the call out for people was very true to what you're seeing on the mural.

The process of designing the mural has certainly been unlike anything I've ever worked on before. We started in April 2022. There was a massive call-out from the club. They obviously had people that they wanted to be involved like families of legendary players, such as David Rocastle's daughter for example. It was an enormous process

Designing *Found a Place Where We Belong*

considering the amount of people who've been consulted. We had fan groups from all over the world, we had meetings with fans in the Tollington Arms pub, relatives, players, ex-players, Gay Gooners, everyone. The thing is that Arsenal are representative of many, many different people and it really felt like everyone was consulted. However, I think what was good was that it wasn't designed by committee because I don't believe in 'designed by committee' in that sense – I feel like that doesn't always work when everyone gets to change things – but certainly from gathering the raw materials to work with, the consultation was so important. For the first time, for example, the Invincibles mural features players from the Arsenal women's team. Arsenal Women are one of the most successful teams in the world. They are the only British team who have won what's now known as the Champions League, and they had Black players such as Rachel Yankey, Lianne Sanderson and Alex Scott. I understand the representation game, but because it's always been there, it's never felt forced.

↑ *Remember Who You Are* Highbury mural.

When Arsenal initially asked me to get involved, it was absolutely terrifying. Maybe because of the scale or just maybe the expectations of the actual club history. It is going to be there for years. There was a lot of attention on Arsenal as the club had started doing well again. It was really exciting, but it was also a big undertaking. But the process always felt really comfortable because it all felt like what I had to work with were the right ingredients.

We have so many football clubs that are still based in multicultural areas of London. But I feel if other clubs did the same thing you'd be making a conscious effort to try and insert multiracialism there because it doesn't chime with what you can see organically in the stands. So, there's something about the natural correspondence between what has been created and what's already there, because what you'd be doing for other clubs would be a recreation of an imagined or hoped-for fanbase or history that isn't really there. But with Arsenal there's no real kind of effort there in terms of trying to present an image

Designing *Found a Place Where We Belong*

of what they would hope to be their fanbase in time or wish to be, but maybe isn't there already. If you look at the Arsenal fanbase and you look at what is on the mural, you're looking at pictures from that span of a hundred years. There are people who have sent in pictures as fans when they were kids or from the nineties or the early 2000s or, you know, back in the seventies or even earlier. I was trying to make it as uniform as possible. There's a red wash over everything, for example, so everything has a similar kind of tonality to it, so obviously you can tell that there are people from different cultural backgrounds and different races, but they all seem at home. It's why the piece is called *Found a Place Where We Belong*, after the Dennis Bergkamp quote. The objective was not even to highlight race or Black identity. It was more about the unity of the Arsenal community. It's like a wall of people, and really it's very moving. The racial makeup is so diverse, but within that there's so many quiet, emotionally charged stories as well. There is a picture on the mural of the poet Michael Rosen and his son who passed away, which was of course extremely sad. We talk a lot about Arsenal and its responsibility to its fans and community, so even that was something that played on my mind. Like, you know, they're coming to the game and they're able to see their relations and their relatives who passed away, which again, goes back to Arsenal and this sense of identification and belonging.

From a fanbase point of view, I've always felt that Arsenal still is a club of the London street, much more than other clubs. It is in part to do with the removal of stadiums from the town centres and the building of new modern stadiums, because if you look at where West Ham United's old Boleyn Ground in Upton Park was, look at where White Hart Lane was and you look at where Highbury was, you had terraced houses stuck to the side of them. You had blocks of flats across the road. Those stadiums felt as part of those communities as possible. But that's changed. It's why I like walking down Gillespie Road to get to the Emirates. I like when you come out of Arsenal Tube station. I love that route because you still get that feeling of 'wow, look at this'.

So much of what the mural captured predates the Emirates, but even the new generation of fans would have kind of caught elements of Highbury culture either through their parents or their older brothers or sisters, so there is still that connection. The Emirates is starting to feel more accepted as home. I think you've got a younger generation who never went to Highbury, never seen Highbury. It was part of the reason why we decided, rather than have one theme and wrap the whole stadium, that we'd have one mural that was dedicated to this chapter of Arsenal's *history*, and another for this chapter of Arsenal's *future*, because for so many they don't know Highbury, but they know who [actors] Micheal Ward and Ashley Walters are. Because of the very nature of football, a decision was made to have no current players represented. Arsenal has an amazing academy and there are several players, like Jack Wilshire for example, who've joined as a child and literally gone right away through the system to the first team and now has become a coach. Bukayo Saka obviously was at the Arsenal Academy and now he's in the first team. He's one of the best players in the world. But who's to say he'll still be here in three years' time? I hope so, but we don't know. Leah Williamson, for example, she'd just won the European championship when we were deciding to design the mural. And she would have been an amazing person to put on it. But again, she might go to another club for some reason. I hope she never would move on, obviously, but there's nothing to say that they can't. So having only past players meant we could avoid situations where we include current players who may no longer be playing for the club in the future.

We see there are Black people spread all over the mural, but I didn't consciously place the Black fanbase in a balanced way like we see. I can imagine that there could have been a temptation to put all the Black players and all the Black fans in one section of the mural. But there was no conscious decision to make sure that there was an even dispersal of black faces and brown faces across the whole of the mural space and not just in one section because we are just replicating what is already present in the stands. Gunnersaurus is probably the only one that needed a bit of consideration because he's massive. There's a little bit of choreography in regard to people's arms and

scarves and obscuring who can afford to be obscured. But if you look at the image of the boxer Michael Watson, he seems quite prominent there. But in the grand scheme of things he's actually quite small. Because if you actually look at it again, I'm trying to actually paint it in a uniform way so that no one really has any undue prominence. You've got to remember how people were largely seeing this mural. They're seeing this on matchday. They're seeing it from the ground looking up and you can only take in what you can take in. There are people I perhaps don't know who I have painted in there and they probably mean the world to someone. A fan who comes to the game, I don't necessarily know who they are. I don't know their backstory, but others may see it and find a resonance with that person, be it personal, sporting or otherwise. So, whether it's real-life fans or players, the prominence comes from the identification of the person looking at it as opposed to being pushed down a certain route visually from the mural.

In many ways, the everyday, unspectacular, subjective and natural points of identification and importance we place on our experiences of players, fans and moments is what is central to Clive Nwonka's Black Arsenal concept, and I would argue that that mural is a reflection of that. It feels like an encapsulation of Arsenal's connection to Black identity, rather than a cultivation of it. ▮

Designing *Found a Place Where We Belong*

21

ARSENAL'S CELEBRITY GAZE

Charting the emergence of Arsenal as a
Black cultural touchstone

SAM MEJIAS

The Premier League era's ascendency in the nineties and early 2000s seamlessly paralleled the rise of both the globalised internet, and naturally, the global celebrity. The United States has for decades been one of the biggest exporters of popular culture, and around the same time that the world began collectively transitioning to globalised online spaces, in England, Arsenal's stylish play and elite, cosmopolitan players made footballing history with the undefeated 2003–04 Invincibles season, going global and in the process attracting the gaze of influential luminaries within Black American culture.

In those early years of the twenty-first century you could see the American attitude towards football begin to evolve, ever so slowly, nudged forward by the US men's national team's surprising performance in the 2002 World Cup in Japan and South Korea, where they reached the quarter-finals before losing to eventual runners-up Germany. Yet in my hometown of New York City, there were still only a few bars where you could actually watch a match; I remember working hard to find the only bar in downtown Brooklyn where I could see Arsenal tragically lose the 2006 Champions League final (although talisman Thierry Henry didn't score, I fully blamed Jens Lehmann for his early red card). But in the early 2000s, when hip-hop culture began to dominate popular entertainment, the link between Black celebrity and Black footballers became much more visible. In the centre of it all was Thierry Henry, a global symbol of Black elegance, success and – after the 2003–04 Invincibles season – even perfection, who became an alluring ambassador of the game and of Arsenal to some of the most recognised names within Black American pop culture.

Two prominent celebrities offer interesting case studies about how Arsenal and, specifically, a kind of individual Black excellence associated with the team, became attractive as a cultural signifier for the Black experience in the US. In the early-mid-2000s, legendary film director Spike Lee and equally legendary rapper and recording artist Jay-Z both went public about their love of Arsenal. Both forged their connections to the club for seemingly the same reason, an appreciation

← *Previous page:* Kim Kardashian and Eddie Nketiah at Emirates Stadium, 2022.

of Thierry Henry in his pomp. Yet their support was expressed in ways reflecting their public personas, showing how the appeal of Arsenal can intimately connect to two distinct performances of Black celebrity. Spike Lee – already known for his passionate and consistent courtside support of his hometown New York Knicks basketball team – adopted a similar approach to supporting Arsenal, becoming a 'die-hard' celebrity fan. Jay-Z's support for Arsenal, however, manifested publicly through entrepreneurial discourse, and eventually, direct investment.

SPIKE LEE: A SUPERFAN FINDS A NEW LOVE

The earliest evidence of Spike Lee's support of Arsenal can be found in February 2004 through a tweet on 28 February 2019 by Arsenal official photographer Stuart MacFarlane commemorating the fifteen-year anniversary of Lee's visit to Highbury, in the middle of the Invincibles year. He is photographed with Henry and Wenger separately, together with both, and on his own in the Highbury stands with the 2003 FA Cup trophy. Spotted at a Chelsea-v-

↑ Arsène Wenger, Spike Lee and Thierry Henry at Highbury, 2004.

Arsenal's Celebrity Gaze

Arsenal match in 2008, Lee explained to a Brazilian journalist that his support for Arsenal 'started with Thierry Henry, and it's continued, even after he went to Barcelona'. In a September 2018 appearance on the podcast *Unfiltered with James O'Brien*, guest host and MP David Lammy, a noted Spurs supporter, while interviewing Lee about his filmmaking career, raised the rivalry between the two North London clubs. When asked how he became an Arsenal supporter, he responded simply with 'Thierry Henry … you can't blame me for that. That was my in for Arsenal, and then we became friends too!' In another 2018 interview Lee shared views on Wenger's retirement and enthused about the 'Spike Lee is a Gooner!' chant that he heard when he attended matches. 'My wish is that one day Thierry Henry will be the manager of Arsenal, that's my whole connection to Arsenal, it was Thierry Henry.' Through these public statements over the past twenty years, and in anecdotes referencing his choice to wear an Arsenal shirt on film sets, Spike Lee clearly established a deep connection to the club as a fan, extending to Arsenal a similar type of fan devotion that he practised with the New York Knicks.

JAY-Z: BLACK EXCELLENCE AS INVESTMENT OPPORTUNITY

Jay-Z's path to Arsenal support also went through Thierry Henry. In an April 2010 exclusive interview with the official Arsenal. com magazine, Jay-Z shared:

When Thierry Henry was at the club I saw him play and I just thought he was an amazing player, ever since then I have been a big fan of the club, following you guys and still today you play the beautiful football that Thierry did … what I really love is when people play sport in a beautiful way, and that's one thing Arsenal do for sure.

In the same interview Jay-Z also said of Henry, 'that is a guy I would like to meet' before speculating about how 'as a businessman … if the right opportunity [to invest in Arsenal] presented itself, then who knows?' He was later quoted as saying 'I have really got into soccer over the last 10 years and I've been saying for some time I want a percentage of Arsenal … I never want to be a back-seat investor. I want to be on the board, involved in the decision-making … I'm at the stage of my career where I am ready for another investment like this.' As it turns out, this wasn't just talk. Jay-Z's sports management company

EXTENDING CELEBRITY CULTURAL PRACTICES THROUGH ARSENAL

For both celebrities, supporting Arsenal represented an opportunity to extend their particular style of Black celebrity cultural practice to a global, cosmopolitan context. Spike Lee's sustained love of Arsenal is clearly seen over the past twenty years through his wearing of Arsenal attire on film sets, his regular attendance at games when in England, and by speaking candidly in the media about his ongoing support, even as recently as 2019 on the red carpet of an Oscars after-party. Jay-Z, on the other hand, publicly showed support for Arsenal in the same manner as he has for the US sporting teams he loves: through financial investment and by bringing Arsenal into his practices as an influential Black celebrity entrepreneur. It is important to reflect on what the worth of individuals, and specifically in this case Thierry Henry – as a player, and as a symbol of global Black excellence – says about how Arsenal as a football club and culture became attractive to such prominent Black American figures. In the early-mid-2000s, as internet culture and globalised information became ubiquitous, discovering Henry as a cultural touchstone for Black sport may have been inevitable. It is unsurprising that an elite, Black, non-

Roc Sports Nation, launched in 2013, currently represents elite athletes in major American sports, but also represents global football clubs and players, including AC Milan, Leeds United and Arsenal Academy players Tyreece John-Jules and Brooke Norton-Cuffy. And on 11 June 2018, Arsenal signed a £1 million a year agreement with Jay-Z's Tidal streaming music platform to provide streaming music services to Arsenal members. While Jay-Z didn't make it to the Arsenal board, he nonetheless manifested his support from the club directly through financial partnership.

↑ Jay-Z and Chris Martin watching on at Emirates Stadium, 2013.

Arsenal's Celebrity Gaze

American footballer resonated with Black American celebrities, whose achievements and cultural influence had at that same time also become global. Henry as a footballer is the very model of an almost utopian Black celebrity: elegant, successful and devastatingly good at their craft. However, what is notable about Henry's role at Arsenal was that this was one of the first visible forms of transatlantic Black stardom, bridging arts and sport, that attracted major celebrities. Arsenal made that impact first, which has legacies to this day.

It is therefore interesting to consider how, through the prevailing symbol of Henry, Arsenal as a representation of global Blackness has become a part of the cultural repertoire of influential Black American artists. While this admittedly continues the grand tradition of locating importance and primary value in the celebrity individual, it brings Arsenal into conversation with fans of both Spike Lee's films and Jay-Z's music (and sports

↑ American Arsenal fans outside O'Hanlon's Bar, New York City.

management), not to mention more recent cultural contributions from Black American artists. In recent years, other prominent Black American celebrities have also embraced the club: the actor Jamie Foxx is a fan and supported the launch of their 2016–17 kit in Los Angeles while supporters chanted 'Jamie Foxx is a Gooner!'; superstar musician Rihanna was famously given a tour of Emirates Stadium in February 2018, and is also a part-owner of Tidal and thus directly involved with Arsenal through their financial partnership.

It is clear that Arsenal have forged an identity in the US pop culture imaginary as an elite club that can generate support from some of the most recognisable Black American personalities on the planet. Jay-Z and Spike Lee may have led the way, but many more will likely make the connection as Arsenal continue to influence Black culture. ■

↑ Kim Kardashian back at Emirates Stadium in 2023.

↑ Jamie Foxx launches the new Arsenal second and third kits in Los Angeles, 2016.

Arsenal's Celebrity Gaze

FOR

22

BLACK HERO. BLACK SUPERHERO

TAYO POPOOLA

Thierry Henry never lost to Tottenham. I like to think that hurts them as much as it delights him every time he crowbars it into a conversation about Them when he's on TV. There's *THE* photo: Thierry, on his knees, in the pose that became the statue outside the ground. After scoring the opening goal of a 3–0 destruction of Tottenham at Highbury in 2002, Thierry runs the length of the pitch, shrugs off every ecstatic Arsenal teammate in his way and knee-slides in front of the Spurs away end, only to cast his gaze downwards. He refuses to look at them – they need only know one thing: they don't matter.

Every time I look at the photo, I look delightedly at every Tottenham fan glaring back at him, giving him their best. Snubbed, ignored, emasculated and desperate for Thierry's attention. They're all there: wanker signs, Burberry caps, middle fingers, furious, pissed-up faces, mostly white. But wait – top right, there's two unusual faces that stand out. Unusual because they remain impassive, not joining in with the vitriol. Unusual also because they're Black. One of them is wearing a very recognisable pork pie hat, though not the shades this time. I can't believe my luck. Arch Spurs fan, my hero. Hello Norman Jay.

The first time I met Norman Jay was in a record shop in Soho. I was working behind the counter when he came in, regulation pork pie hat and shades. I held my breath a bit. Growing up, his show on Kiss FM had made him a hero to me. Listening on my brother's twin-deck Tandy cassette player, hovering over the play and record button, Norman had been a cypher into a musical world that was happening just outside my estate: a Black London just out of reach.

That day in Soul Jazz Records in Soho, I was wearing the 95–96 Arsenal top. JVC logo. The one Wrighty was wearing when he chipped John Lukic at Elland Road. Norman took one look at it, at me, and said loudly, 'Well, I'm not being fucking served by HIM, that's for sure.' He laughed afterwards – not so soon as to stop my embarrassment I'll add, but enough to relax me. He then told me he was only joking and introduced himself. We have remained friendly for almost thirty years, often DJing on the same line ups.

← *Previous page:* Thierry Henry's goal celebration against Tottenham Hotspur, 16 November 2002.

My heroes were always people like Norman – male, Black, older than me. Pretend older brothers and fantasy uncles. Ian Wright, for example, for what he did on the pitch, sure, but also because of what he represented off it. Wrighty was a traditional hero, the 'I wanna be like you when I grow up' kind. Like Norman Jay, Wrighty was accessible, relatable. After all, he'd only turned pro at twenty-three and helped perpetuate the idea that my football career wasn't quite over. A mirage that was still attainable with a bit of luck and hard work. Much like my promised teenage growth spurt, it never materialised.

Thierry Henry was absolutely none of these things. He didn't fit my usual criteria of a hero. Two years younger than me, Thierry didn't feel accessible *at all*. Thierry was from another planet. The ultimate athlete: six foot two, a boxer's build and spring-loaded feet that ran the 100 metres in ten seconds with a ball glued to his boots – or were they ballet shoes? Who knows.

↑ Thierry Henry in action against Tottenham Hotspur.

Black Hero. Black Superhero

Ian Wright called him a 'Black superhero' for a documentary I made – and he was. Thierry was Black pride. Football perfection. He could, and did, do anything he wanted with a football. Watching him was like seeing a generational artist hit their stride – Prince's *Purple Rain* to *Sign o' the Times*, Stevie Wonder from *Music of My Mind* to *Songs in the Key of Life*. Thierry's Golden Period began sometime in 2001 and just snowballed, an avalanche of otherworldly goals from everywhere with assists for everyone. Often, he'd just assist himself – because he could.

And we know about the goals. Those goals are the Thierry we share with the outside world, it was the other stuff that had me in wonder. My favourite part of Thierry was the disdain he had for the opposition. Not an obvious arrogance; it's lazy calling him arrogant because he really was as good as he thought he was.

The knee-slide encapsulates his nonchalance for the opposition. He infuriated crowds because he pretended they weren't there. Thierry could timewaste to perfection. At the Bernabéu, in the fourth minute of injury time, he dribbled the length of the pitch at top speed, looking like he'd just popped out to get a pint of milk. Shrugging off world-class defenders like Sergio Ramos, skipping over Álvaro Mejía, before playing a wall pass off the defender, winning a throw-in and walking away. He doesn't even look back. He knows the corner will be the last kick of the game. The match was won. The disrespect is *gorgeous*.

Ignoring the mob. That is why that Tottenham goal is so special. He ran the length of the pitch, along the West Stand, where I was sitting. Burning eyes, a war cry we will never hear because of the noise in the ground that day, shrugging off Big Sol or anyone else who wanted to stop him in full celebration flow. We saw a fury and anger and elation we'd never thought possible with Thierry. This personification of *elan*, controlled aggression, Black excellence, absolutely *losing his shit* like we had never seen. At that moment, after years as an alien, unrelatable superhero, he was just like one of us. Celebrating the hell out of a goal against That Lot. And he wanted to head down to their end and let them know about it.

I've got a picture of my two heroes in a frame at home – Thierry and Norman together. Many times since, I've spoken to Norman about this photo, and this moment. For all his very real antipathy towards all things Arsenal, it never extended to Thierry. 'How could you?' he'd say. 'There aren't many of Your Lot I'd let myself admire. But he was different.' I think Norman Jay actually ended up DJing at Henry's wedding, you know. Although he did wear a small golden cockerel on his suit as a silent mutiny. ◾

← Thierry Henry with teammates Ashley Cole, Sol Campbell and Rami Shaaban.

→ *Overleaf:* Thierry Henry statue, Emirates Stadium.

Black Hero. Black Superhero

ES STADIUM
Arsenal
ARSENAL MALDIVES
PHILADELPHIA
DUBLIN ARSENAL
ARSENAL CAPE TOWN
FERMANAGH
Arsenal Armed Forces Supporters Club
ARSENAL DELHI
DERRY
ARSENAL YORKSHIRE
SOUTH CENTRAL
ARSENAL SCOTLAND
ASCFR
ARSENAL NIGERIA
NEWRY & MOURNE
SYRIA
ARSENAL
INDONESIA
GERMANY
LITHUANIA
ARSENAL NORWAY
CZECH & SLOVAK
GUNNERS
SOUTH AFRICA
ARSENAL CROYDON
COPENHAGEN '94
IRAQ GUNNERS
KENYA
JAMAICA
SOUTH LONDON
ARSENAL CAMDEN GOONERS ARE MAGIC
ARSENAL FINLAND
ARSENAL WOMEN SUPPORTERS CLUB
COSTA BLANCA
ARSENAL HUNGARY
UKRAINE
PERUVIAN GUNNERS
GOONERS
우리는 잠들지 않습니다.

23

FROM KINGSTON TO NOTTING HILL, VIA NORTH LONDON

Designing the Arsenal 'Jamaica' shirt

CLIVE CHIJIOKE NWONKA

For many of the Black diaspora, Black Arsenal functions as the personal and communal term through which we are able to make sense of and communicate the organic connections that are found in Arsenal. These were often birthed from the period in the late 1980s to the early-to-mid '90s when there was an emergence of a powerfully resistant Black multiculture in the UK that allowed for certain kinds of Black British subcultural practices and expressions, be it Black music, fashion, visual culture or their fusions, to find some kind of cultural and political prominence, connection or home points in Arsenal and certain Black players, but also the fanbase as well. And the idea that a football club served as a Black community affinity space in which Black people felt safe going to games at Highbury given that it possessed a more condensed Black identity within the terraces, which wasn't the case for other clubs even in London, reaffirms not only how Black Arsenal can be understood as originating from Black cultural memory, but the significance of the products and material items that inform and populate our recollections that are in turn animated by the stimuli of television and print media as much as the physical spaces of the stands. This asks for a consideration of the impact of merchandise and the prominence of the sporting brand Adidas, who had between 1986 and 1994 manufactured Arsenal's kits and in the context of Black Arsenal as informed by recollection, retain an associativity with Adidas as the brand in which its Black players, the spectacular and everyday iconographies they created and particular sporting moments were apparelled in.

Thus, there is something inherently evocative about Arsenal's return to Adidas in 2019. One way of looking at the different facets of what Black Arsenal is, has been, could look like or be experienced now, can be found in the spectacle of the Notting Hill Carnival. The area of North Kensington, where the carnival has taken place since its first year in 1966, was throughout the fifties a stronghold of the neo-Nazi organisations the White Defence League and the Union Movement. Subsequently it was the site of a culture of violent racist attacks that would culminate in the Notting Hill Riots

← *Previous page:* Arsenal launched the 'Jamaica' shirt in August 2022, coinciding with the start of the 2022–23 season and Notting Hill Carnival.

of 1958 and the following year by the killing of thirty-two-year old Antiguan Kelso Cochrane by a group of white youths. This would motivate the activist Claudia Jones to organise a series of indoor Caribbean carnivals that would later evolve into what came to be the modern Notting Hill Carnival, second largest in the world, which is attended by over two million people across its two days and is firmly placed as the most significant point of celebration of the UK's Afro-Caribbean community. For those who have attended what is now Europe's biggest street from their young years as an instinctive annual Black cultural tradition, there is nothing at all novel to see Arsenal replica shirts being worn by its attendees along the carnival's three and a half mile route between Westbourne Grove and Ladbroke Grove, and the various, continuous swathes of people that emerge from the nearby Black locales of Harlesden, Kensal Green and Kilburn. The omnipresence of Arsenal jerseys throughout the carnival weekend points to the legitimacy and power of the idea of Black Arsenal as a way of thinking about the connection to a club culture that transcends locality, for despite the carnival being based in and around a location synonymous with Queens Park Rangers, that club has never enjoyed anything close to the widespread visibility Arsenal have asserted over the carnival, which reflects how the gravitational pull of London's Black community to Arsenal has established the idea of Arsenal as essentially Black *London*. So, the launch of the Arsenal 'Jamaica' pre-match shirt that was released by Adidas on 27 August 2022 for the home fixture against Fulham, the Saturday of that year's Notting Hill Carnival, and to be worn throughout the 2022–23 season, invites a consideration of the permeation of Black Arsenal in much broader terms of contemporary brand culture and apparel.

The question of Arsenal's creation of the carnival shirt as a commodifying culture is significant as it asks if in this product we might neglect the recognition of the importance of the Notting Hill Carnival not just as a point of Black and cross-cultural celebration, but as a historical and contemporary site of Black struggle, where we saw not just the criminalising of Black people, but the policing of the most organic modes of Black culture and cultural expression. The cultural and racial meanings being captured by Black Arsenal, despite its heterogeneity, is an extremely delicate and valuable political experience that is being tapped into by branded and commercial culture. How can Black Arsenal as an everyday Blackness and multiculture avoid being pulled into the well-intended but ultimately extractive and accumulative logics of the market? Does it need to? Just as the very concept of a Black Arsenal is a personal then collective social experience that does not, and cannot, have a singular point of expression, it is also true and in many ways acceptable and intriguing that Black Arsenal is inevitably captured within the flows of modernity in which newer generations of young Black people will think, feel, display and enjoy their manifestations of Black Arsenal through the material items of brand and consumer culture, in which Adidas, as any other brand, produce responsive products to capture such cultural expressions.

Here, I talk to Andrew Dolan, Senior Project Manager at Adidas, to discuss the sportwear brand's design principles that informed the Arsenal Jamaica shirt, but also the commercial and social considerations in its production.

CLIVE: The Adidas Arsenal 'Jamaica' shirt, as it's colloquially termed now, has become somewhat of a Black cultural phenomenon that has really transcended its primary function as a pre-match jersey. Could you offer some insight into how the whole project came into being?

ANDREW: I've been working on the Arsenal kits for four years as the product manager. I'm in the Adidas football marketing team and our job is really to come up with these stories and insights and try and find the connection between obviously the club but the fanbase and the community that makes up that fanbase. With the Notting Hill Carnival, this story in particular was one that came through my own personal experience of having lived in London, in Hackney Downs, for three years and my flatmates, one was of Ghanaian heritage and the other was of Jamaican heritage and we used to go to the carnival every year. We would just wear the loudest outfits, like basketball jerseys and shorts with loads of colours, headbands, accessories. Basically, anything we could find.

CLIVE: I definitely see a continuity between the Jamaica jersey and the Arsenal 'Bruised Banana' away kit of '91–93 that coincided with Ian Wright's first season and remains one of the most popular shirts of Adidas's initial period of designing of Arsenal's kits between 1986 and 1994. So, when Adidas signed the five-year kit manufacturing contract with Arsenal in 2019, was there always the intention to create something distinctive that paid homage to Arsenal's historical Black fanbase?

ANDREW: With the Jamaica jersey itself, I don't know if you're aware, but the base graphic that's used was actually shared across different clubs. For example, Manchester United have the same pattern but in a totally different colourway. So, whenever it came to choosing the Arsenal colourway, it's the only club that Adidas did something unique with. The idea actually came when I watched *Rocky and Wrighty: From Brockley to the Bigtime*, the TNT documentary, with a good friend of mine and the designer of the jersey, Aaron Craig, who's also living here in Nuremberg. The documentary touched on Ian Wright being that cult figure at Arsenal who came through in the early nineties with the birth of the Premier League, and he and David Rocastle were such good friends. Then the documentary touched on their heritage and their background and the fact that Ian's family came from Jamaica and Rocky's family were from Trinidad and Tobago. So, as well as the jersey, there's also footwear, and the footwear on one side has the colours of the Jamaica flag and on the other side are the colours of the Trinidad and Tobago flag. It kind of all came together around this time when creating the jersey. We were looking for an insight and then realised at this moment that these two players in particular from Arsenal deserve a story and a moment built around them. So, while other teams have this pre-match Adidas jersey launched on the pitch in April 2022, when we saw this, we saw an opportunity with its colours that its launch timing could be a huge moment if framed around the Notting Hill Carnival and with Ian Wright involved.

CLIVE: So Ian Wright was actually involved in the design and marketing?

ANDREW: Yes, he was personally involved, especially in the footwear side. If you see the shoes, a ZX 420, one has Ian Wright on one of the labels on the tongue and David Rocastle on the other. There's obviously already a partnership between Adidas and Ian Wright, but to partner with David Rocastle, we worked with the foundation that his family set up and are involved with since his death. The idea was developed really organically, just through a lived experience of knowing that this is something Arsenal fans care about. There is an unusually high amount of Arsenal jerseys worn versus other London clubs at the Notting Hill Carnival and it just felt like a natural fit. And the fact that it resonated so well is, I would say, has been half luck but also built on that insight – and obviously working with Ian and him being such a great guy to work with and just deserving of this kind of product and storytelling around him.

CLIVE: I could sense immediately when the shirt was launched that it would be powerfully resonant with Black Arsenal fans and Black people in London who go to the Notting Hill Carnival, because historically there's always been the image of people wearing Arsenal shirts at the carnival, given that the carnival falls on the last Bank Holiday of the summer that also coincides with the opening weeks of the new season in August. Having these more specific design shirts that resemble Jamaican colours and all the celebrations of the carnival would naturally have a powerful impact on Black Arsenal fans and beyond. So, beyond luck, I think it's also just an inevitable outcome of both the design and the timing of its release as well. So, thinking specifically about the print marketing campaign, it's an interesting range of backdrops. There is one image where a young Black boy is in the barber shop having his haircut and another one where two people are posing in a tropical location. Did you actually go to Jamaica to shoot the marketing campaign?

ANDREW: We have a communications team in London that worked on the print campaign's imagery. I unfortunately didn't get to travel myself, but the comms team did travel to Jamaica where we shot these images so it was as authentic as could be with the print campaign around it. We used a Jamaican-based agency and used largely local talent and photographers. We then shot with some of the players [Gabriel Jesus, Emile Smith Rowe and Gabriel Martinelli] in and around North London and contrasted that with fans and models in Jamaica to help illustrate the link, with the pre-match jersey being the common thread across all content.

CLIVE: There's a connection to observe here between Jamaica, London, the carnival and Arsenal. West London is in many ways the epicentre of post-war Windrush immigration from the Caribbean, at least in Notting Hill, but the jersey seems to imply that we can also find an obvious point of reference for Black people and those of Jamaican heritage in North London. These are very, very interesting points of cultural interaction, but again they all speak to the kind of global and trans-local impact of Black Arsenal.

↑ → Stills from the 'Jamaica' shirt campaign, 2022.

ANDREW: Yes, definitely and just to give you another insight on why I mentioned the friends I lived with who are of that background and that heritage, one of them mentioned to me when he first saw the design that we'd only used the colours of Jamaica. We'd not used the colours of any other Caribbean country and Notting Hill Carnival is for everyone. But it was actually a limitation within the design itself – we could only print a certain number of colours. That was something that when it was coming out, I was really worried there could even have been a backlash against it, where people feel excluded by it despite the fact that the story is about inclusivity, and it is about appreciating Black players and their background. So just the fact that it has gone down so well, is half a relief.

CLIVE: I think again it really symbolises what's specific but also precarious about Black Arsenal. It's so capacious as an experience that when it naturally moves from a historical Black identification to say, commercialisation and merchandising, more nebulous but important contemporary situations can emerge, which as you say requires an additional sensitivity and ethical consideration around what we would identify as the interaction between branding and promotional culture, fashion and race, ethnicity and Black identity. With that in mind, are there plans for like a second or third iteration of the Jamaica jersey?

ANDREW: The fact that it went so well and resonated so well with the community, I think it would be an oversight to not look at doing a follow up to it, whether that's this year or the next. That's to be seen, but yeah, definitely. There is a fanbase that we have connected with.

CLIVE: I grew up in north-west London and many of the people I grew up with or around either supported Arsenal because their parents had an affinity with David O'Leary or Liam Brady, you know, that kind of Irish diasporic allegiance, or for the Black diaspora, through Ian Wright, Patrick Vieira and later, Thierry Henry. And it's allowed for the terraces, stands, streets and physical locations to become spaces of a natural multiculture and integration. Just as Black Arsenal is an experience of multiculture, the Notting Hill Carnival is historically a space for Afro-Caribbean celebration but has in time also become a space for cross-racial and cross-cultural integration as well. And I think there's something about how the Arsenal fanbase congregated around the shirts that kind of embodies the multicultural ideal that we're seeing as being quite instinctive to Arsenal. So, thinking towards the work of Adidas with the Jamaica shirts, did it make your job a lot easier just knowing there's an immediate multicultural fanbase that could be responsive to the jersey and the campaign?

ANDREW: It's not like it was, say, identified that because this is Arsenal, this is definitely going to work. It was that we were definitely aware of the diverse background of the fanbase and how mixed and varied it is. And like you mentioned, there are a lot of Irish fans based on previous Irish players, a lot of Afro-Caribbean fans because of Ian Wright and David Rocastle.

CLIVE: Despite the widespread positive response to the shirt's release, there were some who may have seen the Jamaica jersey as an example of commercial exploitation. Was this a consideration for Adidas, and if so how did the design and marketing teams navigate those ethical considerations?

ANDREW: When we pitched the idea, cultural sensitivity was a massive thing. We have a cultural oversight team within Adidas, so we don't want to be seen to be doing any sort of cultural appropriation or exploitation of a fan group or anything. There's a fine line between doing something that resonates for the fans and exploiting their loyalty. We never want to cross that line. So again, the fact that the story was really properly communicated well and launched at the carnival was a joy. I mean, even days after the carnival, I was getting so many people sending me Tik-Toks and Instagram stories of people who were just walking around the carnival, spotting people in the jerseys. You know, it was just relentless, it was almost unbelievable. I didn't get to go that year [2022], but I would love to have been there just to see how many there were and I'm sure in the following years there's still going to be people wearing that jersey. ■

24

BLACK ARSENAL AND BRITISH ASIANS

ANAMIK SAHA

attended my first Arsenal game in October 1985, the day after my eighth birthday, a home game against Ipswich Town. I had been an Arsenal fan for about a year, following a brief and very random dalliance with Brighton & Hove Albion. Growing up in a multicultural suburb of north-east London, most of my school followed West Ham, our local team, though the Jewish kids generally supported Spurs, and the Asians, Liverpool. Wanting to be different and influenced by my best mate Craig Pearl who came from a family of Arsenal season ticket holders, I decided to follow the Arsenal.

Back then, Black people and Asians mostly experienced football through television, the radio and newspapers. Racism was rife on the terraces and the streets surrounding the dilapidated stadiums, with West Ham-supporting skinheads an occasional, though very visible presence where we grew up. As such, despite our love for our football clubs, physically going to a game was something we never countenanced. While I would denounce my Liverpool-supporting Asian mates as *glory-hunters* (Liverpool were by far the dominant team from that period), I understood that

their support for a team so far away reflected the lack of attachment we had to our own local area, where racial hostility felt like background noise. Thus, when my dad told me that my birthday present was going to an actual Arsenal match, my immediate reaction was both jubilation and terror, a strange concoction of emotions that I only ever experienced once more, when my wife first told me we were having a baby.

English football has a serious problem with British South Asians. Despite the huge popularity of football among the British Asian population, and the thousands of Asians who play for local teams, there is an inexplicable dearth of Asian players in the professional English leagues. It is difficult to read this situation as anything other than systemic racism. In this context, Asian fans have found a particular identification with Black players. While coming from a very

← *Previous page:* Anamik Saha, Emirates Stadium.

↑ Anamik Saha as a child.

Black Arsenal

254

different culture and having a very different experience, Black people also had to deal with racism like us. Their struggles in Britain felt the same as our own.

Arsenal was not the first team to have Black footballers, or Black fans for that matter. By the mid-1980s many teams had Black players who had entered their folklore. But Arsenal felt like they had their own special relationship with the Black community. In the match against Ipswich Town that I attended, Arsenal fielded three Black players: Viv Anderson, Chris Whyte and Paul Davis. Davis would shortly be joined by David Rocastle, Michael Thomas and eventually, Ian Wright, who together made up a very special cohort of young Black players from South London. We could identify with them because, while they obviously looked different, they *sounded* like us Asians born and bred in the capital. Ian Wright had a particular significance; the earlier generations of Black players had to conform to the whiteness of the changing room to greater or lesser extents, but Wright was defiantly Black. This was the time of what cultural theorist Stuart Hall called *new ethnicities*, where a new generation of Black and Asian artists, writers, musicians and filmmakers were articulating new ways of being British that did not deny or play down their racial or ethnic identity. A little later, with the arrival of French manager Arsène Wenger, a new wave of Black heroes arrived – Patrick Vieira, Nwankwo Kanu, Thierry Henry, Kolo Touré – who brought a global, cosmopolitan Blackness to Arsenal. On 28 September 2002, Arsenal fielded nine Black players – the most in a competitive English game. To repeat: Arsenal were not the first club to have Black players, or to even laud its Black players, but Black Arsenal is unique with its own distinct history.

This translated into the fanbase. The Arsenal crowd is the most racially mixed in the league. This is no doubt a reflection of the liberal multicultural corner of North London within which the club resides. But Highbury & Islington was not always like this. Legend has it that a vital Black figure from the Arsenal terraces in the 1980s – Dainton 'The Bear' Connell – helped ensure that Arsenal was never infiltrated by the far right like other clubs. While Asians remain absent on the pitch, they are very present in the Arsenal crowd, and this produces an immense feeling of belonging, a rush I get at every match I attend. I can take my daughters to a game knowing that they will see other fans who look like them.

I do not remember seeing any Asians, or even Black people, when I went to my first game on that warm, sunny day on 19 October 1985. I do remember wincing when my dad asked a young white man with short, cropped hair for directions to the ticket office, and the feeling of relief when no racist abuse ensued. But once sat in the heights of the Upper West stand, seeing those three Black players on the pitch below, I felt an immediate connection. I knew then that this was going to be my team for ever. This was confirmed when our tough yet elegant midfielder Paul Davis scored the winning goal. The final score? One-nil-to-the-Arsenal, of course. 🟨

Black Arsenal and British Asians

25

THE VISUAL CULTURES OF BLACK ARSENAL

CLIVE CHIJIOKE NWONKA

n the opening moments of the film *Declan Rice* by Arsenal and Adidas, released online in August 2023 to mark the signing of the West Ham and England midfielder, we see an aerial view of Emirates Stadium, which captures not just its immediate surrounding areas of Islington but the wider skylines and horizons of London. However, our next image is not of the actual player of focus, but of Micheal Ward, the Black Jamaican-British actor noted for his performance in Steve McQueen's film *Lovers Rock* (2020), part of his West Indian anthology *Small Axe*, but more significantly, for playing the cult character of Jamie in Netflix's East London-set series *Top Boy* (2011–23). Here, Ward is dressed in an Arsenal shirt and tracksuit while walking down what we believe to be a nearby street, speaks on his phone about Rice's pending signing in an accent and dialect that purposely makes no distinction between his performance here as an everyday Arsenal supporter and his on-screen character in the Black urban drama. Intertextuality, the way in which we can identify the interplay, cross referencing and relationships across different texts, media and narratives, often through characters, allows the film to make a natural association with Arsenal fandom and Black identity, here drawn from the most popular examples of Black urban multiculture. There are of course many other cameos of different social and cultural identities featured throughout the minute-long online film, all dispersed across different settings as they discuss the transfer, predominantly through digital modes of communication; the sports presenter Laura Woods within a radio studio, Ian Wright on a phone at a restaurant, the grime artist Stormzy is captured leaving a voice message, before we finish on the image of Rice in the Arsenal changing room, behind him the banner 'We are The Arsenal'.

What exactly 'The Arsenal' is in this film, framed around the signing of Declan Rice as a cultural event, is a unified and integrated cultural experience of difference where the news of a new signing produces a cross-platformed interaction among its diverse fans. Equally, the film's use of Micheal Ward and Stormzy is a reference to a Black urban identity that displays a unique reliance on digital technology, not just in the film's motif of mobile phones and social media comments, but the ways

← *Previous page: Top Boy* actor Micheal Ward appearing in a film released online to announce the signing of Declan Rice from West Ham, 2023.

in which its fanbase interact with the club and each other, and how a new, digitally native fanbase, decidedly but not exclusively young and Black, are being identified and increasingly catered for through the creation and circulation of digital brand culture. Whereas in previous chapters I draw attention to the significance of television and the unexpected spectacle of Black iconic moments in the construction of Black Arsenal in its earliest examples, here, I am interested in how the strategic creation of digital content by Arsenal has contributed greatly to the representation of and interaction with Arsenal's Black fanbase who demonstrate support through cultural and material consumption. Here, Black Arsenal is identified through the branded creation of Black content and Black cultural identity in a competitive marketplace of both fandom and the attention economy, and how the novel combination of football, music, fashion subculture and technology appeal to a new generation of Black and multiracial fans whose allegiance with Arsenal is determined as much by the association of Blackness with the club through various kinds of cultural production as with their proximity to the area.

Much of what has been observed here as Black Arsenal through visual culture should be understood as the outcome of Arsenal's kit manufacturing contract with Adidas, which has produced a notable culture of

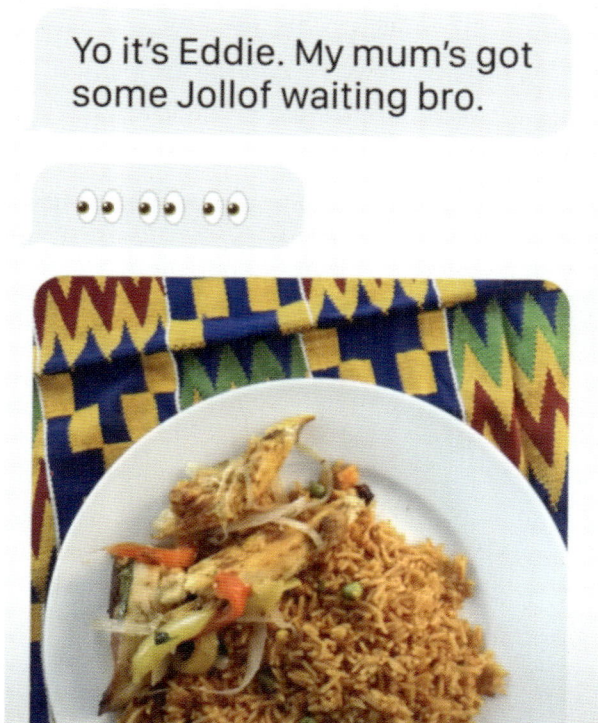

↑ A still from *Declan Rice*.

↑ *This is Home*, 2018.

The Visual Cultures of Black Arsenal

branding and merchandise that has proved opportune for the commercial use of Black identity through the creation of online promotional content. These have been predominantly framed around the theme of North London as a specific location where Arsenal as a club have asserted a cultural dominance. This concept of North London as synonymous with a multiracial Arsenal is seen in the film *This is Home*, launching the new Arsenal/Adidas home kit in 2018, which consciously encapsulates the idea that Arsenal's culture accommodates the global identities that comprise the club. Here, Arsenal's numerous players drawn from abroad such as Pierre-Emerick Aubameyang (Gabon) Mesut Özil (Germany) and Sead Kolašinac (Bosnia), are seen talking in North London's Arsenal-adorned local communal spaces, the barber shop, greasy spoon cafes, streets and press conferences, where their voices are dubbed over with local accents representative of the various demographics and cultures of North London. However, these are not the primary windows through which we understand Arsenal as 'home', and we identify an iteration of Black Arsenal in how, just like London's Black youth subcultures, the film presents Arsenal as a natural expression of convivial identity through a specific appeal to a Black urban authenticity. This inheriting of the 'dialect' of Arsenal, expressed to the soundtrack of Black urban music, attempts to mirror the everyday vernacular of multiracial North London as the territory of a multiracial Arsenal, but held together by the unified idea that to be an Arsenal supporter is to be a Londoner, and this is to be embedded in a certain expansive idea of the local, be they from Spain, Germany, Gabon or beyond. And the prominence of the local Black urban accent among what could be described as the atypical white

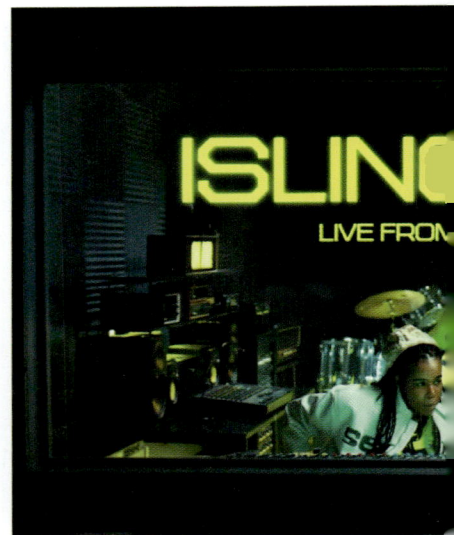

↑ *Islington FM*, released to launch Arsenal's 2023–24 away kit.

working-class voices present suggests that even within the diversity of the people who are in it, their youth identity, like Arsenal itself, is informed by Black London urban culture as a convivial, integrated culture. In other words, for *This is Home*, and its representation of Black Arsenal, read 'This is our music. These are our locations, and this is our accent.'

A similar sense of the representation between the local and the global, and Arsenal and Black identity's place within it, is found in *Islington FM*, the two-minute film launching Arsenal's 2023–24 away kit. For Arsenal's branding team, the key conceptual question that informed the film was 'How do we tell a story of like what makes Arsenal *Arsenal* and taking all the best parts of Islington and North London. But with it being an away shirt, a shirt that we're going to wear on our travels all around the country, how do we capture that essence of it as an experience, what it means to be from North London and try and export this to the world? I think what became clear very quickly was that if we wanted to tell a story that takes the best of North London and export that globally, the best manifestation of that was music and music culture.' The film can be interpreted as a conurbation of different kinds of identities and cultures within the sphere of North London. Here, Arsenal becomes a shorthand for North London and its sense of a distinctive fan culture which is then broadcast around the world through music as a valuable way of tracing Arsenal's global permeation as much as the circulating physical shirts themselves. However, the telegraphing of this culture through Black music and Black people makes a natural association between Arsenal and racial difference, that also finds connections with the history of the Caribbean presence in London in the

The Visual Cultures of Black Arsenal

promotion of Arsenal's away kit through a reliance on music culture, presented through a fictional North London pirate radio station and the expressive Black subcultures that have emerged through them. Throughout, a range of rapid sequences that open with Bukayo Saka in the back of a team coach asking the driver to 'tune into Islington', display a Black representational density that attempts to place Arsenal at the centre of a vibrant Islington-born Black creative expression, Lava La Rule, *Scratcha DVA and SHERELLE* to the AntsLive track 'Number One Candidate' playing across 188.6 Islington FM's airwaves. Indeed, the first six faces across its opening four scenes are all Black, before we see Martin Kemp, the Islington-born actor, Spandau Ballet bassist and radio host. From here, we are taken through a number of cameos by players and Arsenal-supporting cultural figures such as Wolf Alice's Theo Ellis and *Sex Education*'s Asa Butterfield, and the film concludes with a live jam session with ten Black musicians within the Islington FM studio.

It is somewhat understandable that such an approach was taken by the creative agency Weirdo, given that Adidas's away kit design mimics the map of Islington and in doing so resembles radio waves that, like Arsenal's away games, travel across the world but maintain links to N7, for it is certainly the case that Arsenal's supporter bases within Europe and parts of Africa and their connection with Arsenal, at least for Black people, have been developed from particular Black cultural iconographies, be

it Patrick Vieira throughout the 1990s or Thierry Henry in the 2000s. Here, we find an imaginative representation of Arsenal that finds immediate connection to Islington but permeates worldwide. This is particularly salient for Black Arsenal as a concept, for it is something that begins in North London, but finds routes and connections nationally and globally. However, while Islington FM is conceived here as a cultural experience that resonates out from North London, it equally draws people back into the parameters of Islington, and within this, Arsenal as both fan culture and equally, community, through featuring the many elements of Black cultural production and urban music. The presence of Ashley Walters, the Black British actor most notable in recent cultural imagination for playing the lead role of Dushane in *Top Boy*, has a particular relevance within the aesthetics of Islington FM specifically, and the idea of Black Arsenal more broadly. Walters is someone who can represent and signify certain elements of Black popular culture in its broadest understanding, being a Black British cultural icon who first began his career as a youth actor, then becoming involved in music (Walters was a member of the successful South London UK garage collective So Solid Crew, as well as a solo artist) and then returned to acting. Thus, as we see in the various examples explored throughout this book, Black Arsenal is an experience felt not through just one form or point of identification or expression, but something that transcends different kinds of visual media. Again, in a similar form to the promo, figures of intertextual Black cultural identification and iconography further align Blackness and Arsenal as natural, unified experiences. Despite Islington FM's sequences spreading across a range of races, nations, settings and music genres, it is Black cultural identity that is the basis upon which other identities become adjoined. For example, fashion culture is so heavily implied throughout Islington FM and its creative talent, for the music produces subculture, which also involves clothing and the increasing visibility of Arsenal's kits as everyday streetwear within the multicultural city. As the closing sequence reminds us, 'North London's Never Far Away', and both Islington FM and the Arsenal shirt it celebrates becomes a way to access the authenticity of is Black urban expressions.

The variety and accessibility of in-house-produced content on Arsenal digital platforms demonstrate a cultivated approach to the visibility of Black cultural identity. Notably, David 'Frimmy' Frimpong has developed a cult figure status within Arsenal's visual culture, not simply through his formal role as the club's Host and Content Editor, but through the Colony Carpool series, where Frimpong is filmed conducting comical interviews with staff, former and current players while driving around Arsenal's London Colney training ground in a golf buggy. These seven-minute features allow for a certain proximity to players in a much less formal setting and tones than the traditional, heavily guarded pre/post-match interview.

However, a crucial aspect of the continuing circulation of Black Arsenal has been the emergence of AFTV, the fan-based YouTube channel established by former BBC Radio reggae DJ Robbie Lyal in 2012, that has provided Arsenal supporters with a form of direct access and expression through the availability and provision of online content. The channel, which in ten years has amassed over 1.5 million YouTube subscribers and over a billion views across this and its social media platforms, has firmly positioned itself at the forefront of the expanding sphere of fan-led TV. This being so, AFTV remains a highly polarised part of Arsenal's fan culture, with some insisting that the platform has given a previously denied visibility and voice to what can be described as the traditional, unheard 'terrace' supporter, however misinformed, fickle, inaccurate or vitriolic these perspectives may be. For others, despite the credibility gained through its more recent studio-based content which has featured in-depth interviews with former players such as Ian Wright and Paul Davis, Labour Party leader Keir Starmer and the former Arsenal chairman David Dein, AFTV's generally perceived tone of 'entertaining' content cannot provide any kind of serious or relevant representation of the Arsenal fan opinion. Finally, and at the very end of this spectrum, given the channel came to prominence within a period of underperformance and organisational

The Visual Cultures of Black Arsenal

transition that underpinned the at times volatile 'Wenger Out' campaign for which AFTV were a primary visual repository, many (including Arsenal's own players) have claimed that the channel serves no function beyond easy clickbait through the unhelpful creation and capturing of negativity. Even so, it is impossible to look at any AFTV video interviewing a group of fans around Emirates Stadium on matchday and not observe the density of Black people articulating quite passionately about what they feel about the game, the players or any other aspect of Arsenal's club, or a group of multiracial fans gathered behind. There are of course differing intentions, production values, stylistic approaches and visual tones between AFTV and the highly stylised content to be consumed on Arsenal's own digital platforms. However, there remains little fundamental distinction between an AFTV interview or feature and an Arsenal/ Adidas kit launch that's more choreographed and deliberate, as both are committed to an influential and lucrative visual culture that contains, gives visibility to and builds upon the existing and expanding Black fanbase.

The ability to create a two-minute film launching the signing of a player or a new kit is of course in no way specific to Arsenal. What is specific and worthy of exploration, is how the combination of these is instinctively reliant on the visibility and popularity of Black youth identity,

↑ Fans react on AFTV.

subcultural practices and consumerism as the essential value to be found in the production of Arsenal-branded creative visual culture. It is also the case that Arsenal benefit from their location in North London and the multiracial specificity of its geographic space, which we have seen across all of the content produced through the Adidas Arsenal X brand and its various collaborations, for example with the clothing brand Maharishi in 2023, which attempts to combine London streetwear with the cultural power of branded sportswear. This is a task made more convincing by the promo's filming within the gritty but real and authenticating surroundings of a tower block, football cage and a launderette.

The ease through which Black identity, culture and subcultural practices bleed into the branding, marketing and commercial strategies of Arsenal through visual content renders Arsenal's promotional features as an important signifier of contemporary Black urban culture. Thus, the identification of a Black density within Arsenal's digital content strategies, transposed here into a two-minute film concerned with the signing of Declan Rice may seem novel, but to those who understand the importance of branding and creative content in the increasingly congested marketing landscape where club fandom is just one variant of a lucrative sporting economy, the promotion of players' club merchandise in many ways

↑ A group of Arsenal fans.

The Visual Cultures of Black Arsenal

necessitates a creative approach where there is equal emphasis on the consumer cultures of the Arsenal supporter based either locally or globally, or where the young fan in possession of a smartphone is as important economically as the older fan in possession of a season/match ticket.

All these various visual images and narratives of Black cultural expression so central to these online content approaches remain important for us in understanding Black Arsenal as an idea that is comprised of paradoxes. The changing ethnic and demographic face of London, and the power of football as a global economy, have encouraged leading clubs within multiracial cities and societies to develop marketing strategies that appeal not to the general but the specific, conveyed through a certain visual language. This may not be the language of a previous generation whose natural mode of 'engagement' with the club may not be through the consumption of stylised creative content, but of a digitally native generation who will be multiracial, most likely Black, and among whom the presence of 'coolness', realness and 'credibility', the primary language of youthhood and modernity, remains important commodities for brands so invested in engaging with Black identity as representing a racialised, marginalised and therefore politicised existence, and Black culture as representing a simple but highly lucrative share of the global sportswear market. In either case, the medium of online content is a crucial aspect of the branding of Arsenal as Black multiculture, and the branding of Black identity as consumer culture. ■

↑ ABOVE: Ashley Walters in the Arsenal 1994–95 away shirt. BELOW: Arsenal 424.
↗ ABOVE: Arsenal kit launch, 2019.
BELOW: Chunkz, Arsenal Original Essentials.

The Visual Cultures of Black Arsenal

ABOVE: A group of fans celebrate after Arsenal's victory over Chelsea in the delayed FA Cup final in August 2020.
BELOW: Idris Elba on the set of 'This is Home'.

Ian Wright, Wretch 32 and Kano.

Aston Mack at a Black Lives Matter Protest in Orlando, USA following the police killing of George Floyd.

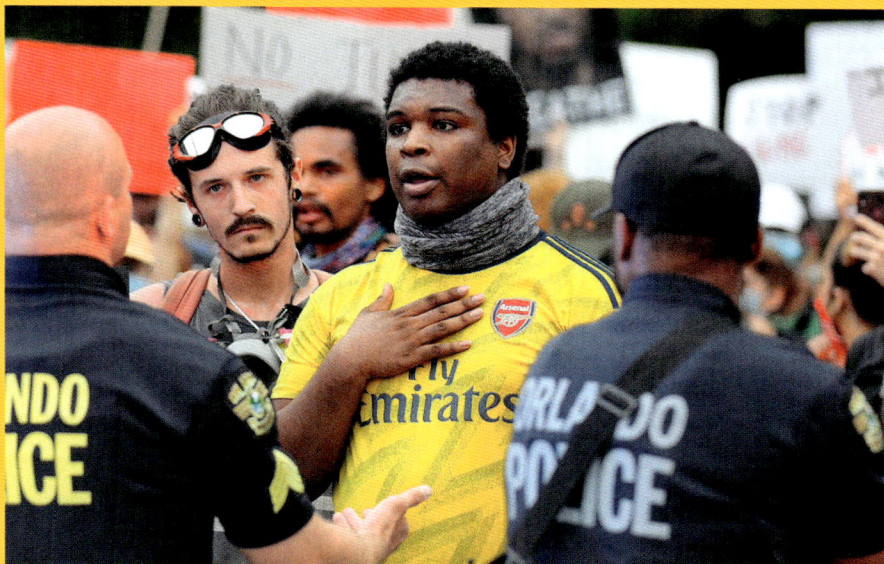

A still from the 2021 film *Pirates*, set within the late 1990s London garage music scene. The film was written and directed by Arsenal fan Reggie Yates.

ABOVE: NBA star James Harden and Reiss Nelson launch the Arsenal 2019–20 kit.

BELOW LEFT: Pierre-Emerick Aubameyang takes a knee in support of Black Lives Matter.

BELOW RIGHT: Daniel Kaluuya recording the voiceover

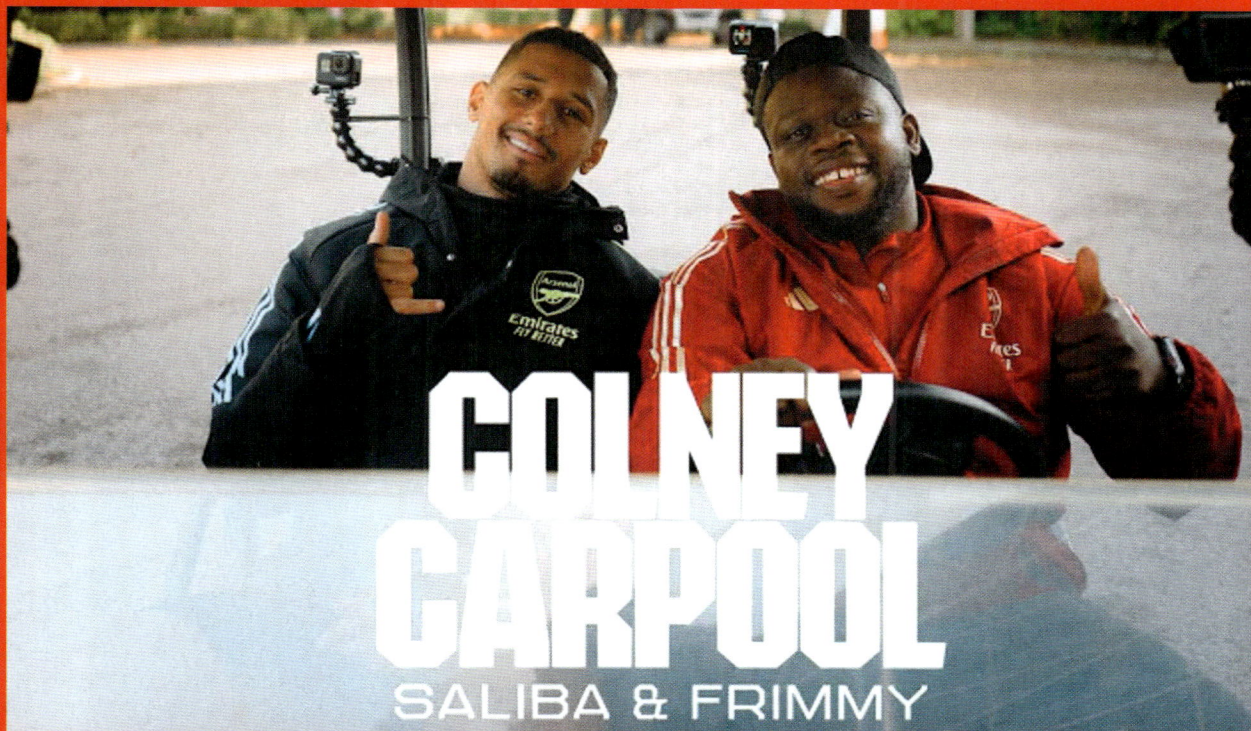

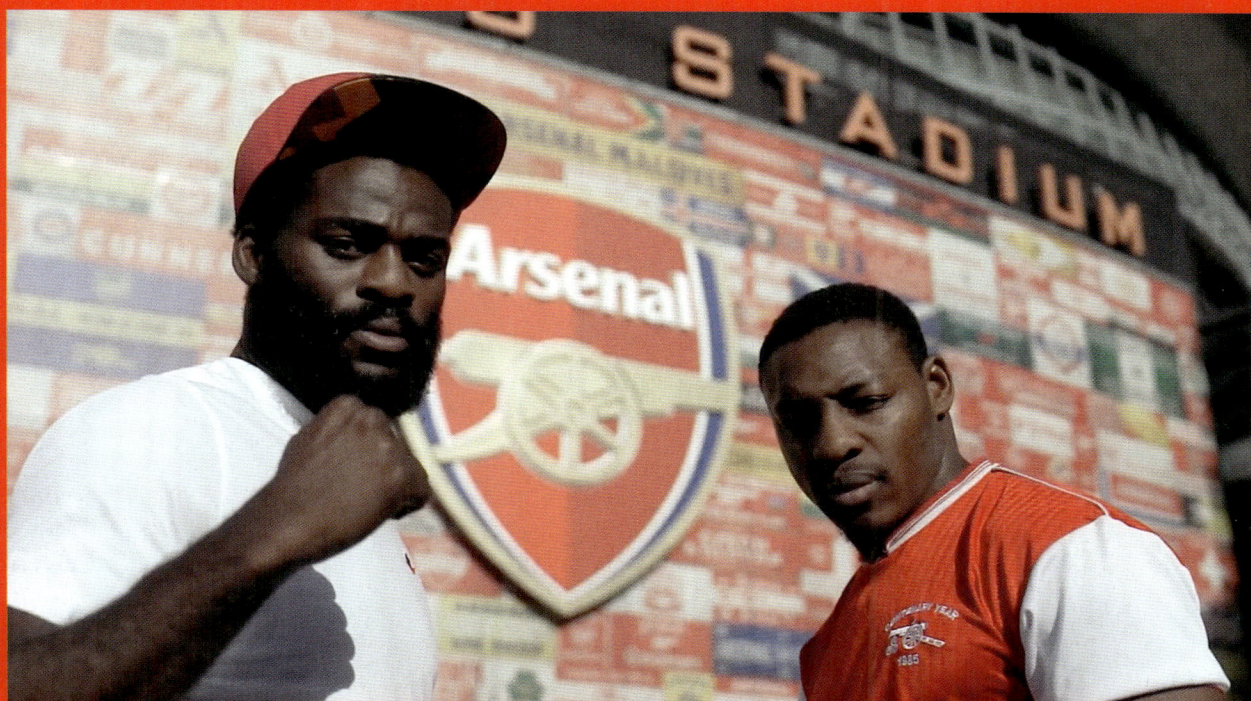

ABOVE: William Saliba interviewed for Arsenal's 'Colney Carpool' Series hosted by David 'Frimmy' Frimpon.

BELOW: London boxers and Arsenal fans Joshua Buatsi and Dan Azeez pose outside the Emirates Stadium to promote their British Light Heavyweight and Commonwealth Light Heavyweight Title fight at the OVO Arena, February 2024.

Eddie Nketiah celebrates after scoring a hat-trick v Sheffield United on the day of Arsenal's Black History Month celebrations.
Opposite: Arsenal's Black History Month Programme guest edited by Dr Clive Chijioke Nwonka.

BLACK
HISTORY
MONTH

ARSENAL

GABRIEL
6

SHEFFIELD UNITED
SATURDAY, OCTOBER 28, 2023 • 3PM

Emirates   adidas   VISIT RWANDA

Arsenal Women's team photo, 2023–24. Arsenal drew criticism for having no Black players or staff in their women's first team.

Opposite: Arsenal supporters hold up a banner during the Premier League match between Arsenal FC and AFC Bournemouth at Emirates Stadium on 4 May 2024 in memory of fourteen-year-old schoolboy Daniel Anjorin who was murdered in a sword attack in Hainault, east London that week. His image also appeared on the stadium's LED board during a moment of applause at fourteen minutes into the game, with the permission of his family. Daniel was an avid Arsenal fan

26

COMING FULL CIRCLE

MATTHEW JOSEPH

When we talk about Black Arsenal and my interpretation of what that was to me as a young YTS player at Arsenal in the late eighties, it's 'Pops' (Paul Davis), 'Uncle Gus' (Gus Caesar), and then Rocky (Rocastle) and Mickey (Michael Thomas). But below them was also Kevin Campbell, the year below him was Kwame Ampadu and Raymond Lee, and the year below them was Andy Cole, and then me and Mark Flatts. That was a real representation of Black Identity in North London. So, when you were younger, you used to look at them and think, 'right, I can get in. There are people that look like us there.' Mickey and Rocky were established in the first team, as was Paul. But when we first joined as kids, Kev was in the youth team. He was the one that while we were there hadn't made it yet, and then did make it. I remember watching him in the FA Youth Cup final, and then he gets through to the first team and there's an even greater connection. Then Kwame makes his debut, and the connection grows stronger. And then Cole is coming through, and we would go and watch him play when he was on loan at Fulham and when he got sold to Bristol City, going watching him there. We were always around each other. I remember when I got released from Arsenal and went on trial at Leeds United. Rocky had joined by then and was absolutely brilliant with me. That's how we were; we all came through in the same period and supported one another.

Stoke Newington was where I grew up, and I went to school in Islington, and that's how I ended up being at Arsenal because I played for the District and County teams, which was the route in at the time. And then a scout who was there for Arsenal came and spotted me. But it was very different times then and I had a couple of years away from the club, because in those days there were no academies as we have now. So the 'best' players went to the FA School of Excellence at Lilleshall, which is where me and Mark Flatts went to when we were fourteen. Andy Cole was the year above. Rod Thomas was another trailblazer at Watford who was there before us. Bryan Small was also above us in terms of age groups. So, in my year was Mark Flatts, and at the time there were players like Trevor Sinclair, Garry Flitcroft, and then the year below me was Andy Myers from Chelsea. Junior McDougald, who was attached to Tottenham, was a good friend of mine and came a couple of years after me at Lilleshall with Sol Campbell, Nick Barmby and Darren Caskey. I went to Arsenal primarily because of the location. I was a local boy from Stoke Newington, and it was the closest club. My mother didn't drive. When I played grassroots football, access and transport was always a challenge. So, for me, location and being more of an Arsenal supporter was part of the reason. I never, ever thought about going anywhere else. I joined Arsenal when I was thirteen, and by the time I was fourteen I'd gone to Lilleshall. But I always knew I was coming back to Arsenal.

Paul Davis was really important for us coming through. He has always been the same. Really quiet. But a steely assurance, you could not mess around with him. He spoke with authority. And when he spoke, you listened. And he was very much inclusive of us, of us always being around. But if you weren't behaving or you weren't doing what you're supposed to do, he would tell you in no uncertain terms, although he won't scream and shout at you. But it almost felt like we didn't want to disappoint him. Once you've been at Arsenal and you understand what the place is, it's quite unique. I spent three years at Arsenal. I came back to Arsenal from Lilleshall at sixteen until I was nineteen. I've got lifelong friends that I made in those three years, over thirty years later, just because you understand the place.

It's ironic that the phrase that is so synonymous with Rocky is 'Remember who you are, what you are, and who you represent.' If you speak to anyone who was at the club at the time, they could quote you that. Because that's what it is. You need to be really sure of who you are. That there are others who looked like you, and not just in terms of race but realising who you are among your peers. You are The Arsenal. That's important. And you have to think about who you represent. Are you representing just yourself, your family, the next generation? The supporters? That's a big thing because it was really clear to us. The Emirates is a fantastic place, but to me, because of my time there, it's not quite Highbury. When you go through the glass doors into the concierge and you go up the steps and you're on the marble floors in front of the Herbert Chapman statue, that's Arsenal. You go in there and you know it's a different standard. Some might say I'm biased, but it was the only club I've ever known, where even to this day, people of a certain generation call it The Arsenal. It's held on standards; it's held on behaviour. This is what you have to be.

I came back from Lilleshall and went straight back into the youth team at Arsenal. It was the best youth setup in London, and one of the best youth setups in the country. At that time Manchester City were very strong with Paul Simpson, David White, Paul Lake, Andy Hinchcliffe and others, but we were strong, so if you came back and you got to play in Arsenal's youth team, that was a big thing. You had to earn your right to get into that youth team. And of that youth team, quite a few went on to play first-team football at Arsenal, and many went on to play professional football which was not at all guaranteed. That tells you the standard. After school when we would go in there would be the JVC Indoor Training Centre under the North Bank stand and we would watch the older teams play. They were so good. We actually once bunked off school just to watch Kevin playing in the FA Youth Cup final at Doncaster Rovers in 1988. The youth setup was really multicultural, but it didn't always matter. There were definitely Black players around, but there was never any kind of issue because at that time we had players from all over. We would have had Steve Morrow in there who came from Northern Ireland, Dino Connolly who was Scottish, as were Paul Dickov and Scott Marshall. There were a lot of Irish and Scottish kids that came over to play in my youth team, so everyone was kind of just fitting in.

I don't think anyone was established enough or felt confident enough to start throwing stones at anyone else. So, there was a real bond and a camaraderie. I think what might have been different for us is that the people who were playing in the first team when we arrived were also really young. They were no more than three or four years older than us. You're seventeen or eighteen and Mickey and Rocky are twenty-one and Kevin is about eighteen or nineteen. There's not a massive age gap, so the music you listened to was probably similar. The places you went to were probably similar, so you would come into the car park in the morning and hear people playing similar music or dressing the same way. There was not a distinct age gap between us and Kev, who was sort of the younger guy of that whole group of David, Tony Adams, Rocky, Mickey, Paul Merson, Gus. Maybe if the gap was bigger, it might feel different, but to us it was just the same. They would come in and have a conversation with you and it was no different. You knew you were going to different pitches to train. But they wouldn't ever not come in and say hello. The best way to describe this is in comparison to George Graham. If you walked in through London Colney and George Graham was coming your way you had to say, 'Morning, Mr Graham', regardless of whether he acknowledged you or not as he walked past you, and most of the time he did. It was almost like there was that hierarchy in terms of who you said hello to. And that was what it was like from the day you walked into Highbury or London Colney. There's a respect to be earned, it's attainable, but don't run before you can walk. But with these guys, you didn't have to say, 'Morning, Mr Rocastle. Morning, Mr Thomas.' They'll come and say hello to you. And that was really it. It was just organic, there was no hierarchy. It's just you in a moment with them talking to each other, then we go our separate ways. You weren't their mate, because you weren't training with them, but on the other hand you felt like they would look out for you. Whether they did or not,

I don't know. But that's how you felt. Because they would come and say good morning to you and not all the players did. But *they* did. So from the players' point of view, there was no hierarchy in there. But we had characters as well. In my youth team we had strong characters like Paul Dickov and Ray Parlour. The hierarchy was respected. But if those players in those positions decided to mingle with you, that happened, and it was very organic. Often you just learnt who you need to say good morning to in a formal way and who you can be more informal with.

We had to go to the first team games at Highbury. I know it's definitely changed because of different rulings that are in place in terms of contact time, but back then the youth players had to go to every game. When we finished our game in the morning at London Colney, we'd cleaned up the changing rooms, the training ground and then got a coach to the game. You sat in the paddock behind the dugout, and you watched the game. And then once the game finished, your job was to go and clean both the changing rooms. So, I didn't notice at the time that the fanbase was quite multicultural because in my head, I just played the youth game in the morning, went to watch the game and at that moment, all I'm looking at is Lee Dixon thinking, 'What do I have to do to be better than him? What do I have to do to get in the team?' That team won the title twice in three years. I mean that 1991 team – I think we lost one game all season, to Chelsea, and

probably should have done the double; we lost against Spurs in the FA Cup semi-final. They were so good. So, at the time I didn't realise the significance of the Black fanbase as you're sitting there trying to watch the game, thinking how to get in the team.

Ian Wright was very different. He's very loud in a nice way. He joined in September 1991, so we only had one season where we were both there. But it was just the character of the man. I remember him doing the bogle on the pitch. I remember Aswad singing about him in their song 'Shine'. I remember the Nike boot adverts; I remember the great celebrations. I think with all the other guys, they were brilliant people, brilliant players, aspirational role models in the footballing world. But when Ian turned up, he probably transcended Arsenal to the point where there were people who didn't support Arsenal but loved Ian. Rocky, Mickey and Davo might have had it in a different way. But people loved Ian despite who he played for. And it probably grew even more because he came from a really multicultural team in Crystal Palace with Andy Gray and Mark Bright, but I don't think there was that cult Ian Wright thing at Palace. But there was when he came to Arsenal and that happened really, really quickly.

I got released from Arsenal in 1992. It was of course very hard to leave. Because ultimately you only really leave Arsenal for two reasons – you leave on your terms, or you leave on their terms. I left on their terms in that I was deemed not to be good enough at that time. There's that part of being hurt because that's the first club you know, it's my club, and having spent so much time there and still know people from that period years and years later. So that was hard. And I remember when I had my interview here [for academy coach], one of the questions I got asked was if I was an Arsenal fan. And I said it was a difficult one to answer. It's difficult to support a club that broke your heart. I will always look out for Arsenal and it will always be my club, more than any other club, and it's probably in my blood. It was thirty years ago, and it still hurts. But the football part of it is you have to be good enough to play and generally, if you dig deep enough, there's generally one person's opinion that you are or you are not. And I suppose for me personally, I'd wish I'd played at least one game. Just one, so I could have said I've played for The Arsenal. Because there is such an amount of work that would have gone into that one appearance. But I think for anyone, be it Paul, Rocky or Mickey, there's always the romantic way to go, but in football that doesn't happen very often. So, it can be quite hard when you have given your heart and soul to playing football at a place like Arsenal. That's always going to be hard, because there's a bit of you that isn't there anymore, just a little bit of you that is lost. Because you've given it up. That's hard.

So, to come back to the club thirty years later as Arsenal's Academy Coach Developer at Hale End is in many ways quite the fairy tale. When I got released from Arsenal,

I went on and played for about ten years. I went to Cambridge United and then Leyton Orient, so those are the two I played the longest at. I was unfortunate. I'd signed for Gillingham, but then they had an embargo on them. I was to sign a contract at Watford. That didn't happen. I went to Northampton, then they had a transfer embargo as well, so couldn't sign there. It was a tough time, but I ended up playing about ten years and then I went to work for the FA, so I've been lucky in terms of going full circle. Paul Davis came to the FA afterwards, so it was quite good to come back to connect with him. If we think about it, between fourteen and sixteen I played for England and then twenty years later I come back working with England as a coach educator. I did that for about fifteen years and then towards the end of that I was lucky enough to work with Greg Lincoln and take the Under-16s, having previously played for that group. I'm proud of that, and then just as that is taking off, this opportunity at Arsenal comes up. There aren't many clubs I'd have left the FA for, but Arsenal's definitely one of them. So as much as there's that little nagging bit from having to leave in 1992, for me Arsenal is the place to come to without a shadow of doubt in terms of how I feel connected to the players, how I feel about the club, how now I'm older I've got a better understanding of how it feels to different communities. I'm much more aware of that than when I was a seventeen- or eighteen-year-old.

For me, generally there's only a few reasons why you support a club. You're told to by your parents or siblings because they are a lifelong supporter of a certain club and they're going to take you along to those games and that's that. Then you form your own opinion, so you might have gone to a club and thought, 'Actually, this is not for me.' Or it might be connected to where you live. But for lots of people of Arsenal – I'm talking about the Black community – they support Arsenal because it's who they identify with. That's a really powerful way to support a club. So, they don't necessarily support the club because they live nearby or because of any particular affinity, but because they can identify with somebody in that club who makes them feel represented or the way they represent themselves. That's a really powerful way of connecting with a club because the thing that's got you into Arsenal still exists.

I can't remember too many Arsenal teams that haven't been culturally or ethnically diverse. So even if there hasn't been a Black player, there's been someone from a different country. That means a different type of culture. I don't know if people supported Tottenham because Ledley King was there. But I do know people loved Arsenal because of Ian Wright. I do know people loved Arsenal because of Patrick Vieira. Yes, they're fantastic players. But look at what and who they represent? There is a big part of the African community that loved Vieira. That's what is meant about people being able to identify. That there are lots of second- or third-generation Caribbean and African people in Britain that looked at them and

thought, 'Yes, they represent me, *and* they wear that badge.' Bukayo Saka is probably the next one.

It's probably becoming more common now just from having a look around the Premier League clubs in London, but the high number of Black players that we see in one Arsenal Academy team is a representation of Arsenal across any age group at any time. It could have looked like that at the time I left the FA in 2022, if you look at the national teams. And the younger age groups look like that. But it's quite synonymous with Arsenal. It still almost feels like an inclusive place. You're not dissuaded. You can be whoever you like and support the club. If you're good enough, you can play and I think for me, as I get older now and I think back, we were lucky that in our youth team in that period we had Pat Rice. I didn't always agree with and like him at that time when I was a kid, but I definitely do now I'm older. And I made a point of going and telling him that he had a massive impact on my career. I just didn't realise that at the time. He was always like, 'You have to be good enough to represent the Arsenal badge.' He didn't care if you're Black, white or anything. You must be good enough to wear the badge. That was always the thing that Arsenal had, that was what was most important. Are you good enough to represent The Arsenal? Because people are always looking in and wanting to find an identification. So, if you're part of that club, whether you want the responsibility or not, people are looking at you and you're part of their identity. You're part of what The Arsenal is. You're part of what people expect Arsenal to look like. If there was ever an Arsenal team that wasn't diverse, I think people would question it.

Of course, it still can be better in terms of coaching, in terms of cognitive, cultural and ethnic diversity; everywhere can be better. But again, if you were going to Highbury and you walked through the concierge and the glass doors and the marble floors, everyone looked at us here as the benchmark. We're almost trailblazers now.

↑ Matthew Joseph, Arsenal Academy training, Hale End.

But that's what Arsenal has built up over a period of time. It's not always right, but in certain communities it can be a benchmark. We're always going to have these people at the club. Where those people end up and how long they're here for and the long term is a different conversation, and not just for Arsenal, but lots of different clubs, in lots of different places. We're talking about diversity and inclusion, because I'm very much in and around that from my time at the FA. Looking at Arsenal, is there enough representation of lots of different things that represents the community that it's in? Yes. And we have to be mindful of that because there are many clubs who are not as diverse. But then you have to look at the demographic and where they are. If you're asking if a club is representative of the community, I would always argue that Arsenal is representative of *its* community. I would also argue that outside of that, Arsenal is representative of its fanbase, and the fanbase isn't just the local community any more. It used to be, but there's a bigger global fanbase. So, among this bigger fanbase now, if you say to ten people to name me an Arsenal player, five out of ten will say Saka. He has the identity of a home-grown, exceptional player. Well spoken. Diverse. Dealt with adversity and trauma on the back of Euro 2020. I can't imagine many other players being on the end of that as an Arsenal player and getting a round of applause at Tottenham Hotspur. So, when you're talking about someone who can transcend the badge that they're wearing,

Black Arsenal

but still represents the club, you know that's powerful, and Arsenal have been able to do that for a period of time. For me, as a youth player who didn't quite make it first time around and has come full circle as a coach at Arsenal, it's a privilege to see it happening again. ▪

↑ Arsenal Academy training, Hale End.

Coming Full Circle

27

STARBOY: BUKAYO SAKA AS DIGITAL CULTURE

JAMES McNICHOLAS

When Bukayo Saka volleyed Arsenal level during their 4–2 win over Aston Villa in February 2023, he celebrated by leaning with insouciance on the nearby corner flag. What appeared to be an instance of casual improvisation had deeper cultural significance. It was a moment that simultaneously alluded to Arsenal's Black heritage, and connected it through Saka to their present and future. Social media duly went wild.

The celebration was, of course, a tribute to Thierry Henry. Saka was, as he confessed in his own tweet, 'honouring The King'. The Arsenal winger had previously celebrated by replicating Henry's iconic knee-slide. That he had opted for this less exuberant, more nonchalant pose seemed indicative of a player arriving at the peak of his powers. The season 2022–23 was when Arsenal's starboy became a star man.

Over the remaining weeks of the season, Saka's form granted him the opportunity to replicate the corner flag moment several times. It became a concerted campaign in iconography, a self-conscious attempt to establish that silhouette as his own. It was

part of separating Saka from the pack, of carving out an individual identity. In an age dominated by video games such as EA's *FIFA* series, the bespoke modelling of a goal celebration is something that denotes a player as special. It was a moment destined, from the start, to become a meme.

Saka is arguably Arsenal's first-born digital Black superstar, and his development within the club's academy was concurrent with the emersion and explosion of social media. Although Saka has become a star in a relatively nascent media landscape, he already belongs among Arsenal's other legendary Black icons. Saka's cultural impact is so great that he was the only current player seriously considered to be included on Arsenal's 2023 renewal of the murals that adorn the exterior of Emirates Stadium.

The winger's own use of social media has helped form his perceived identity. Saka's Instagram bio – simply, 'God's child' – while doubtless intended as an uncomplicated statement of faith, lends itself to the ongoing depiction of him as a paragon of purity. The god's child sobriquet, coupled with being Arsenal's anointed 'starboy', fosters

← *Previous page:* Bukayo Saka, Arsenal v Wolverhampton Wanderers, 28 May 2023.

the idea of there being something almost preordained about Saka's rise – 'Burdened with glorious purpose,' as Ian Wright put it, quoting Marvel's Asgardian deity Loki – and further cementing links between Saka and pop culture.

Emulating Henry is just one of the ways in which Saka has demonstrated an awareness of his place in Arsenal's lineage. Another is in wearing the number 7 shirt which will be forever associated with David Rocastle.

Saka has long been aware of Rocastle's legacy. A graduate of Arsenal's Hale End academy, Saka would have grown up training in the sports hall named in his predecessor's honour, the David Rocastle Centre. On the twentieth anniversary of Rocastle's death, Saka took part in a club photoshoot wearing the 2020–21 home shirt, with 'Rocastle 7' emblazoned on the back. Saka shared the images to his Instagram story, captioned simply, '#RememberingRocky'.

Saka has also been embraced by Rocastle's good friend – and the archetypal quintessential 'uncle' of Arsenal – Ian Wright. 'You know what I love as well is that you, coming through the academy like you have, blasting onto the scene,' Wright told Saka in a YouTube video created by Arsenal's media team. 'Somebody that loved the club, somebody that's wearing the number 7 … You wearing that shirt and the fans singing his name, and you being as integral to us as you are now – it's amazing.'

Saka's rise has gone beyond taking his place in Arsenal's Black history. He has had a

role in the cultural reshaping of the England team – and, as a corollary, arguably the national identity.

It has been a difficult path. When Saka missed the decisive penalty in England's Euro 2020 final defeat against Italy, he was inundated with online racist abuse. It was a shameful episode, one that has since been retold through more traditional forms of media too, depicted in the National Theatre's production *Dear England* – the stage flooding with red as the racist attacks pour in.

Saka, then just nineteen, responded to the torrent of abuse with remarkable courage and maturity. He used his own platforms to call upon social media companies to take greater responsibility.

↑ Bukayo Saka is consoled by Gareth Southgate following England's defeat in the UEFA Euro 2020 final by Italy.

To the social media platforms Facebook, Instagram and Twitter [he wrote in a statement shared on Instagram]. I don't want any child or adult to receive the hateful and hurtful messages that me, Marcus [Rashford] and Jadon [Sancho] have received. I knew instantly the kind of hate I was about to receive and that is a sad reality that your powerful platforms are not doing enough to stop these messages.

There is no place for racism or hate of any kind in football or any area of society and to the majority of people coming together to call out the people sending these messages, by taking action and reporting these to the police and driving out the hate by being kind to one another, we will win.

While English football's fight against racism is ongoing, Saka has become a symbol of equality and meritocracy. In 2021–22, he was named England's Senior Men's Player of the Year – an award decided by an online supporters' poll.

Throughout the highs and lows, Arsenal has proved his refuge. By the time Saka returned to training after the Euros, the club had collated letters, cards and banners – all from supporters, all professing their love for Saka. It was a perfectly analogue response to the abuse Saka suffered online. He was visibly moved – and the strength of the connection between Arsenal and Saka deepened, solidified by a new long-term contract in the spring of 2023.

↑ Bukayo Saka reading the wall of letters sent to him following the UEFA Euro 2020 final defeat.

Arsenal's latest Black icon continues to build his own legacy. It will be fascinating to see how the evolving social media landscape intersects with this young star's ascendancy. Saka will be more visible, across more platforms, than footballers from previous generations. Online influencer culture means more emphasis is placed on the individual than the collective. He has the potential to build an audience that are Saka fans first, Arsenal fans second.

And with time, we may begin to build a more multifaceted picture of this young man – one that goes deeper than his A-grade GCSEs, diligent faithfulness, winning smile and astonishing talent. Saka appears to be a private person, but as he matures may want to wield his cultural cachet a little more freely, either for commercial gain or creative satisfaction. Saka is already well on his way to being established as a football icon. In the social media age, it's perhaps a matter of time until he is a pop culture icon too. ■

↑ Bukayo Saka greeting fans as he arrives at the Emirates Stadium, 2024.

→ *Overleaf*: Bukayo Saka, 2024. Bukayo Saka wearing David Rocastle's number 7 shirt.

28

BLACK ARSENAL

Potentiality of being and becoming

GAIL LEWIS

INTRODUCTION: MOVING WITH MY FRIENDS

Whatever route I take on home matchdays, many people accompany me to the Emirates. I go with my love, and sometimes my nephew. I always go (well, these days at least) with 60,702 or three others, in addition to my love and my nephew. We stream in, flow after flow navigating the surrounding streets, going through the Arsenal songbook as we move: 'red army, red army, red army' or 'Zinchenko, always believe in your soul, you're unforgettable …', 'Allez allez, allez, we won the league at Anfield, we won it at the Lane …', 'do do dodo dada, d do dodo, owowohhoo … Saliba!'. Or it might be in a kind of hush as if we are approaching a temple, readying ourselves to make prayer and show devotion, a deeply familiar repetition yet still not quite sure what to expect. Whatever the prevailing atmosphere, we flow into the twisting funnel of removable barriers that navigate us to bag inspection and on through the turnstile, at J Block for me, and into the concourse vestibule that is the inner circle of the stadium. People gather – lining up for the toilets, or for a beer or pizza, or even, for a few, a tea or coffee or Coke.

Breathe. Breathe. Breathe.

Or it might be: park the car in Liverpool Road or maybe Highbury Station Crescent. Walk for a short while along Liverpool Road and merge into the streams in Holloway Road near the Turkish food shop. Check out what fruit they have to buy after the match, waft into the mounting tension as we merge into the chorus of bodies flowing into Fieldway Crescent or the bottom end of Ronald's Road, where my love lived when we first met, next to Joyce, a woman from the Caribbean whose seat is a few rows back from ours, one bank of seats to the right; her son's, a few rows even further back. If it's a weekday evening, stop for egg and chips and a strong tea at Veli's, nod to some of the faces in mutual recognition. Sid comes up as usual, to chain his bike to the railings and chat about predictions for the match today. He goes off, luminescent yellow vest setting

← *Previous page:* Rachel Yankey with a young fan in the late nineties.

his tall, brown-skinned body aglow. Eat up and cross the road by the concrete letters of A.R.S.E.N.A.L. that edge the road at the bottom of the Danny Fiszman bridge and walk over, opening our jackets/coats for inspection by the string of black and brown security men and women that span out across the bridge: 'Jackets and bags open please, ladies and gents, open jackets, that's it ...'

Breathe. Breathe. Breathe.

Once upon a time when I lived at the top end (the Archway end) of the Holloway Road, when the not-yet-imagined-or-built Emirates was still a huge industrial and waste disposal site, walking down the Holloway Road on matchday felt like putting your life in your hands, especially if Chelsea or a few other clubs were the opposition for that day, when the likelihood of anti-Black and/or homophobic threat was palpable. Then, I couldn't have imagined joining in the expectant throng, cheering The Arsenal as *my* club, being part of 'Who's that team we call The Arsenal, who's that team we all adore. They're the boys in red and white ...' My identification genderless until the 'Martin Jol' line when black feminist sensibility mutes me, even for an implicit reference to the hated Tottenham!

Breathe. Breathe. Breathe.

If I've arrived via Tube on a weekday evening, the joy of gathering with fellow Gooners can be matched by an anxious feeling of too many people, too many people trying to get up the stairs and onto the escalator and out onto the concourse of Highbury & Islington station, where at last there is air. A sense of vulnerability lurking the whole time between platform and street as images of the King's Cross fire of 18 November 1987 (we played at home on the 21st, losing 0–1 to Southampton) hovering just at the edge of consciousness, pressing apprehension into my mind. Making it out into the top end of the Holloway Road with a sigh of relief.

Breathe. Breathe. Breathe.

Any of these arrivals press me with the need to breathe. It catches me almost as a gasp and in this I am connected to all the invisible but vibrantly present others who accompany me to the Emirates – something like Essex Hemphill's queer evocation of black collectivity in *Heavy Breathing* (1988), whispering at the edge of consciousness but conjuring the shouting of unfettered, unashamed desire for that connection. Gooner family in black mode – drawing upon and connecting to all the modes of black life and blackness that manifest at Arsenal, at the Emirates. The blackness that emerges through what Clive calls the 'alchemistic' character of Black Arsenal, that 'exists and remains outside definition' and resists location as a 'source of origin' (Nkwonka, 25 October 2022, Barbican). Blackness that is interstitial, existing in and through the contradictory cauldron of global capital flows as harnessed to the EPL and 'global soccer' (and, for us, signalled in the very name *Emirates Stadium*); black experience fashioned by multiple modes of anti-blackness, including violent physical attack by state agents or private individuals;

Black Arsenal

and blackness as 'otherwise' (Hartman, 2019; Crawley, 2017). Otherwise in the sense of naming 'plurality, … [a nomination that] bespeaks the ongoingness of possibility, of things existing other than what is given, what is known, what is grasped' (Crawley, 2017:24). The otherwise that resides in a 'quiet', interior place (Quashie, 2012), that is 'a stay against the social ideas of blackness' (Quashie, 2021:20) and yet, 'despite its name, [bespeaks an] interior [that] is *not un*connected to the world of things (the public or political or social world)' (Harper, 1996, cited in Quashie, 2021:20, my emphases). Or what Clive calls the 'personal' which he conceives as 'the site of resistance to assimilation into the capitalist logics' of Arsenal Football Club.

All of these ideas, and the black life they summon, accompany me on match day – a day of exhilaration and anticipation, hope and disappointment – and, just as on match day, I walk with them into this piece of writing as I attempt, via three scenes, to evoke some of the magic of the stadium where we find ways to 'live together', to riff off of a statement so often repeated by 'Super Mick Arteta'.

SCENE 1. ON 'DEMONIC' GROUND: THE UNIMAGINABLE SUBJECT IS CONJURED

I never saw you play live. I never saw you play live. I never saw you play live yet … you opened a space for this black woman to become a Gooner. Making and holding space was familiar to you. At least in my imagination. At least if you are regarded through a certain way of conceiving blackness as fugitive moves; as a force that unsettles the normativities which enclose racialised/gendered identities as fixed and known entities; blackness as an ongoing process of becoming beyond the traumas of endless misogynoir.

At eight years old you crafted and made space for your own desire to play football by parsing your black girl body under guise of a boy's. You did this for two years – honing your skills and ability to see the game that would become supreme as an adult black-woman-in-becoming on the pitch. At Fulham (2000–2004) you became the first woman professional football player and in the 2004–5 season you won Nationwide International Player of the Year. That was around the time I went to my first match of the men's first team. At Highbury. I can't lie. I was as much scared as thrilled. Scared that there would be no place for me as a black woman at a London football ground. Thrilled that at last I'd get inside the hallowed ground. And I knew there was you – Rachel Yankey. Player in womanly blackness who would become an Arsenal Women's Legend. Who, across two spells as an Arsenal player (1996–2000; 2005–2016) would make 198 league appearances for the club; score fifty-one goals in her two spells and win the FA National Premier Women's League six times; FA Women's Cup nine times; FA Women's Premier League four times; FA Women's Super League twice; and the UEFA Women's Cup with a goal from Alex Scott in 2007, the year when Arsenal Women won the quadruple without losing a single game en route. The other Invincibles. And you were for a time *the* most capped football player for England – most capped of either women or men. Just the most capped.

And I never saw you play live.

But I know what you gave, what you bequeathed – it was to open and hold space for blackness as potentiality embodied as a black woman to enter football even while this domain of cultural life was just one more of the off-limits spaces of violence – symbolic and at times physical. Spaces that still – despite the rise of some of the black men players to iconic status, despite Paul Davis, despite Arsenal fielding nine black players in 2002, despite Rocky Rocastle and Michael Thomas and Ian Wright – deemed black presence among the women's teams as 'space invaders' (Puwar, 2004). The football player who was a black woman represented a gendered/racialised invasion of the space of MEN, a category of person, whom on the register of colonial thought and its afterlife (Wynter, 2003), neither male nor female bodies marked as 'black' could occupy.

In a whisper then, and almost without (perhaps) consciously knowing it, you embodied what former enslaved and pre-figuring feminist Anna Julia Cooper (1886/1997:563) declared:

Only the Black Woman can say when and where I enter, in the quiet, undisputed dignity of my womanhood, without violence and without suing or special patronage, then and there the whole [Black] race enters with me.

Or more pointedly, not 'the whole *race*' whose members are divided into men and women, but a whole panoply of people characterised through the prism of black feminism wherein the construction and meaning of black femininity and womanhood is the effect of a spectrum of genders, bodies and positions. An approach that recognises that 'female bodiedness can constitute a range of gendered subject positions, even as we also acknowledge that female bodiedness is not a prerequisite for womanhood' (Cooper, 2015:17). Neither a binary divided 'race', nor a 'race' transparent and 'known' through the logics of either the colonial or the neo-liberalism of contemporary global capital flows, but a range of potentialities of being that marks a mode of living termed 'blackness'.

Black Arsenal

RACHEL YANKEY.
RACHEL YANKEY.
RACHEL YANKEY.

If this was a door opening, a space-making to allow the meeting of souls in the London constituency hailed by Jazzy B's Soul II Soul, who themselves had opened doors of black cultural possibility and becoming, yours was more expansive than any 'simple' essentialised opening, as your quiet and yet insistent travels through gendered locations in pursuit of your ambitions and desires and honed into the skills with which you graced Arsenal – or better still Arsenal-community-in-becoming, showed. It was more in the lines of, following Wynter (1990) what might be termed a 'demonic' presencing of a heretofore *unimaginable* figure – that of the black woman – now embodied as footballer. The figure of the 'black woman', understood in the plural ways suggested by Cooper above, signals a mode of personhood whose presence pushes to the very limits of the frameworks through which human population is categorised, made intelligible and valorised. The entry of the erstwhile unintelligible, unthinkable figure 'the black woman' requires development of a way to think this!

Rachel Yankey, your presence was enormous and symbolised an undoing of sorts, not in (or only) to indicate an unravelling or falling apart under the strain of the pervasive anti-blackness known as misogynoir (Bailey, 2021), but an 'undoing'

(or interruption of) all the processes and practices (material and symbolic) of time-space that produce the sociological black woman/man subject and the modes by which they are known as an essentialised, fixed identity, and instead ushers in a mode of black being irrupting into simultaneous visibility and opacity. The visibility and opacity of you, in your number 11 shirt, dancing and skipping and criss-crossing down the wing to either score or assist. A magic of black womanhood in process of becoming even as she is material and fleshy technical majesty. As you cut through and down the sides of the opposition, pulling defences out of shape, you also cut through any settled subject-position of 'black woman' as rendered intelligible in misogynoir.

SCENE 2: VOICING BLACK AUTHORITY: WALKING THE LINE

You never know what's going to happen when you walk through the J turnstiles and make your way down to Lower East, Area 18, and edge along to your seat. It's true that these days, three years into Mikel Arteta's regime, the atmosphere is always buzzing – expectant as ever but now edging more toward expectation of victory, yet still … you never know. But songs are being sung as there is a vibrant milling, people (men mostly) drinking beer, eating a hotdog, sharing sweets, finding mates, or running into the toilets. Navigating our way to our seats, nodding to those you recognise but cannot name, as you squeeze by: 'hello', 'how are you?', 'what'd you reckon… two-nil, three-one?', ''scuse us, cheers'.

You never know what's going to happen.
You never know what's going to happen.
You never know what's going to happen.
But you enter anyway.

An entry repeated over and over and over with every home game.

In the repetition an uncanny space is conjured as if we are all lifted into and suspended in a perpetual 'now', that is both anxiety producing and thrilling. A kind of 'in thrall-ness' that registers on and in the body and is felt both haptically and emotionally. And a 'now-ness' where today is tomorrow, is place-holder for the 'future', i.e. the end of the season in the hope that *this* time it will be ours, this time the Mikel Arteta that we've got (as the song says) really will know what we need to win the league. The repetition of songs, of arrivals, of suspension in anticipation manifested as repeated 'now' anticipates a future becoming – becoming champions, Cup winners, Champions League contestants. Repetition carries dreams and hopes. Repetition forestalls pain and anguish …

… It also carries the past – or at least the inherited – an inherited of repetitious racialised and gendered time. Simultaneously, a kind of suspension in the transparency of 'known' identities and a suspension in the opacity of time that might be called 'futurity', following black feminist Tina Campt (2017:17) or which Crawford (2022) links to the question: *What time is it when you're black?*

Clive says that Black Arsenal 'exists and remains outside definition' but as 'continuous experience it is conditioned by [the interweaving] of race, politics, social and [the] cultural but also change, [the] televisual, the European Union'. And in this loop, this web, sometimes the dial gets stuck, unable to move beyond that point that says 'anti-blackness' and positions the black body in another time, a behind time, that robs the black body of authority and value. A stuckness or entrapment in the practices of relating and discourses of modernity that usher a black fractured temporality (Sawyer, 2018: vii) and black experience and ontology is rendered 'Be(ing) out of time'; a Fanonian arrival too late; a fracturing of body and experience and ability for self-authorisation.

On 2 May 2023 we face Chelsea at home (originally scheduled for 29 April).

Atmosphere is very tense. We'd played Manchester City six days before at the Etihad and lost and we'd drawn the three games before that. Our title hopes are rapidly descending and this match, against a hated rival – a cross-London derby – is a must win. The stadium is packed, raucous and edgy, a kind of muted aggression circulating in the air. We're communicating our support for the team – being the 'twelfth man' (sic) in iterative performance – but the fear and dread that we are repeating the 'collapse' right at 'the business end of the season' like last year is evident in our heightened tension, our almost manic performance of support and belief. Ten minutes from kick-off everyone is standing, urging the team on in a kind of desperation, sending shouts of abuse and worse to the Chelsea players. We are all standing – spilling out to the sides of the aisles a bit, shuffling in front of our own seat in the too narrow gap between each one.

The stewards form a line and walk along between the first row of seats and the barrier to the pitch and turn into the steps between the banks of seats. They are all black men today. One assumes a style and posture that particularly irritates the guys around me. He's acting like he's been on a one-day crowd management course. Apparently appealing to fans' rationality and reasonableness – maybe even fellow Gooner-ness – by looking directly at us with outstretched arms and hands open with palms down and lifting his arms up and down repeatedly in a gesture that says, 'Sit down and calm down' and is the ultimate in condescension. But as I look at his face, I hear another message: a message that lets me know, 'I know this is ridiculous and I too know, that for this game at least, standing is the only way to watch'; OR: 'I am really only doing what I'm told to do and I need my job, so maybe just do me a favour … I don't make the rules.'

The more he gestures, the more worked up and agitated the crowd becomes: 'fuck off', 'Sit dowwwn you fucking cunt', 'Stand up for the Arsenal, stand up for the Arsenal' – leaning in towards the aisle and getting more and more angry and threatening. The more they do that, the more pronounced the split between his bodily gestures and what his face, frozen in rictus smile, becomes and communicates.

And I find myself in a movie reel, witnessing as if on loop, the fracturing of the black body in real time that is suspended time: 'Sealed into that crushing object hood, I turned beseechingly to others … I burst apart. Now the fragments have been put together again by another self … I discovered my blackness … and I was battered down by tom-toms … intellectual deficiency, fetishism, racial defects, slaveships …' (Fanon, 1986:112).

It's unbearable to me. I squeeze by all the guys in my row and walk up two or three steps and call the security guy over and talk to him. I tell him his attempt is just making it worse, and that if he and the other security guys leave, everyone will settle down. I say I am a psychologist, including a psychologist of groups which is almost true, and he says, 'OK. You think so?' I say, 'Yes, I do, they'll settle once you stop telling them they must sit, and like, they don't like your gesturing. They'll sit if you go.' He almost brushes my hand – which prompts me to say, 'Anyway, I can see you're kind of caught, go easy brother.' He says 'OK, if you think so, thanks.' He calls his colleagues and they retreat.

I walk back down, retracing my steps through the crush to my seat. The guys around me ask what I said, I give a vague account. One says, 'Well it seemed to get them to go, fucking twats.' They turn their attention away from the security guys and back to the match: 'Arsenal, Arsenal, Arsenal' rings out around the ground and morphs into 'Come on, Arsenal, Come on Arsenal.' The chanting is sustained over minutes, mixed with more abuse to the Chelsea !*!*.

Eighteenth minute: we score — Ødegaard!!! YESSSSSSSSSSSSSSSSSS booms up and ricochets in echoes around the stadium: 'One-nil to The Arsenal, one-nil to The Arsenal, one-nil to The Arsenal …' We'll score two more times in the first half: Ødegaard again in the thirty-first minute, and Jesus in the thirty-fourth. The west Londoners pull one back in the sixty-fifth and the tension gets thick with the fear that we might let them back in for a draw, but we have three goals not the fateful two, so …

It ends with a satisfying win. And we go two points clear of City … But the feeling of being suspended in neo-liberal multicultural time and its haunting echoes of colonialism's racial time shrouds me. I need to breathe but am constricted. I need to be in a space of 'spiralism' (Frankétienne, 2014:7) that offers another way to live with difference outside the categorical (Taylor, 2023:42). I need this space of breath as I move back into the cycle: suspended in hope and apprehension.

Breathe. Breathe. Breathe.

↑ Arsenal v Chelsea at Emirates Stadium, 2 May 2023.

Black Arsenal

SCENE 3: TOWARDS BLACK PRAYER

8 December 2013 – home match against Everton.

It's one of those dank, almost misty London evenings. There is a muted expectancy around the stadium as the fans stream in. The usual round of hellos – varyingly warm, accompanied perhaps with an embrace, or cooler, more a sign of formal acknowledgement that we are here again, than a real sense of unity in Goonerdom. The losses associated with the move away from the beloved Highbury ground haunt. But the arrival of Mesut Özil just as the window closed at the beginning of September, has brought a tiny sense of hope, of possibility – could this be the year? We can still recruit the elite so is this the end of the drought? Are we getting back where we belong? Who knows? But now we just gotta get a win, a knowing and a hope that still cannot shift the atmosphere, which is dull, cut-off and seemingly dispassionate. Until …

… Almost like a whisper, from the Clock End comes the call and response prayer that it seems like we haven't heard or sung for years – since we left Highbury, it feels like. The whisper starts, moving just inside the audible, gathering up behind the goal, rising over it and wafting down the pitch to the North Bank, the call made:

Sotto voce: *We are the Clock End, the Clock End, the Clock End, Highbury!*
In reception and echo
We are the North Bank, the North Bank, the North Bank, Highbury!
Back again, summoning louder this time
Mezza voce: *We are the Clock End, the Clock End, the Clock End, Highbury!*
Call and response continues:
We are the North Bank, the North Bank, the North Bank, Highbury!
We are home now, not just in the infrastructure of the Emirates but in the *affect* of home – the affect of Highbury – a place of lost origins vibrantly alive and present in the heart and hope Özil's presence symbolises
Piena voce: *We are the Clock End, the Clock End, the Clock End, Highbury!*
We are the North Bank, the North Bank, the North Bank, Highbury!

And the testifying swells and gathers up, the breath of collective voice displacing, or maybe symbolising the slight miasma of mist that has met the wetness of the grass that makes the ball slide along between the players if the movement is just right, the weight and direction of the pass fine-tuned to perfection, allowing us to move up the pitch in the other direction from the prayer-song from North Bank towards Clock End in a silky move for our first goal.

On the emission of the collective sigh: *YESSSSSSS!* crescendos around the pitch and settles to stillness. The stillness, marking the coming to rest of the sigh, that hints at the possibility that now, Arsenal and its fans, might be on the verge of being able to breathe again, like it did in 1989 at Anfield, or when Henry, and Vieira, and Campbell and Lauren and Kanu, and Pires and Hleb played. When the invincibles became the Invincibles in 2003–04. When they embodied and enabled a shift from the ambiguity of the sigh to the full ownership and release of the breath. A shift that Claudia Rankine (2014, cited in Crawford 2022) suggests is hard beyond belief, yet vital, for black life, since the sigh crafts the 'pathway to breath' (Rankine, 2014:60). Or, we might say, is the dance between the hushed tones of the call-and-response as it suddenly segues into the *whoop* of a goal scored and summoning the Emirates into congregation as if present as Aretha told *Mary, Don't You Weep* at the New Temple Missionary Baptist Church in 1972. A move through and with relief into glory-be aliveness; the prayer of black aliveness fashioned between the will and majesty of the Invincibles and the pulse of black cultural productions rising to the top in urban otherwise living.

14 *February 2016* – home match against Leicester.

Sixty-eighth minute: we are trailing 0–1 and playing against ten men. Vardy's scored on the stroke of half time following a soft penalty against Monreal. All our attempts to break through either saved by Kasper Schmeichel, ruled offside or off target. Frustration and hope sit in tension with each other – yes, they are league leaders (and will go on to win the league this season) but this is Leicester and we're at home, COME ON ARSENAL. Theo's been subbed on. He gets the equaliser following a sharp run in to collect the rebound and drive it home just at the seventieth minute. 1–1!

Still time.

We harry and hustle, trying to make the moves and connections that will allow us to open them up one more time … and then, in the ninety-fourth minute, one of their players – Wasilewski (who had also been subbed on) fouls for a free kick.

Mesut takes his place on the right-hand side of the North Bank goal. He's twenty-five yards out. Composes himself as the team gathers in the box. We see his chest slightly rise as he opens his palms upwards, slightly tilts his head upwards and backwards, making that patch of the Emirates a sacred place of prayer for thirty seconds. Movement in stillness. Opportunity in quiet. Belief at the edge of time.

He assesses the distance and in the grace that flows through him he calibrates and executes the most perfect of kicks, length and weight and height supreme and possible for only one head to meet: Danny Welbeck's as he lifts his body in what seems like slow motion and rises above all others, swivelling his neck and head to glide the ball into the top left-hand corner of the net! 2–1 to The Arsenal in the ninety-fifth minute and with almost the last kick of the match.

Our prayers are answered. From the prayer of the call and response of the 'Clock End/ North Bank' song. Through the embodied prayer of a footballer who believes, meeting the prayers of 60,000+ fans and together meeting the black head of a substitute player whose self-belief didn't falter, the impossible is made to happen, fashioning space and time when neither seemed available.

'Black flesh knows something of the truth of elaboration and elongation, about expanding within loopholes of retreat, about movement and vibration against the strictures of cramped time and space,' Ashon Crawley (2020:33) tells us.

And in this impossible win, it's as though we've all been invited to witness just such a manifestation. The prayer of Mesut's body in 'quiet' (Quashie, 2012) contemplation of his task, summoning spirit as interior-exterior force, or perhaps more accurately Rūh al-qudus [the Holy Spirit], to guide him.

And after the goal so exquisitely guided by Danny's head, the whooping prayer of fans and players alike, morphing into a quivering and spinning and jumping and hugging congregation in echo of black life in the pew or on the dance floor.

Choreography and orchestration of Arsenal as black and Black Arsenal as the point of intersection of 'black cultural memory and black politics' (Nwonka, 25 October 2022), black (feminist) futurity, and black multiplicity and becoming. Making joy and congregation by seeking 'the quarter tone' that lies between the flatted and the unflatted and moving in the space not yet known or become.

Black Arsenal.

Breathe. Breathe. Breathe. ◼

↑ Danny Welbeck, Olivier Giroud and Theo Walcott celebrate Welbeck's goal during Arsenal's 2–1 win over Leicester City, 2016.

REFERENCES

Bailey, Moya (2021) *Misogynoir Transformed: Black Women's Digital Resistance.* New York: New York University Press

Campt, Tina M. (2017) *Listening to Images.* Durham, NC: Duke University Press

Cooper, Anna Julia (1886) 'Womanhood a Vital Element in the Regeneration and Progress of a Race', in The Norton Anthology of African American (1997). Edited by Henry Louis Gates and Nellie Y. McKay. New York: W.W. Norton and Company, pp.553–569

Cooper, Brittney C. (2015) 'Love No Limit: Towards a Black Feminist Future (In Theory)', *The Black Scholar, vol.45, no.4, Winter, pp.7–21*

Crawford, Margo Natalie, (2022) 'What Time is it When You're Black', *South Atlantic Quarterly, vol. 121: 1, pp.153–172*

Crawley, Ashon T. (2017) *BlackPentecostal Breath: the Aesthetics of Possibility.* New York: Fordham University Press

— (2020) 'Stayed|Freedom|Halleujah', in *Otherwise Worlds. Against Settler Colonialism and Anti-Blackness.* Edited by Tiffany Lethabo King, Jenell Navarro, and Andrea Smith. Durham, NC: Duke University Press, pp.27–37

Fanon, Frantz (1986) *Black Skins, White Masks,* London: Pluto Press

Frankétienne (2014) *Ready to Burst.* Archipelago Books

Hartman, Saidiya (2019) *Wayward Lives, Beautiful Experiments: Intimate Histories of Social Upheaval.* New York and London: W.W. Norton and Company

Hemphill, Essex (1988/1992) 'Heavy Breathing', in *Ceremonies: Poetry and Prose.* New York: Plume

Nwonka, Clive (2022) 'Black Arsenal: Race, Cultural Memory and Black British Identity', Talk at the Barbican, 25 October

Puwar, Nirmal (2004) *Space Invaders: Race, Gender, and Bodies Out of Place.* London: Berg Publishers

Quashie, Kevin (2012) *The Sovereignty of Quiet: Beyond Resistance in Black Culture.* New Brunswick, NJ: Rutgers University Press

— (2021) *Black Aliveness, or a Poetics of Being.* Durham and London: Duke University Press

Rankine, Claudia (2014) *Citizen: An American Lyric.* Harmondsworth: Penguin Books

Sawyer, Michael E. (2018) *An Africana Philosophy of Temporality: Homo Liminalis.* Cham, Switzerland: Springer Nature

Taylor, Foluke (2023) *Un/ruly Therapeutic: Black Feminist Writings and Practices in Living Room.* New York and London: Norton Professional Books

Wynter, Silvia (1990) 'Afterword: Beyond Miranda's Meanings: Un/Silencing the "Demonic Ground" of Caliban's Woman', in *Out of KUMBLA: Caribbean Women and Literature.* Edited by Carole Boyce Davies and Elaine Savory Fido. Trenton, NJ: Africa World Press, pp.355–372

— (2003) 'Unsettling the Coloniality of Being/Power/Truth/Freedom: Towards the Human, After Man, Its Overrepresentation – an Argument', *CR: The New Centennial Review, vol.3, number 3, Fall, pp.257–337*

COPYRIGHT

ILLUSTRATION CREDITS